Contents

L<small>IVING THE</small> W<small>ORD</small>
S T A F F

Editor-in-Chief, Jim Wallis

Editors, Aaron Gallegos, Bob Hulteen

Managing Editor, Karen Lattea

Art Director, Ed Spivey Jr.

Associate Editor, Brett Malcolm Grainger

Assistant Editors, Julie Polter, Jim Rice

Editorial Assistants,
  Sandra Maben, Richard Vernon, Anne Wayne

Publisher, Joe Roos

Director of Marketing, David A. Wade

Director of Development, Hugh E. Brown III

Production Manager, Cynthia J. Martens

Business Manager, David D. King

Special thanks to Rev. John Hulden for first conceiving the idea of a regular lectionary column in Sojourners *and for special consultation on the creation of this resource.*

Illustrations by Julie Delton.

LIVING *the* WORD

CYCLE A

Recollect the Journey

*S*o much around us fo-
cuses on moving for-
ward, making
progress, racing ahead, a
linear pull to bigger and
better things. But our
story, creation's story, the
story of God-with-us,
seems more accurately de-
scribed by a spiral,
swirling from familiar territory to unexplored fron-
tier, not tossing off the old,
but seeing it in ever-shift-
ing new light, moving
higher, deeper, wider, a
steady unfurling through
eternity. Advent calls us to
recollect this journey, our
story as God's people, the
where we have been, the
where we are, and the
where we will be.

It is a season of prepa-
ration and penitence; of
acknowledging darkness
and deliverance; of anticipating judgment and joy.
The fences we put up to
guard ourselves—from
promises that are too big
and hurts that are too
deep—shudder and begin
to fall. Hope blows in, a
wild wind; we realize that
the love of God is a persistent squatter, camped in
our backyard all along.

—Julie Polter

First Sunday of Advent

Awake! Salvation is Near!

PSALM 122 • ISAIAH 2:1-5 • ROMANS 13:11-14 • MATTHEW 24:36-44

"AWAKE FROM YOUR SLUMBER!" I think of my own transformation, my death,
and of the world's transformation, the coming "kindom" of God, the end of life as we
know it.

We live in neighborhoods where death comes quickly, unannounced in a spray of
bullets. We know each time we say goodbye may be the last. We live our usual lives,
yet in the background is always the thought that death may come before nightfall.

In our neighborhoods we see the decay and disintegration of our economic and political systems. At Mary's House here in Birmingham, I watch people search franti-
cally for minimum wage jobs, to find that there is no public transport to take them to
the jobs once found. Collapse may come at any moment.

Time of decay, of transition, of hope and despair, death and birth. The Advent
readings call us to see the birth usually buried under decay: No one knows the day or
the hour, so watch! We teeter on the edge of a new year; if we live these days in God's
Spirit, perhaps we will be able to see the coming of the kindom at last.

I no longer part easily from a friend if our friendship is marred; this may be the
only time left to repair those bonds. I no longer take life's necessities for granted; this
may be the end of the system that brings them to my neighborhood. Then what? After
my death I'm still in God's hands. My world is in God's hands too, but God claims
my hands to uncover God's new work.

—Shelley Douglass

Second Sunday of Advent

Anticipation

PSALM 72:1-7, 18-19 • ISAIAH 11:1-10 • ROMANS 15:4-13 • MATTHEW 3:1-12

TREMENDOUS LONGING for justice suffuses these readings—a yearning, a pleading for a time when we will live in love of God and of each other, when all creation
will be reconciled. "They will not hurt or destroy on all my holy mountain" (Isaiah
11:9). Read that in Birmingham, which had 22 homicides in August alone.

When I was about 9, living in Switzerland with my parents and attending local
schools, I used to make-believe to lessen my homesickness. Walking home from
school each day, I would tell myself that when I rounded the last corner I would see
in the distance my grandparents' old black Chevy parked in front of our Swiss apartment building.

Every day I would turn the corner more than half-expectant—the car would be
there, and with it my grandparents and the restoration of our family community. The
car was never there; my grandparents didn't make the trip. I've never forgotten the
heart-stopping sense of anticipation that any day they MIGHT be there. I would like
to have that sense of the possible in my yearning for the coming of God's kindom.

John the Baptist must have had that feeling about the coming of his Messiah: Any
day now he could round the corner and reveal God's presence. John knew just what
God's agent would do—wreak vengeance on the evil-doers, burn the chaff. Repent, or
bear God's wrath! It's right around the corner.

—Shelley Douglass

Third Sunday of Advent

Redeeming the Chaff

LUKE 1:46-55 • ISAIAH 35:1-10 • JAMES 5:7-10 • MATTHEW 11:2-11

NO WONDER JOHN was doubtful. He was in jail, and Jesus was acting in a most peculiar manner. Instead of sweeping the chaff aside for burning, Jesus was trying to make wheat out of it! He invited tax collectors—collaborators with the hated Romans—and other sinners into the new community. Instead of a powerful army of the righteous, Jesus was gathering a community of the weak, the outcast, the foreign.

Jesus' response echoes Isaiah: Tell John what you have seen. We are being healed. The highway for God's people is open, and no fool (not even me) is lost. We are returning, singing for joy. Returning where? To God's holy mountain, where there is more rejoicing over one repentant sinner than over all the righteous.

I'm struck by the Magnificat, a song of victory accomplished, juxtaposed with the longing in Isaiah's words: When will this day come, Lord? Like John I am confused. I look around, I read Mary's words, and I think: "Yeah? The hungry filled? The rich realize their emptiness? Where?"

I look again, like John's disciples, and I do see. The hungry are filled in a small way, here at Mary's House. The rich come empty and are filled. The powerless are lifted up and celebrated. Maybe the kindom comes most days, in little ways.

Isaiah's dream couldn't be achieved by separating wheat from chaff; the chaff must be transformed. The fire is our own repentance, burning away the impurities until we can love God and each other unreservedly.

—Shelley Douglass

Fourth Sunday of Advent

Humble Understanding

PSALM 80:1-7, 17-19 • ISAIAH 7:10-16 • ROMANS 1:1-7 • MATTHEW 1:18-25

IN THESE FINAL ADVENT READINGS, we move from desperate pleading ("How long, Lord?") to the child named Immanuel in Isaiah, to triumphant theology in Paul, who dares to extend God's favor even to Gentiles. In a few paragraphs we move through centuries of pain and joy, to the final summation of Paul's faith, which answers the psalmist's cry: God has given us life!

And then abruptly to everyday pain: a young woman untimely pregnant, a man's decision to be merciful, to "dismiss her quietly." Then Joseph's dream, and God is with us again in our human pain and fear. Back and forth through centuries of political and personal upheaval, but always, "God is with us!"

In the end theology is too high for me. I can understand Advent best in humble human terms. When someone I love is away there is a break in the circle; our sharing and affection are missing. When that person is about to return there is a sense of excited anticipation: The loved person will come home. The listening and caring and knowing of each other will go deeper. It reminds me every time of being a child at Christmas, awaiting surprises and family reunions with joyful anticipation.

The return of a beloved friend completes the circle again. God with us completes our circle, reminds us as we go on that we are always surprised, cared for, and known, whatever place of tears and violence we may inhabit.

—Shelley Douglass

Christmas Day

When God Starts Humming

PSALM 98 • ISAIAH 52:7-10 • HEBREWS 1:1-12 • JOHN 1:1-14

WHEN MEL TORME penned those familiar words, "Chestnuts roasting on an open fire, Jack Frost nipping at your nose," his Christmas song was little more than a faint echo of a version brought into the world centuries before. Torme's rendition of the song evokes nostalgia and sentimentality. The original version heals the sick, raises the dead, and causes rivers to clap their hands.

While the original would never make *Billboard*'s Top 50 seasonal songs of all time, it is continually sung by the multitude of the heavenly host and was the soundtrack for the creation of all things. As light broke forth from nothing, this was the tune God was humming.

The hope and joy of Christmas lies in a return to newness. Now, you may ask, how can you return to something that's new? If it's new, doesn't that mean it hasn't been around before? Why would you call something a "new" song if it had been sung since the beginning of the world?

This is the same mystery that puts a baby in a manger and acknowledges that the world was created through this infant. It's not logical. "The light shines in the darkness, but the darkness has not understood it." Words became flesh. Creation bursts into singing. Ruined cities dance like Fred Astaire. Either Christmas has been staged by Monty Python or a new way of seeing and being has come to be, calling for us to learn to celebrate.

In all seriousness, these scriptures all point to a Christ that is transcendent—a Christ that embodies a truth and a reality greater than any we have known. While all things have been created through him, the creation he birthed is marked by justice, joy, light, and peace. In the midst of the biblical writers' lives, this was a foreign reality. Their world was marked by violence, poverty, tyranny, and darkness—not altogether different than the world we live in today.

So then this Christ points to a world we have never known, and promises a return of that reality over our current and historical despair. This is the song that is Christmas—hope. "The hopes and fears of all the years are met in Thee tonight." The song we sing at Christmas is that of strangers in a strange land. "He came to his own, and his own knew him not." But it is not a song of lament and loss, but rather of longing and of promise. This mysterious tune, odd and out of place, heralds a world not of our making but rather one made through him, one outside our experience but hidden in our hearts.

In the manger lies an ancient dream, a melody composed at the beginning of time, remembered only in snatches and pieces. But now, in Christ, it comes into its own, fully scored and orchestrated. The hope promised from the start appears, and we are called into the chorus. That which was old has become new, that which was in darkness is bathed in light, that which was hopeless now rejoices. This is the song of Christmas.

—David A. Wade

First Sunday After Christmas

Down and Dirty

PSALM 148 • ISAIAH 63:7-9 • HEBREWS 2:10-18 • MATTHEW 2:13-23

THE CHRISTMAS CAROL LYRICS describe "angels we have heard on high," but the more accurate point seems to be that not just angels but God as well has always gotten down and dirty. It was the angel of God's presence that sustained and redeemed the people of Israel throughout their rough and rocky history—not a remote-controlled spiritual fix-it job, but hands reaching down into the rubble of Israel's (often self-imposed) failures to pick them up and carry them on.

We forget sometimes that the people in scriptures were real, once-upon-a-time, not just Bible character cutouts moving stiffly across a pastel-colored map of the Holy Land. Maybe some details have gotten shuffled with the retelling of the stores, but nonetheless at some point there were real hearts pumping fast with fear and joy, hands doing their work, minds fretting and plotting. Matthew has neatly summarized the escape of Mary, Joseph and Jesus to Egypt and their return to Nazareth so that it seems to be no more fuss than an impromputu trip to the park But slow it down, fill in the gaps with the worries Mary and Joseph must have had. How will we live, eat, and shelter ourselves in Egypt? How will we protect our boy from all the dangers of the world? Will we make it safely?

When scripture proclaims God's presence in our affliction and our suffering, it's not just a presence in our "spiritual" struggles—it's God-with-us in daily life, whether it's filled with the routine or the extraordinary, small victories or great tragedies. The incarnation of Jesus is a mystery, surely, but it is a mud-splattered and humble mystery.

We may think the only trick is to remember and believe in the grandeur of God, the miracles, the road to Damascus conversions, and the angelic choirs. Perhaps the harder trick is to remember and believe in the steady, sturdy part of salvation, the work-roughened hands holding us up.

—Julie Polter

The Flickering Light of Epiphany

*A*s the winter yellow grass holds up gray-black branches, silently testifying to the annual season of death, we make our way with the flickering light of Epiphany. We still hold one arm around unconsolable Rachel, whose arms are empty and whose tear-filled eyes are looking back over her shoulder. Another arm is wrapped around Mary, whose arms are filled with the fragile promise of new life, and whose hopeful eyes are looking ahead. This journey into Epiphany is made slowly, for neither Sister Grief nor Sister Promise can walk quickly.

Christmas proclaimed the presence of the light. Epiphany calls us to spread the light on the journey. Epiphany means "manifestation." We see the light of Christ as it is manifest from the crib of Jesus in Bethlehem to all the nations. "A light for revelation to the Gentiles" (Luke 2:32) is the Bible's shorthand way of saying that Christ's mission is to the whole world. Epiphany stories reach out to the world through the coming of the Magi, Jesus' baptism by John, the call of the first disciples, and the beginning of Jesus' ministry.

The welcome mat is set out. The front porch light is left on to welcome foreigners, local fishermen, city priests, Roman soldiers, and Greek tourists. There are no limits placed on this love born at Christmas.

—Nancy Hastings Sehested

Epiphany Sunday

God's Glory Still

PSALM 72:1-14 • ISAIAH 60:1-6 • EPHESIANS 3:1-12 • MATTHEW 2:1-12

BROTHER JOHN is a 73-year-old friar who escaped World War II Poland by walking cross-country on bare and bleeding feet. He was a laborer in Hitler's Germany, where he was paradoxically safe, warm, and fed—and where he outwitted the authorities repeatedly.

He told me one day about walking through a devastated city after the Allied carpet bombings. It was all rubble, he said, and there was a thick mud that stuck to his boots, so that every few steps he had to stop and scrape it off. There was a stench. Eventually he realized that he was walking on human debris: the remains of people killed in the bombings. Almost nothing could be recognized, just a piece of bone here and there.

Brother John said that he never forgot that experience: "They were human beings too," he said. "They were people like us."

At Epiphany we remember that we are all human beings together, and all made in God's image. The glory shining in the Christ child, beckoning the wise; the glory smashed into the mud under Brother John's feet—the same glory. God's image, still being smashed, still there to be recognized.

—Shelley Douglass

First Sunday After Epiphany

Drenched in God

PSALM 29 • ISAIAH 42:1-9 • ACTS 10:34-43 • MATTHEW 3:13-17

IN MY TEXAS BAPTIST Sunday school class, several of us third graders surmised that Jesus was a Baptist because John the "Baptist" baptized him. Such an assertion fit well within a religious ghetto that encouraged the claim that we Baptists were the best of all the rest. What further proof did we need than for Jesus to be one of us? Years later, my enlightened seminary education confirmed my earlier Sunday school insight. Jesus' baptism was a sign that he was "one of us" all right. He was one of us Gentiles, an outsider to the faith.

Jesus was a full-blooded Jew. As a Jew, his baptism by John carried significant political implications. Long before John, baptism was practiced as a ritual cleansing for Gentile converts to Judaism. John the Baptist blustered on the scene with a prophetic word that all God's people, Jews and Gentiles, needed the baptism of repentance. For Jesus to be baptized by John was a sign that declared the tearing down of the walls of religious nationalism and elitism. Jesus was one of us, one of us Jews and one of us Gentiles, who was baptized into God's movement of peace and justice for all.

With Jesus' baptism, his public ministry began. The event acted as his service of ordination and installation. Jesus received affirmation as God's beloved, God's chosen one. He also received the call and commission to his prophetic ministry empowered by the Holy Spirit. With one sweep of the holy hand, Jesus was touched with divine approval and appointment. His baptism was not a private act for private purification or private devotions. It was public, publicly recognizing and affirming immersion in the historic family of God.

Immersion is the preferred method for baptism among the Baptist branch of Christendom. I know that it is not the amount of water that is the saving grace. However, I must admit that I favor the excess of water among Baptists.

To be seized as one of God's beloved sons and daughters is to be drenched in God. Baptism confirms our chosenness as well as our vocation, buried with Christ in the likeness of his death, and risen with Christ in the likeness of his resurrection. It is grace that propels us to fulfill our vocation as Christ's resurrection people. As baptized believers, we follow the Christ who "does not fail or get discouraged until justice has been established in the Earth" (Isaiah 42:4). Baptism is an intimate sign and wonder that God has not yet given up on us or this world.

—Nancy Hastings Sehested

Second Sunday After Epiphany

Beholding the Lamb of God

PSALM 40:1-11 • ISAIAH 49:1-7 • 1 CORINTHIANS 1:1-9 • JOHN 1:29-42

I KEEP THINKING of Christmas and the glory of God's image in us, the incarnation among us. "Look, here is the Lamb of God!" (John 1:29).

Alex came to Mary's House for two weeks. His caregiver was on vacation and he stayed with us during the hottest part of Alabama's summer, nurses attending him 24 hours a day. Alex is 9. He is a spina bifida child and cannot see or control his movements; he is fed through a tube, and he spends his days sitting in a wheelchair or an infant seat. "Look, here is the lamb of God!"

Before Alex arrived, I wondered how I would feel about him, how it would be to have someone so handicapped here at the house. As Alex stayed and we came to know him, I realized that here indeed was a lamb of God.

Alex's face would shine when he heard a familiar voice, felt a gentle touch. He loved music, and would be perfectly still for hours at a time listening to tapes. He especially liked Johnny Clegg and Savuka. When he was unhappy or in pain Alex had a way of letting us know, with moans and cries that reminded me of the psalmists. When he was happy his face radiated his joy.

Alex was a lamb of God in the simplicity of his suffering and his joy. I wonder how many times I have missed God's lambs because I haven't looked carefully for them. How many times have I kept looking, when Jesus was right in front of me? I want to be like Peter, a rock—but like Peter, I turn away from the suffering Jesus.

—Shelley Douglass

Third Sunday After Epiphany

Repeated Repentance

PSALM 27:1, 4-9 • ISAIAH 9:1-7 • 1 CORINTHIANS 1:10-18 • MATTHEW 4:12-23

"REPENT," JESUS SAID. "Drop everything and follow me. The kingdom of heaven—the reign of God—is at hand." Sometimes we do just that. After we do it, we begin to argue about who has the right road map, and where this realm is, and what it looks like, and what we need to take with us. Who baptized you, and whose teaching did you receive? Not as good as mine! I'm closer to God than you are!

What happens to the first impulse to follow where we are led, not to let anything get in the way? Repentance is always needed, daily. (Hourly, even.) I find that I'm frequently distracted from God's work, from God's image in my neighbor, by my own selfishness and my own prejudices. Jesus is always calling me back to repent, to follow, to open my eyes as Brother John did, and see the image of God in my enemy, in my friend—in the one baptized by a different teacher.

—Shelley Douglass

Fourth Sunday After Epiphany

The Sunday before Ash Wednesday is Transfiguration Sunday. If Ash Wednesday falls in this week, skip to the readings for Transfiguration Sunday, page 16.

Being Blessed

PSALM 15 • MICAH 6:1-8 • 1 CORINTHIANS 1:18-31 • MATTHEW 5:1-12

THE MOST POWERFUL LIFE at Mary's House so far was one that ended here. Laura died just over a year ago, just after Christmas, in one of our upstairs rooms. In Laura these scriptures were lived out before my eyes each day, the weak and foolish becoming the strong and wise in the process of dying.

Laura came to us an angry street addict and prostitute, her face turned to the wall, her hand raised against everyone. No one, nothing, could please her. Laura was touched by God's saving power, by the love of community, and when she left us she was at home, at peace. In her life the mourner was indeed comforted, the thirst for righteousness began to be satisfied, the poor in spirit came into the kindom of heaven.

It was nothing we did. It was God's doing. God gave her to us, and God gave us eyes to see the gift and hearts to accept it joyfully.

When I read the beatitudes, or when I read these passages from Paul, I think of the hard and strange things God asks of us sometimes: going to jail, nursing someone with Alzheimer's or AIDS, accompanying people to court, changing diapers, and cooking meals and washing floors! I think of the blessings that are contained in these tasks, the transformation of suffering into joy, so that we embrace the odious gratefully, and wonder why people are surprised.

I think of Brother John, of Alex, of Laura, of myself, and realize that in our struggles and our sufferings we are somehow caught up in God's wisdom. We are indeed blessed.

—Shelley Douglass

Fifth Sunday After Epiphany

The Sunday before Ash Wednesday is Transfiguration Sunday. If Ash Wednesday falls in this week, skip to the readings for Transfiguration Sunday, page 16.

If the Salt Has Lost Its Savor

PSALM 112 • ISAIAH 58:1-12 • 1 CORINTHIANS 2:1-16 • MATTHEW 5:13-20

"YOU ARE THE SALT of the earth. But if the salt has lost its savor, with what will it be salted? It is good for nothing and is thrown out and trampled underfoot by humanity" (Matthew 5:13).

In today's gospel from Matthew, whom does Jesus mean by "the salt of the earth"? And what is the savor without which the salt becomes good for nothing?

The preceding verses of the Sermon on the Mount provide the key: "Blessed are those who are persecuted for righteousness' sake, for theirs is the reign of heaven. Blessed are you when people revile you and persecute you and utter all kinds of evil against you falsely on my account. Rejoice and be glad..." (Matthew 5:10-12).

When we understand the salt of the earth in this context, do we begin to lose our taste for it?

The salt of the earth are those who are persecuted for their active pursuit of justice. The salt's savor is action that inevitably provokes suffering on the actor. Suffering for justice, suffering for Jesus' sake, suffering for the Beloved Community.

"You"—we—are expected to be the salt of the earth: the persecuted for the sake of justice. Without the savor of active love and suffering, we are good...for nothing. Thrown out and trampled underfoot by humanity.

Is that a ruthless perspective from a source where we'd prefer a soft glow on faith?

Jesus' modern disciple Mahatma Gandhi had a similar emphasis on salt and suffering love. Gandhi identified Britain's monopoly on salt as a symbolic key to India's freedom. Every villager needed salt. By marching to the sea and breaking the imperial law by picking up a pinch of salt, Gandhi chose persecution, redemptive suffering, and freedom. His people followed his example. Millions of them made, bought, and sold salt in defiance of British law. Hundreds were beaten as they advanced on salt works, tens of thousands including Gandhi were jailed, and Britain's rule over India was in effect ended.

On the eve of this freedom campaign, Gandhi said, "Mass civil disobedience will not come if those who have been hitherto the loudest in their cry for liberty have no action in them. If the salt loses its savor, wherewith shall it be salted?"

—Jim Douglass

Sixth Sunday After Epiphany

The Sunday before Ash Wednesday is Transfiguration Sunday. If Ash Wednesday falls in this week, skip to the readings for Transfiguration Sunday, page 16.

Is My Anger Innocent?

PSALM 119:1-8 • DEUTERONOMY 30:15-20 • 1 CORINTHIANS 3:1-9 • MATTHEW 5:21-37

NOTHING TESTS ONE'S faith more than belonging to a community of faith. In today's readings Paul and Jesus speak to the issue of conflict, especially in faith communities.

For Paul, the question arises from one leader being set off against another: "One says, 'I belong to Paul [substitute here the name of a leader you prefer, A],' and another, 'I belong to Apollos [and here the name of a competing leader, B]'....What then is Apollos [leader B]? What is Paul [leader A]? Servants through whom you came to believe, as the Lord assigned to each. 'A' planted, 'B' watered, but God gave the growth. So neither the one who plants nor the one who waters is anything, but only God who gives the growth" (1 Corinthians 3:4-7).

Jesus raises the stakes of conflict by (absurdly?) linking murder with anger: "You have heard that it was said to those of ancient times, 'You shall not murder'; and 'whoever murders shall be liable to judgment.' But I say to you that if you are angry with a brother or sister, you will be liable to judgment" (Matthew 5:21-22).

Can we believe it? Judgment on our anger? That makes me angry! Wasn't Jesus angry himself? Who is he to judge?

In a recent discussion of youth homicides, it was pointed out that an insult which a generation ago might have provoked a counterinsult or a fistfight may now inspire a gunshot. We are living in a world where anger passes quickly into murder, and not only among armed teen-agers.

In a country possessed by its guns, is my anger innocuous?

Jesus' way out of the impasse puts the need for a disarming reconciliation before everything—before worship and before dealing with the question of who exactly is to blame in a conflict: "So when you are offering your gift at the altar, if you remember that your brother or sister has something against you, leave your gift there before the altar and go; first be reconciled to your brother or sister, and then come and offer your gift" (Matthew 5:23-24).

—Jim Douglass

Seventh Sunday After Epiphany

The Sunday before Ash Wednesday is Transfiguration Sunday. If Ash Wednesday falls in this week, skip to the readings for Transfiguration Sunday, page 16.

The Foolishness of God

PSALM 119:33-40 • LEVITICUS 19:1-2, 9-18 • 1 CORINTHIANS 3:10-11, 16-23
• MATTHEW 5:38-48

AS PAUL PUTS IT, the gospel passage for today is filled with the "foolishness" of God: Turn the other cheek? Hand over your cloak? Walk the extra mile? What is this madness?

One thing it's not: Jesus isn't talking martyrdom here (although that was the fate of a number of his hearers). What he's offering is transformation, both practical and theological. He's calling us to active, creative, nonviolent resistance. As Walter Wink points out in his book *Engaging the Powers*, Jesus is offering a way for poor, humiliated people to take the initiative against their oppressors, allowing them to restore a sense of dignity while putting their oppressors off balance—and at the same time offering them opportunities for conversion.

If that isn't enough, Jesus is also transforming the very definition of "us and them." For ancient peoples—and perhaps even more so for the Hebrews—the world was divided into the people of God and the "other," the sacred and the profane. The instructions in Leviticus are given "to the whole Israelite community" (19:2) and are primarily (but not exclusively, as we will see) about how to deal with family, neighbors, and tribe. Don't "defraud your neighbor" or "slander your kin," "hate your sibling" or "bear a grudge against any of your people."

Jesus affirms the love of neighbor, but takes it a colossal step further: Love (even) your enemies, that you may be children of God—who, after all, is creator and lord of all people, bad and good, just and unjust. With that, Jesus takes the concept of "our people" and expands it to include all the children of God—that is, he makes sisters and brothers of all peoples.

But back to Leviticus. There's something else here that can't be ignored. God does more than describe "gleaning," where the poor can collect the leftovers from the harvest. The mandate is that producers *intentionally* leave a portion for the benefit of those in need. The assumption is that they have a right to sustenance; this is about justice, not charity.

And here's another surprise: It's not just the poor among "thy people" that have a claim to a portion of the harvest, but also the alien, the foreigner. God's bounty extends beyond human boundaries; the lines that Jesus later obliterates are already being stretched. The "wisdom of the world" yields to the perfection of God.   **—Jim Rice**

Eighth Sunday After Epiphany

The Sunday before Ash Wednesday is Transfiguration Sunday. If Ash Wednesday falls in this week, skip to the readings for Transfiguration Sunday, page 16.

A New Set of Priorities

PSALM 131 • ISAIAH 49:8-16 • 1 CORINTHIANS 4:1-5 • MATTHEW 6:24-34

RIGHT AT THE HEART of Jesus' greatest sermon lies this profound—and oft-trivialized—passage. Despite its context and its clarity, not many of us seem to take this message too seriously. It is, we are told, "poetic" imagery, or perhaps an "impossible ideal," not attuned to our modern sensibilities or realistic for those of us living in the fast-moving '90s. Who, after all, could live like the birds of the air or the lilies of the field?

But like most hard sayings, we ignore this wisdom at our own peril. The passage is as much a pastoral word about how to achieve quiet of the soul (Psalm 131:2) as it is a laying down of the law (although it is that, too).

We are not, the gospel says, to "serve" wealth—if we do, we cannot also serve God. To serve wealth is to be a slave to it, to be in bondage to it. Jesus illustrates with metaphors from the natural world—birds and lilies most certainly don't aspire after material things in the way humans do. It is the non-Jews, the pagans, who "strive for" these things; people of faith have (or ought to have) a different set of priorities.

Perhaps the emphasis here should be on the striving. The root of the Greek word (*epizeteo*) connotes a craving, almost an obsession with the things of mammon. Jesus is aware, of course, that we have material needs (Matthew 6:32), but his point is one of priority: We are to seek *first* the kingdom of God and its righteousness. We are called, in fact, to strive for, to crave, the things of God. The rest will then be added unto us.

The passage ends with an exhortation straight out of the 12-step program: One day at a time. Most contemporary translations render Jesus' words as "do not worry about tomorrow" because "today's trouble is enough for today" (6:34). In the King James version ("Take therefore no thought for the morrow....Sufficient unto the day is the evil thereof"), Jesus acknowledges the presence of evil—which carries more spiritual weight than "troubles"—but still calls us not to be anxious or distracted from our focus on God.

And lest in the midst of troubles we fear that God has forsaken us, Isaiah reminds us that God's love is as unfailing as a woman's for her nursing child, and more (Isaiah 49:15). With that kind of steadfast care, what reason have we to be anxious?

—Jim Rice

Transfiguration Sunday
(Sunday before Ash Wednesday)

God's Turning Point

PSALM 99 • EXODUS 24:12-18 • 2 PETER 1:16-21 • MATTHEW 17:1-9

THE TRANSFIGURATION IS God's turning point. In each of the synoptic gospels, after Jesus predicts his death and prescribes the way of the cross for his disciples, he takes Peter, James, and John up the mountain. There God confirms in a vision Jesus' decision to walk into suffering and death.

As Jesus is transfigured in clothing "white like the light," a symbol that fuses martyrdom and divinity, a bright cloud overshadows him, Moses, and Elijah. Through it God says, "This is my Son, the Beloved; with him I am well pleased; listen to him!" (Matthew 17:5).

Listen to him, and see the transfiguration.

Listen to him in the soldier who turns away from war; see the transfiguration.

Listen to him in the unmarried woman who chooses to give birth to her child; see the transfiguration.

Listen to him in the citizen who refuses to pay taxes that pay for nuclear weapons; see the transfiguration.

Listen to him in all who choose their own suffering and death for the sake of others' lives; see the transfiguration.

The transfiguration is God's turning point in Jesus' story and our story. It is God's confirmation in history that suffering love is a divine choice. Humanity's inner life in God is revealed in the light that extends down the mountain to the cross.

Matthew says that as they were coming down that mountain, Jesus ordered Peter, James, and John, "Tell no one about the vision until after the Human Being has been raised from the dead" (Matthew 17:9).

Only by living through the suffering, death, and raised life of Jesus would the disciples be able to say with understanding what they had experienced on the mountain.

Listen to him. And see the light of God in a new humanity. **—Jim Douglass**

The Cross of Forgiveness

These reflections cover Lent, Holy Week, and several weeks after Easter—times ripe for self-reflection and repentance in our tradition. In the midst of our Holy Week readings, there is an evil legacy identified with one verse in particular—from Palm Sunday's gospel: "And all the people answered, 'His blood be upon us and upon our children!'" (Matthew 27:25).

Scholars have suggested that the author of this gospel molded his passion narrative, and composed this verse in particular, to dramatize a theological explanation in the 80s for the destruction of Jerusalem in the year 70. We know the centuries-long descent into the night of Auschwitz which the deeper twisting of that theology was used to justify. If this passage is read aloud on Palm Sunday without acknowledging its evil history, we are once again complicit in the Holocaust.

Yet the cross is the place at which Romans, Judeans, and today Americans and all others have been forgiven our (ongoing) ways of killing: "Father, forgive them for they know not what they are doing" (Luke 23:34). Certain manuscripts lack this verse. Is it because copyists, sure of God's judgment on someone, couldn't believe Jesus said it?

Can we pray Jesus' prayer of total forgiveness? Or are we as hard of hearing as his early disciples when he tells us that loving our enemies is precisely what makes us children of our enemy-loving God (Luke 6:35)?

—Jim and Shelley Douglass

First Sunday of Lent

In the Wilderness With Jesus

PSALM 32 • GENESIS 2:15-17; 3:1-7 • ROMANS 5:12-19 • MATTHEW 4:1-11

LENT IS A WALK INTO the wilderness with Jesus. In today's gospel, Jesus' 40 days in the wilderness symbolize Israel's 40 years, and however long our wilderness may last. The scriptures that Jesus cites in response to the devil's temptations refer back to Israel's trials...and ahead to ours.

Jesus' counter to the first temptation, to turn stones into bread, is, "One does not live by bread alone, but by every word that comes from the mouth of God" (Matthew 4:4). The way to our daily bread (Israel's manna in the wilderness) is to follow God's will in the desert—40 years of prayer, pilgrimage, and patience.

Our first temptation is to escape hunger by accepting whatever compromise is necessary for the security of turning stones into bread. An economics of Providence is in any case, Satan argues, insane.

The devil's second proposal is, "If you are the son of God, throw yourself down [from the pinnacle of the temple]," relying on God's angels "to bear you up" (Matthew 4:6). In Matthew's gospel this challenge foreshadows the mockery of the chief priests, scribes, and elders at the cross: "...let him come down from the cross now, and we will believe in him. He trusts in God; let God deliver him now, if he wants to; for he said, 'I am God's Son'" (Matthew 27:42-43). But God's way of transformation is not spectacle but the patient, enduring suffering of the wilderness and the cross.

Our second temptation is to seek God in the spectacular, not in suffering and dying.

Jesus' and our third temptation is to power: "all the kingdoms of the world." If we will only worship the voice behind that power, "all these I will give you" (Matthew 4:8-9).

Accept the military contract....
Swear to the loyalty oath....
Support the execution....
Trash the poor....
March to the beat of war drums....
"And all these I will give you."

But Jesus said, "Away with you, Satan! for it is written, 'Worship the Lord your God, and serve only God'" (Matthew 4:10). Then the tempter of security, spectacle, and power left him—and will leave us as well, if we pass through that wilderness with Jesus and give the same response.

"And suddenly angels came and waited on him" (Matthew 4:11).

We can expect their help, too.

—Jim Douglass

Second Sunday of Lent

"...that the world through him might be saved."

PSALM 121 • GENESIS 12:1-4 • ROMANS 4:1-5, 13-17 • JOHN 3:1-17

WHAT DOES IT MEAN to be saved? In John's gospel the question of sight is crucial. "Come and see!" Jesus invites. "You do not see!" he mourns. "We speak of what we have seen," says John's Jesus, "and you do not receive our testimony." Perhaps to be saved means to see anew, with this new sight given by a new birth.

Nicodemus, a leader of Israel, does not see or understand. He misses the point.

"You are a teacher from God," he says. "We know, because we have seen your signs." What signs? Before this chapter in the gospel, Jesus has been baptized by John, has called some disciples, has attended the Cana wedding, and has cleansed the temple. Nicodemus, having alluded to these signs that are intensely pragmatic, ignores them for an abstract discussion about second birth. Why? Perhaps because these signs point to a vision he does not really want to accept: a vision of justice and compassion and of the doing of God's will before all else.

To be born anew through the Spirit means to begin to see with the eyes of Christ, not to condemn but to save. How many times do we look aside and ignore money-changers in our temples because we don't want to be troubled? And how many times do we look with eyes of judgment rather than compassion at our sisters and brothers?

—Jim Douglass

Third Sunday of Lent

The Samaritan Apostle

PSALM 95 • EXODUS 17:1-7 • ROMANS 5:1-11 • JOHN 4:5-42

PREACHERS AND BIBLICAL SCHOLARS have treated the Samaritan woman like another woman gone wrong. After all, didn't Jesus tell her, "You have had five husbands, and the one you have now is not your husband."

But the Samaritan woman is a spokesperson for her people. She speaks eloquently as a national theologian on behalf of "our ancestors" to a man she sees as a representative of his people. They address each other in the Greek plural.

She: "*You people* say that the place where it is necessary to worship is in Jerusalem."

He: "The hour is coming when neither on this mountain nor in Jerusalem will *you people* worship...."

In light of her representative nature and their dialogue on nationalism and worship, who might the five former husbands be?

Could Jesus be alluding not to her personal sex life but to Samaria's past, in which five nations have colonized and intermarried with Samaritans (2 Kings 17:24-34)? And could "the one you have now who is not your husband" in fact be Rome, a colonial power with whom the Samaritans lived (more intimately than with Judeans) but did not intermarry as much as with the previous five?

The author of the fourth gospel identifies this Samaritan woman as the first apostle to her people. Like the apostles in the synoptic gospels who left nets, boats, parents, and a tax station, the Samaritan woman leaves her water jar at the well and goes off to evangelize her city.

But then might not Jesus' scandalized male disciples, astonished to find him speaking with a woman, be the author's allusion to her own church and some of its male members' wonderment at the women disciples alongside them to whom Jesus was continuing to speak?

Who in fact is the anonymous author of this fourth gospel in which a Samaritan woman, Martha and Mary, and Mary Magdalene have such leading roles and such extraordinary conversations with Jesus? Would a male disciple have even been able to write such dialogues?

Or in terms of a gospel proclaimed by the Samaritan apostle, are such limits just as outdated as the division between Judeans and Samaritans?

—Jim Douglass

Fourth Sunday of Lent

"Surely we are not blind, are we?"

PSALM 23 • 1 SAMUEL 16:1-13 • EPHESIANS 5:8-14 • JOHN 9:1-41

THE FORMERLY BLIND MAN makes it very simple: I was born blind, and now I see! Having experienced this miracle of healing, he cannot fathom why the leaders of the people quibble over inessentials—why he was born blind, that he was healed on the Sabbath. God's action breaking into history is no respecter of human laws, and the crucial point is simply this: I SEE!

This sight that we gain through Jesus is a dangerous thing. In John's gospel we see the blind man's parents distancing themselves from him because to claim Jesus—to see him as Lord—is to be declared a sinner by the community, and forced out of the synagogue. At the same time, Jesus (the Christian community) declares that if we CLAIM sight, we will be judged as though we do in fact see. To claim Jesus is to open ourselves to Jesus' message—from that point on, our own lives should begin to reveal the same signs seen in Jesus' life. Dangerous indeed.

As we walk through this Lent we ask ourselves a dual question: How often do I quibble with inessentials to avoid facing the gospel? And how often does my vision of Jesus become clouded over by selfishness, by our culture, by fear—so that though I claim sight I am in fact still blind?

—Shelley Douglass

Fifth Sunday of Lent

Resurrection Again

PSALM 130 • EZEKIEL 37:1-14 • ROMANS 8:6-11 • JOHN 11:1-45

DEATH. DRY BONES in Ezekiel's valley. Can these bones live? Stench rising from Lazarus' tomb. "Lord, if you had been here, my brother would not have died." And Jesus' response to Martha: "Your brother will rise again."

Martha misunderstands: "I know that he will rise again in the resurrection on the last day."

But Jesus means life for Lazarus now: "I am the resurrection and the life. Those who believe in me, even though they die, will live, and everyone who lives and believes in me will never die. Do you believe this?"

Do we believe this? Do we believe in him who is one in love with the One who so loved the world as to send him? Do we believe in the resurrection and the life now?

Do we believe what happens next, that Jesus' faithful love brings life out of a four-day-old corpse? Do we believe that God's faithful love in us through Jesus can do the same thing, and even more?

Fast forward to Jesus' promise at John 14:12: "Very truly, I tell you, the one who believes in me will also do the works that I do and, in fact, will do greater works than these, because I am going to the father."

The site identified as the tomb of Lazarus is in the Palestinian village El 'Eizariya, identified with Bethany, on the outskirts of Jerusalem. One day I went down the tomb's almost vertical shaft. In the shadows at the bottom of the rock pit, I imagined the depth of faithful love necessary to bring life out of the decomposing corpse of my life, country, and world.

And when even the corpse seems to have rotted away, as in the decades since Martin Luther King Jr.'s assassination, can these dry bones still live?

Because Jesus went to the One who is Love—and into the center of our communities of faith—we can love with his love, the Spirit, and "do greater works than these."

Imagine what those might be. Resurrection. Here and now.

"I *am* the resurrection and the life."

Do we believe this?

—Jim Douglass

Palm Sunday

"You have said so."

PSALM 31:9-16 • ISAIAH 50:4-9 • PHILIPPIANS 2:5-11 • MATTHEW 26:14-27:66

MUCH OF THIS PASSION Sunday gospel revolves around questions of responsibility. Within the gospel itself Jesus repeatedly reminds people of their responsibility for their actions: "You have said so!" He says this to both Judas and Pilate.

Jesus stands in marked contrast to those who evade consequences. He does not argue against his accusers; he claims his truth and his actions. How can he do this? Not, I think, because he knows that he is God and will suffer and rise again. He is able to claim his actions for a much more human, perhaps more painful, reason: He has accepted his own death.

In the garden at Gethsemani, Jesus faces the consequences of living the life he has been called to live. He agonizes over his impending arrest and execution—and then accepts them. In accepting this ultimate price, death, he becomes free to be fearless and to acknowledge his own identity and his history.

Other characters in this narrative refuse their responsibility: Judas, who betrays Jesus and then commits suicide; Pilate, who allows an unjust execution to take place; Peter, who denies his leader and Lord. In each case, fear of death, disgrace, humiliation, or responsibility itself prevents the doing of right. In Judas' case I wonder if the terror of facing his own responsibility for an innocent death did not ultimately lead, not to repentance, but to annihilation.

I think of my own refusal to accept responsibility, and of the pain that can cause others, and sometimes myself. As we pass through this Holy Week into Easter, I pray for the grace to accept my own coming death so that when the price must be paid I can offer it freely.

—Shelley Douglass

Easter Sunday

Mary and the Corpse

PSALM 118:1-2, 14-24 • ACTS 10:34-43 • COLOSSIANS 3:1-4 • JOHN 20:1-18

IN THE 20TH CHAPTER of the fourth gospel, Mary Magdalene is dismayed by the absence of Jesus' dead body. "They," she keeps repeating, "have taken away my Lord, and I do not know where they have laid him." Her obsession with a missing corpse carries over even to her encounter with the living Jesus. "Stop clinging to me!" he tells her.

Don't sentimentalize Mary. She is one of the oppressed seeking the body of her teacher who was executed by a hated colonial power and its client rulers. I have met quiet, determined women in similar circumstances. Had Mary in fact discovered a dead body, it could have led to anything. In Belgrade, Zagreb, and Sarajevo over the past two years, I have seen the victim's grave become the blessed point of departure for the next murder. Beloved corpses function as inspirations for slaughter. The death penalty lies in waiting in our hearts.

Theological propaganda has isolated the resurrection of Jesus from the event it followed. The crucifixion was an atrocity, standing for all the atrocities committed against loved ones from then until now. We are liberated from bondage to that parade of corpses by the resurrection of all our beloved victims into the forgiveness of the living God.

—Jim Douglass

Second Sunday of Easter

"Blessed are you who have not seen, but have believed."

PSALM 16 • ACTS 2:14, 22-32 • 1 PETER 1:3-9 • JOHN 20:19-31

THIS BLESSING IS FOR US: We are they who have not seen the physical being of the Lord, yet have come to believe, and so are blessed. The paradox here is similar to others Jesus expounds in the gospel: Having believed without seeing, we now see with the sight of believers.

Even in the earliest days of the church there were those who had seen, and those like Thomas, who had not. As time went by, the number of those who had not seen grew, and yet the presence of Christ and the Spirit enabled them to see. Those early saints accepted the consequences of their faith-given sight, often going to death for their belief in Jesus' Lordship.

It should be noted that the consequences of this Lordship were many: the sharing of one's goods, living in community, remaining in prayer, and—though not listed in Acts—refusal of incense to the emperor and of military service. All this accepted by those who had not seen, but who, like us, had experienced the Lord. The saints have for centuries made the Lord present to us, and we in turn in our own small ways make the Lord present to others.

I saw with my own eyes the Selma to Montgomery march; I experienced the sacrificial love of people jailed for peace; I heard with my own ears the voices of women begin to reflect their experiences; I share the bread of the poor, the tears of the forgiven, the joy of the healed. I see daily the presence of the Lord and of God's kindom. He is risen indeed.

—Jim Douglass

Third Sunday of Easter

The Way to Emmaus

PSALM 116:1-4, 12-19 • ACTS 2:14, 36-41 • 1 PETER 1:17-23 • LUKE 24:13-35

MODERN SCHOLARS HAVE DEBATED inconclusively the physical location of the Emmaus in Luke's resurrection story. But is there a symbolic intent in the gospel's identification of this village?

Judas Maccabeus led his rebel army to a historic victory over Gentile forces at Emmaus, according to the book of 1 Maccabees (3:40, 57; 4:1-15). This popular nationalistic text of Jesus' time cites Judas' speech to his soldiers, urging them to cry to heaven that God crush the enemy army lying before them at Emmaus: "Then all the Gentiles will know that there is one who saves and liberates Israel" (1 Maccabees 4:11).

On their way to Emmaus, the disciples explain to Jesus in similar terms why they are despairing over their dead Jesus: "But we had hoped that he was the one to liberate Israel" (Luke 24:21).

A little more than a generation earlier, the hope to liberate Israel had also motivated a guerrilla attack on a Roman company at Emmaus by the popularly acclaimed king Athronges. In retaliation, Roman legions burned Emmaus (Josephus, *Judean Wars* 2,4,3; 2,5,1). Jesus warns repeatedly in Luke's gospel of just such a sequence of events for Jerusalem.

The road to Emmaus is the way of messianic violence and self-destruction. So long as the disciples are on it, their eyes are kept from recognizing Jesus, as he tells them why the messiah must suffer and die, not kill.

Only at the table are their eyes finally opened, when his breaking of the bread recalls the recent breaking of his body—and suddenly transforms their violent messianic vision of Emmaus into one of suffering love.

—Jim Douglass

Fourth Sunday of Easter

"The sheep follow him because they know his voice."

PSALM 23 • ACTS 2:42-47 • 1 PETER 2:19-25 • JOHN 10:1-10

TODAY'S GOOD SHEPHERD READING from John follows directly in sequence the fourth lenten reading on the man born blind. In the gospel, 10:1 continues on from Jesus' words in 9:41: "Now that you say 'We see,' your sin remains." In the lectionary, this reading is paired with an idyllic description of the life of the early community, and an exhortation to bear suffering as Jesus did, accepting it out of love and commitment to the truth.

How do we put all this together? The story of the man born blind contrasted the simple truth seen by a newly sighted man with the obfuscations of the learned who wanted to avoid the obvious. Now John's Jesus adds that he is the gate, and that his sheep will follow him out of love for his voice. And out of his love for us, he leads us to have life abundantly.

What will his voice sound like? In 1 Peter, we learn that Jesus suffered abuse unjustly and did not return violence with violence. In Acts, we see the other side of this nonviolent life: the joyful sharing in community love. Jesus' voice is the voice of love in communal sharing, in acceptance of suffering. When a voice leads us to joy through sharing and suffering, we can discern Christ's spirit. Where are those voices heard today? Follow them—they are leading to abundant life.

—Shelley Douglass

Fifth Sunday of Easter

Beyond Believing

PSALM 31:1-8, 15-16 • ACTS 7:55-60 • 1 PETER 2:2-10 • JOHN 14:1-14

THE JOURNEY that we take from betrayal and death to resurrection and new life is a search for community, spiritual vision, and the reconstruction of a new humanity, our own included. To follow Christ is to recognize that we are not captive to the old order; that we are not surrogates of systems that are not working; and that we are not authored by credentials, achievements, or possessions. Rather, to follow Christ is to embrace the path that offers compassion, vulnerability, justice, covenants, and relationships.

In 1 Peter 2:9-10, we are affirmed as the daughters and sons of God, created and shaped in God's image. God's mark and spirit are upon us. We are not God's elite or God's favorite or pampered people, but are claimed by God for God's purposes. This is about obedience and faithfulness.

In Acts 7:55-60, Stephen is stoned for proclaiming that Jesus is the Messiah. The temple leaders, who had condemned Jesus to death for blasphemy, are willing to accept him as the son of Abraham but not as the Son of God. The temple leaders claimed to be believers, but they refused to become disciples.

Believers give lip service without obedience. Belief demands a radical break from life as we know it and live it. It is freedom from our limited perception of things and from the lifestyles and life agenda that those perceptions engender. If God's Spirit is to breathe through us, belief involves a radical break from the gods of militarism, nationalism, and materialism.

However, those who choose to follow in the way of the crucified and risen Sovereign will always be in trouble with the authorities.

Jesus creates a crisis with the authorities because he transcends the rules of the scribes who manage the tax system, the priests who manage the rituals, and the Pharisees who manage the morality. He lived in the world by different definitions. Jesus offers us a new and different notion of what it means to be a powerful person—it is the power to serve but not to master, to die but not to kill, to bring order but not to dominate.

—Yvonne V. Delk

Sixth Sunday of Easter

More Than Charity

PSALM 66:8-20 • ACTS 17:22-31 • 1 PETER 3:13-22 • JOHN 14:15-21

BEING LOVED IS the most powerful motivation in the world. Our experience to love is often shaped by our experience of love. We usually love others as we have been loved.

In John 14:21, Jesus said that his followers show their love by obeying him. Love, however, is more than lovely words. It is commitment and conduct. The demand that we love is more than a call for charity or sloppy sentimentalism. It is to care so deeply that there are things we are simply not willing to live with.

This is a boundless love that reaches out to all. It is an active love—not from a distance, but close at hand. It means opening ourselves up to each other, to be touched and to become vulnerable. It is weeping together, walking together, and witnessing together.

To speak to those living in poverty about the love of God, one must embody the words in action that give answers to the questions arising out of the life they are living now. To speak of the love of God and to act otherwise is to take God's name in vain. To preach good news to the poor is to say by word and deed that God will not leave them in the condition of poverty. Charity is not sufficient; the demand is for justice-based love in which the "first" are to take last place in our consideration, and the "last" first.

In the fourth gospel, when Jesus finishes instructing his disciples, he doesn't give them a law; he gives them a gift of new space, rooted in relationship and covenants. He says, "Love one another." Then he says that when you do so, you had better know that the world is going to hate you. The world cannot tolerate people freely loving each other, because it destroys all the barriers, definitions, and stereotypes that keep us captive and enslaved to the old world order.

—Yvonne V. Delk

Ascension Sunday

In some traditions, the Ascension Sunday texts are used in place of the Seventh Sunday of Easter.

Not of This World

PSALM 47 • ACTS 1:1-11 • EPHESIANS 1:15-23 • LUKE 24:44-53

THE UNFORTUNATELY LOW LEVEL of biblical literacy within many of our churches makes Ascension Sunday a mystery to many Christians. For others in America's spiritual counterculture, the ascension is too often associated with fashionable "near-death experiences" or the so-called "ascended masters."

However, today's scripture readings make it plain who ascended (Psalm 47:5, Acts 1:11), where he went (Psalm 47:8, Ephesians 1:20-21), and—perhaps most important for the church—why (Luke 24:49, Acts 1:8).

Today's believers aren't the first ones perplexed by the act of Jesus rising up through the clouds. After sharing three years of Christ's ministry and witnessing his death and resurrection, the disciples ought to have a clue about the nature of God's kingdom. Still, Luke records them making the same old assumptions that God's reign is equatable with earthly power (Acts 1:6)—an assumption that a good many Christians still make today. Rather than become another clog in the world's political machinery, Jesus Christ ascended "far above all principality, and power, and might, and dominion, and every name that is named, not only in this world, but also in that which is to come" (Ephesians 1:21).

Of course, Christ could have stayed on earth and restored the kingdom of Israel if that had been the plan. God, however, had something much more comprehensive in mind. In passages of both Luke and Acts, Jesus Christ, moments before he ascends from this planet in his bodily form, gives his followers last minute instructions to "wait for the promise of the Father...until you are clothed with power from on high."

Similar to the poignant story of "Jacob's ladder" of Sunday school fame (Genesis 28:12), Christ's ascension opens up a pathway for the "power" of God to flow between heaven and earth. Yet this passage isn't to be traversed by mere angels, as it was in Jacob's time, but by the Holy Ghost—the Spirit of God in believers. Jesus claimed this Spirit to be so important that it was "expedient" for him to leave and make room for it (John 16:7).

In the realized promise of the Holy Spirit, Jesus left his followers with real power effectually to transform themselves and the world; yet not according to the ways of the world, but in harmony with God's true spiritual purpose.

So why are so many of us still standing there looking into the clouds?

—Aaron Gallegos

Seventh Sunday of Easter

In some traditions, the Ascension Sunday texts are used in place of the Seventh Sunday of Easter.

From Private to Public

ISAIAH 68:1-10, 32-35 • ACTS 1:6-14 • 1 PETER 4:12-14; 5:6-11 • JOHN 17:1-11

POWER FROM THE HOLY SPIRIT involved taking the resurrection to the streets. Before the Pentecost experience, the disciples were in the upper room. After, they were in the streets. The Spirit of God was breathing through them and moved them. Acts 1:8 describes an ever-widening circle. The gospel was to spread from the upper room to the streets of Jerusalem, into Judea and Samaria, and finally to the whole world.

The ministry of Jesus was clearly not private, confined to households or even temples. It was in the streets, on the hillsides, in the marketplaces, and throughout all public places where people lived, moved, and had their being. For the most part, Jesus' public ministry was to the crowds and the multitudes of the society—the poor, the diseased and afflicted, tax collectors, and sinners.

We are called to come out from behind our stain-glassed walls and dwell where mothers are struggling, children are hungry, and fathers are jobless. As long as innocent children continue to die in tenement fires; as long as families have to live in winter without heat, hot water, and food; as long as people are forced to live in poverty, the gospel must be heard in judgment against the inhumanity of society.

To be alive to the Spirit is to experience personal and public freedom.

—Yvonne V. Delk

Breathing Space

We are a people on a journey from the season of betrayal and crucifixion to the season of resurrection and Pentecost—a time for receiving the Spirit that will revive, renew, and empower.

For me this is a breathing time—a time for tapping into the open and free space of God's Spirit, where our despair is released into speech, our brokenness healed, our betrayals forgiven, and where there is deep movement from fear and denial toward a new vision of community.

The movement of the Spirit is never private, yet always personal. The power of God's Spirit touches our hearts and longs to be engaged with our bodies and voices in public witness. As you use this lectionary, I suggest the following:
• Center yourself in prayer—"Let thy Spirit breathe through me."
• Engage in a time of meditation and reflection.
• Engage in a time of action that flows out of your meditation.

—Yvonne V. Delk

Pentecost Sunday

Standing Together

PSALM 104:24-35 • ACTS 2:1-21 • 1 CORINTHIANS 12:2-13 • JOHN 7:37-39

ACTS 2:1 STATES "that when the day of Pentecost had come, they were all together in one place." Significantly, the empowerment of the Holy Spirit took place only after the people were all together. This time the empowerment would not just be for a privileged few, but for all, so that they might then set about building a community of faith and justice.

A divided community undermines the credibility of a message that is to break the barriers of language and nation, gender and race, religion and social class to unify all of God's creation in one human family. However, it is also important to note that themes of both unity and difference are built into the reality of Pentecost.

Standing together in one place did not mean that all were singing the same song or even from the same page. The Pentecost experience revealed that each spoke in their own language, maintaining individual linguistic identities and selfhood. What is important to note here is that they were able to understand each other. This is a partnership model, built upon the recognition that others also know and must be heard. It calls into existence a community where the contributions, capacities, gifts, and talents of all are woven into collective effort.

The presence of the Holy Spirit is an imperative to go out for the sake of inclusivity. We in the West have often reduced the cross and the Holy Spirit to introversion and exclusivity. Even when we have been extroverted in our missionary activity, we have not empowered people to understand the message and power of the gospel in their own languages, but forced them to speak our language as a precondition for their understanding.

Standing together in one place can be interpreted as people working together, speaking together, in order to understand and to be understood, and engaging in covenants for moving toward the city that God intends for all creation. This is truly the new space called forth by Jesus.

—Yvonne V. Delk

Trinity Sunday

Renounce and Enjoy

PSALM 8 • GENESIS 1:1-2:4 • 2 CORINTHIANS 13:11-13 • MATTHEW 28:16-20

PSALM 8'S WONDER at God's creation has been re-created in English by Francis Patrick Sullivan. His final verses read:

> *When I see how the sky*
> *moon and stars*
> *flow from Your fingertips,*
> *what are we,*
> *children's children, that You*
> *bring us up,*
> *not as demigods, but*
> *little less,*
> *as those You can honor*
> *and respect,*
> *charged with creation,*
> *its carpet*
> *of beasts, big, small, wild, tame,*
> *birds aloft,*
> *fish below crisscrossing*
> *the sea roads,*
> *God, our God, beautiful,*
> *everywhere!*
> —*Lyric Psalms: Half a Psalter*, by Francis Patrick Sullivan

Gandhi in effect united the wonder of Psalm 8 with the most fundamental prayer of his life, the *Isha Upanishad*. He did so a few hours before his death, in a conversation with Vincent Sheean.

Gandhi told Sheean, citing the *Isha Upanishad*, "The whole world is the garment of the Lord."

God, our God, beautiful everywhere!

Gandhi added from the same *Upanishad*, "Renounce it, then, and receive it back as the gift of God."

It is a simple and transforming prayer, the revealed secret of Gandhi's life.

Renounce and enjoy.

—Jim Douglass

Everyday Miracles

*T*here's nothing ordinary about what's known in the lectionary as "ordinary time." Not Christmas, not Easter, not Pentecost, but the everyday miracles of God with us, of life on earth.

Everyday evil also, the ongoing oppression of God's children, the anniversary of the bombings of Hiroshima and Nagasaki. Everyday miracles: the human family being fed and healed, corrected and forgiven.
Everyday evil: the human family starving, murdered, suffering, exploited.

Ordinary time is the time when we try to understand and live the teachings of Jesus. Nothing ordinary about that—a lifetime worth of challenges instead.

—Jim and Shelley Douglass

Sunday Between May 29 and June 4

(if after Trinity Sunday)

No Other Gods...

PSALM 46 • GENESIS 6:11-22, 7:24, 8:14-19 • ROMANS 1:16-17, 3:23-31
• MATTHEW 7:21-29

ON THE DAY of the 1993 Los Angeles earthquake, near the end of the summer of the Midwest floods, Pat Robertson suggested these events had occurred because the nation had strayed from its intended path. As a nation we were suffering the consequences.

I was challenged. I disagreed with his examples of waywardness and the vision he painted of God's intended world, yet was drawn to the core of his argument: When we leave our designed path, we suffer...and by extension the world suffers.

But I cannot go far beyond that basic truth. I do not really know what God's righteousness looks like. The God of my mind and heart is far more human, far more petty, and far less sovereign than the God of the Bible. Today's passages remind me—in the voice of Yahweh's roaring waters, David's joyful praise, Jesus' stark proddings, and Paul's emphatic pronouncements—that God alone is God, and that the god I create in my image is a stilted image of the Master of the Universe.

God looks out over creation, sees how far from its original state it has come, and with a heart full of pain grieves having made it in the first place. On comes the deluge and, by an act of God, things are made new and the covenant restored.

In Psalm 46, God, our source of strength and comfort, weaves through the city, never abandoning us. God is again described as active. His acts of desolation are acts of restoration; he destroys the means of destruction.

Jesus' words bite at the heels of our self-reliance and presumed understanding of the way of God. I hear him saying "never claim that you know what it means to know me; obey my commands to love one another; build your lives around that, not around what you can achieve." Another act of desolation, this time destroying our assumptions and judgments.

Paul shifts our image of God and God's righteousness yet again—we are all on equal ground; we have all sinned and fallen short; we are all made new by an act of God, and nothing else.

We live in desperate times, as did Noah, David and the Israelites, the Jews to whom Jesus spoke, and the early church. We have much to despair over, and much abuse to bemoan. And we exhaust ourselves by living as though we were God; as though the whole of creation rests upon our shoulders.

The Hebrew phrasing of "be still (and know that I am God)" can be translated "Enough!" God stops us in our tracks, tells us to let go, and commands us to build our lives on nothing less than the sure foundation of his lovely being. God will be with us in his fashion, which, if I have my eyes open, will bring me to my knees; and God will, we are promised, bring our nation to its knees. **—Kari Jo Verhulst**

Sunday Between June 5 and 11

(if after Trinity Sunday)

Rain and the Dawn

PSALM 33:1-12 • GENESIS 12:1-9 • ROMANS 4:13-25 • MATTHEW 9:9-13, 18-26

I GET UP EARLY and sit in our quiet living room to pray. Most mornings it's dark, and when I sit with my breviary I'm aware of the growing light, the swell of birdsong, sometimes of the rush of rain against the window.

Hopeful readings! Light and the rain come gently, unobtrusively; they come to all.

God, who is merciful, desires mercy. Jesus comes not to the righteous, who don't need him, but to sinners who do. His mercy, like the rain and light, is for everyone. Like rain and light it heals, frees, nourishes, and gives life.

In Matthew we have a healing within a healing. Each one brings new life and hope: to a girl already dead, to a woman who had hemorrhaged for 12 years. Both women, both unclean. Each touched by Jesus or touching him—which would make him in his turn impure. Each healed. Mercy, not righteousness; Jesus is not reported to have purified himself after touching them.

Jesus embodies for us (literally) the radical mercy of God, reaching beyond the boundaries of social sin, disease, even of death, and healing where we are most hurt. Who among us has not felt after years of pain that some wound had healed, some flow of our life's blood stanched? Having felt that, can we deny it to our sisters and brothers? Can we lack hope that the rest of our wounds can be healed?

The earth belongs to God, and God invites us into mercy by extending mercy. We are not ordered to be merciful. We are healed by mercy and left with the light and the rain as our teachers. Be merciful, as God is merciful.

—Shelley Douglass

Sunday Between June 12 and 18

(if after Trinity Sunday)

Another Go at the Gospel

PSALM 116:1-4, 12-19 • GENESIS 8:1-15 • ROMANS 5:1-8 • MATTHEW 9:35-10:23

"PREACH AS YOU GO saying, 'The kingdom of heaven is at hand.' Heal the sick, raise the dead, cleanse lepers, cast out demons" (Matthew 10:7-8).

Jesus' commission to the 12, whom I take as representatives of us all, is in my case a rebuke.

While I have preached that the kingdom of heaven is at hand, I have never had the faith to heal the sick, raise the dead, or cleanse any lepers. Maybe the nearest I have come to casting out demons was to pray uninvited at nuclear weapons bunkers. But again my faith was smaller than a mustard seed. The bombs, and the demonic assumptions behind them, are still there.

Jesus' command that we simply live out our faith, with God doing miracles of healing and exorcism through us, is profoundly disturbing. Jesus says plainly at the heart of the gospels that a nonviolent transformation of reality through a living faith is possible. The reign of God is truly at hand—no farther away than my hand moving this pen, or your hand holding that page. Our faith and our hands equal the means to a new reality.

The best way I have found to bridge Jesus' vision of that reality and my own shallow faith is by Gandhi's "experiments in truth"—or better, "experiments in faith." The truth in question is the faith of the gospel.

One such experiment in faith is to join friends going to Iraq, taking medicines in the hope of saving a few lives and breaking an evil law. If our faith is deep enough, totally reliant on our Loving God, anything is possible. Faith exceeds calculation.

Every experiment in faith is another go at realizing what Jesus said is true.

—Jim Douglass

Sunday Between June 19 and 25

(if after Trinity Sunday)

Walking Into the Wall

PSALM 86:1-10,16-17 • GENESIS 21:8-21 • ROMANS 6:1-11 • MATTHEW 10:24-39

THESE ARE FRIGHTENING READINGS. They prepare us for the Holy Spirit and for God's movement, a movement of mercy and compassion that will put us, like Jeremiah, in conflict with our world.

When we have experienced God's mercy and love, we see those around us with God's loving eyes. We are forced to speak words of justice, words of peace. We have to act on those words.

Somewhere in this process we walk smack into a brick wall: our fear, our friends' opinions, our family's security. Something is too important to risk. A choice: We can be silent and feel our very bones burn with the fire of God until we are misshapen, or we can endure the burning of truth in our selves.

These readings are meant to reassure us, but they fail: Who wants to lay down their life? Baptismal death is comfortably symbolic; we'd prefer to leave it that way.

To REALLY lay down our lives, we risk what is most precious to us. It is a real risk. Marriages end, parents and children are estranged, livelihoods are lost or damaged—not to mention jail sentences served, beatings endured, lives lost. Jesus doesn't promise to keep our lives comfortable. He promises just the opposite: We will walk into the wall.

The comfort is not that we won't die, but that if we die for his sake we will live again. Like Jesus we will live a transformed life. We cannot know as we begin to act what the outcome will be. We can only know that as we respond to the mercy shown us by showing mercy, we invite the death of our former selves. And we believe—sometimes barely—that when the dust has settled we will be acknowledged by Jesus, and will regain our lives.

—Shelley Douglass

Sunday Between June 26 and July 2

"When you need something, just talk to me."

PSALM 13 • GENESIS 22:1-14 • ROMANS 6:12-23 • MATTHEW 10:40-42

"WHOEVER WELCOMES you welcomes me, and whoever welcomes me welcomes the one who sent me" (Matthew 10:40).

Clarice South welcomed everyone, and God has welcomed her.

She died last October in Santa Clara, California, at the age of 90. I had known Clarice South since the 1950s, when her daughter Claire and I went together. In my boarding school years, Mrs. South and her family opened their home to me. The warmth of their lives in my young life was a sustaining, enduring presence.

Decades later when I periodically returned to Santa Clara, it was always a gift to wait expectantly at the door on Fremont Street for what I knew would be Mrs. South's warm welcome. I was never disappointed. She knew how to love.

Claire gave the eulogy at her mother's Mass of the Resurrection last fall. She sketched simply, beautifully the portrait of a woman who to the end of her life loved and served others down to the smallest detail in their lives. God then gave her a wisdom of faithful love that she shared with the group of family and friends gathered around her hospital bedside.

Claire recalled: "Mom exhorted us, 'Keep your faith. Stay close to each other.'

And then she said, 'From now on, when you need something, just talk to me.'"

Like Mrs. South's always welcoming smile at the door, I shall remember especially, through her daughter's eulogy, those final words echoing Jesus.

Keep your faith.

Stay close to each other.

From now on, when you need something, just talk to me.

—Jim Douglass

Sunday Between July 3 and 9

Children Sitting in the Marketplace

PSALM 45:10-17 • GENESIS 24:34-38, 42-49, 58-67 • ROMANS 7:15-25
• MATTHEW 11:16-19, 25-30

I REMEMBER WHEN MY children were little, tired, and cranky. There was literally no way to please them. Whatever I did was wrong and led to tears and tantrums. Neither could they please themselves: crayons broke, shoes stumbled, books tore—all their perfect dreams came to nothing.

I could have a nightmare about it: a hot, sticky, humid day; feeling end-of-the-rope tired; knowing what I want to create—and then a stupid mistake, a word come from nowhere, and all is lost and in ruins. I could have a nightmare, but I don't need to: It happens all too often in real life that the loving gesture hurts, the perfect gift falls flat, and the best hopes and dreams are smashed through my own blindness or lack of care. One very good reason to go slow in a good cause! "I find it to be a law that when I want to do good, evil is close at hand."

So here I am, bearing the burden of my self, my failures, my missteps and misdeeds, nothing right, nothing pleasing. And this man walks up to me and says, "Come to me and learn from me; take my yoke; my burden is light."

A cool washcloth over a dirty face, tears dried, a breath of air, relief. Forgiveness, pardon, healing. The easy yoke, the love that cherishes the broken vessel, and the picture where we went outside the lines. Children can sense it: We are loved. We forget it, and we judge. When I want to do good, evil is near— but love will have the last word.

—Shelley Douglass

Sunday Between July 10 and 16

The Good Soil of Iraq

PSALM 119:105-112 • GENESIS 25:19-34 • ROMANS 8:1-11 • MATTHEW 13:1-9, 18-23

IN JESUS' TIME a yield of seven-and-a-half-fold was an average harvest. A tenfold yield was good. How are we to interpret, then, the harvest from the seeds sown on good soil—a hundredfold, sixty, and thirty?

The sequence of the three failures in the parable sets the stage for a shattering of expectations. The eaten, withered, and choked examples give way to the overwhelming yield of the seeds sown on good ground. The reality of God shatters anything we can expect or even hope for.

When the conclusion of this parable has struck home, it seems I have experienced only the seeds eaten, withered, and choked. Matthew's allegorical interpretation of the failures fits my life only too well. I don't need such examples! But what can I possibly make of a hundredfold harvest? What on earth is Jesus talking about?

I remember a church in Qarah Qosh, in northern Iraq, where I had the grace of praying during a recent Holy Week. In a country devastated by the world's economic sanctions, the people in this village were desperately poor. I saw more than 2,000 of them trying to squeeze into the Syrian-rite Church of the Virgin Mary. Others crowded the windows or peered over one another at the doors. On the steps of the altar, children sat watching and listening, as the priest glided among them.

Then on both Holy Thursday and Good Friday, for three to four hours, the people chanted and sang the words of the gospel back and forth across the packed church, in both Syrian and their native Aramaic. Jesus was there as I had never seen him, from his very language to the pure faces of his people—a people that flowed out from the church beyond counting.

The good soil of Iraq.

—Jim Douglass

Sunday Between July 17 and 23

Groaning for Adoption

PSALM 139:1-12, 23-24 • GENESIS 28:10-19 • ROMANS 8:12-25 • MATTHEW 13:24-30, 36-43

"WE DID NOT RECEIVE a spirit of slavery to fall back into fear, but a spirit of adoption."

"A spirit of adoption": to become one of the family, to be at home. There are relationships in which we're at home, and relationships in which we live in fear. Each of us knows the difference: When our inmost self is affirmed and accepted, we are at home. When we are not accepted, we live in fear, a kind of slavery to someone else's preference, to rules, to caprice. We do not trust because we are not loved.

Paul shows us ourselves and our world trembling on the brink of that knowledge: God knows, accepts, loves, adopts us. We tend to think of loving as hard work, but being loved is hard work, too, a discipline of trust. And knowing ourselves to be loved is a gift of grace that transforms our lives and makes us, in our turn, channels of love.

Several months ago I sat in a labor-delivery room in a Boston hospital admiring my first grandbaby. Beautiful, infinitely precious, Maddy arrived into a large and loving family surrounded by the best in medical technology. Truly a member of the family. As I rocked her, I couldn't help thinking of the Iraqi babies Jim was seeing, children as precious as Maddy who are somehow "outside" our family, who are cut off from medical help, who die hungry.

In our world only some of us have a right to life. Wealth, education, race, gender, nationality, political expediency—all determine our membership in the family. We haven't realized our own membership; we do not recognize our brothers and sisters. Our lack of vision orphans us.

About the gospel: I wonder if, come harvest, the servants might not discover that wheat and weeds together are culled, each for its own proper purpose. Perhaps at maturity each is seen in its own way to be part of the family.

—Shelley Douglass

Sunday Between July 24 and 30

A Parable of Corruption

PSALM 105:1-11 • GENESIS 29:15-28 • ROMANS 8:26-39
• MATTHEW 13:31-33, 44-52

A DIALOGUE ON JESUS' Parable of the Leaven: "The kingdom of heaven is like leaven, which a woman took and hid in three measures of flour, until it was all leavened" (Matthew 13:33).

This parable is about as digestible as leaven swallowed whole.

What's your problem? It's just Jesus' hopeful vision. Like leaven, the reign of God will spread rapidly from within. Amen to that!

But for Jesus leaven was a symbol of moral corruption. In those days leaven was made by storing bread in a damp, dark place until it molded. In Exodus leaven symbolized the unholy (Exodus 12:19). Paul understood leaven as symbolic of the morally corrupt. He twice cites a proverb, "A little leaven leavens the whole lump" (Galatians 5:9; 1 Corinthians 5:6-8), whose meaning by his application is the same as our own saying, "One rotten apple spoils the whole barrel." Jesus shows the same understanding when he warns against the leaven of the Pharisees and Herod (Mark 8:15). His parable begins with the common assumption: Leaven equals moral corruption.

But that's nonsense! How can God's reign be morally corrupt?

It's worse than that. Do you know how much "three measures" of flour was? About 50 pounds. Enough to make bread for more than a hundred people. The leaven of God is far more corrupting than a rotten apple.

You make Jesus' parable sound...

Subversive? Yes, like his character—a woman, probably a poor one. One of the oppressed. This far cry from a king turns one's sense of "kingdom" upside-down.

So does this parable get still more corrupt?

Consider the woman's action. She doesn't just put the corrupt leaven in the flour. She *hides* it. She has to sneak in God's tiny corrupting power.

You're making a case that every detail of Jesus' parable is corrupt and subversive. So does that mean God's reign is corrupting our society? Spell it out, this "parable of corruption."

How about this? The reign of God is like a tiny, corrupt substance, which a shrewd woman took and hid in a huge amount of flour, until it accomplished a transformation.

It almost makes you remember Dorothy Day...when the Catholic Worker was beginning.

Yes, not a safely dead saint but a living gospel threat—to our conscience.

What was it we used to call her?

A communist.

—Jim Douglass

Sunday Between July 31 and August 6

Jesus Had Compassion

PSALM 17:1-7, 15 • GENESIS 32:22-31 • ROMANS 9:1-5 • MATTHEW 14:13-21

WHAT DO WE DO when evil triumphs? When hundreds of thousands of people are killed in the first atomic explosions, what do we do? When John the Baptist is beheaded for speaking truth to Herod's power, what do we do? More than 50 years ago, our own country used atomic weapons on human beings; since then systemic evil has claimed millions of lives.

When Jesus hears that John is dead, he tries to go into the wilderness to pray—

perhaps even to realize his own impending death. But the people follow with their needs and their suffering; he relents and teaches, heals, feeds.

He has gone to pray, and 5,000 men followed (plus women and children), perhaps expecting a declaration of revolution. In a way they get it: Jesus heals and blesses them; they feed each other. The kingdom suddenly comes in the shadow of John's death.

I'm reminded of a Quaker friend, Floyd Schmoe, who went for years to Hiroshima to help rebuild after the bombing. In the face of ultimate violence we have only kingdom weaponry: prayer, healing, bread, our lives. As we reflect on this anniversary of Hiroshima and Nagasaki, perhaps we can take stock of our kingdom weaponry, those counters to death in the world.

—Shelley Douglass

Sunday Between August 7 and 13

"Lord, save us!"

PSALM 105:1-6, 16-22 • GENESIS 37:1-4, 12-28 • ROMANS 10:5-15
• MATTHEW 14:22-33

JESUS' WALK ON THE LAKE, and Peter's response in faith and doubt, mingle with my memories of a distant event.

There was once a group of believers in nonviolence who gathered along a waterway in the Pacific Northwest. A giant submarine that could destroy all life on earth was coming. The believers practiced in rowboats how they would blockade the submarine.

They developed two tactics. A first group of rowboaters decided they would be towed on a long rope by a leading sailboat. Then as the submarine approached, they would all let go of the rope. The submarine crew would see them and stop. That would be the beginning of a larger miracle of nonviolence. This was known as the mother-duckling tactic.

A second group of rowboaters also had a mother boat, a trimaran. Their tactic was that the trimaran would run directly at the giant submarine. Then the blockaders would throw their rowboats into the water. They would jump into them and row as fast as they could at the submarine as it came closer. Again the submarine would see them and stop—the beginning of the larger miracle. Some observers called this the kamikaze tactic. Others said that name applied also to the mother-duckling group.

In remembering this experience, I think all the people in the rowboats, whatever our tactics, really had the same faith in nonviolence that Peter had initially in walking to Jesus over the water.

On the day the submarine finally came, so did 99 Coast Guard boats, which the government had assigned to protect its world-destructive weapon. The Battle of Oak Bay, as a reporter called it, was short and decisive. The Coast Guard sank some rowboats with water cannons, crushed others, boarded the mother ships with drawn guns, and tied up the believers in nonviolence like pigs waiting for a roast. The submarine sailed unimpeded to its port.

When Peter became aware of the wind, he got frightened and began to sink. When we were confronted by the Coast Guard, we also experienced fear and got sunk quickly. So, a lack of faith?

I remember, too, though, that when Peter began to sink he cried out in faith to the Lord, who reached out and saved him. I think the real alternatives were posed in our case, like Peter's, by the more enduring question of whether to surrender then to fear or to realize how totally reliant on love we were to continue such experiments in faith. "Lord, save us!" was our way, like Peter's, to continue in the future venturing out on the water in the midst of great winds.

—Jim Douglass

Sunday Between August 14 and 20

"I am Joseph, your brother."

PSALM 133 • GENESIS 45:1-15 • ROMANS 11:1-2, 29-32 • MATTHEW 15:10-28

ONE OF THE HARDEST THINGS for me to do is to look at someone in power and see in him (or her) my brother or sister. I feel like Joseph's siblings, unable to recognize my brother inside that powerful and alien presence steeped in a culture of wealth, making decisions that change lives.

Conversely, when I'm in the more powerful position, I have trouble recognizing the sister or brother who needs my help. I tend to see the power differential first, the kinship second. I'm tired, I don't want to be bothered. Like Jesus in our gospel, I sometimes need a pointed reminder of my own alienation before I can see my relationship to the human family.

Power has an insidious way of insulating us from others. In its most visible form, it takes the shape of fences, weapons, guards, freeways. In our hearts and souls, it becomes apathy, indifference, fatigue. If I'm comfortable myself, I tend not to be so alert to suffering. I'd rather remain comfortable.

That's why most of us working for peace and justice are motivated not by benignity but by pain—the discomfort caused by dissonance between our beliefs and the real world or the pain caused by suffering in those we love. What we learn from Jesus here is to put ourselves in places where our comfort can be disrupted and then to learn from those disruptions.

—Shelley Douglass

Sunday Between August 21 and 27

Pharaoh's Threat

PSALM 124 • EXODUS 1:8-2:10 • ROMANS 12:1-8 • MATTHEW 16:13-20

THE THREAT: INFANTICIDE. "Pharaoh ordered the Hebrew midwives, 'If it is a boy, kill him; if a girl, let her live.'" The beginning of the foundation story of the Hebrew Bible.

The midwives' response is non-cooperation with evil. They disobey Pharaoh's command and let all the newborn live.

Pharaoh is checked but not daunted. He takes up his infanticide threat again, this time commanding all his Egyptian subjects: "Throw all the boys born to the Hebrews into the river, but let all the girls live."

The key response is again non-cooperation. A Hebrew mother places her child in a basket on the river, which is found by Pharaoh's own daughter. Like the midwives she says no to her father's order of death. The fruit of her daughterly disobedience is a child saved, the future liberation leader, Moses; thus a people saved.

The theme at the beginning of our basic story of a people's liberation is non-cooperation with infanticide by a series of determined, child-saving women.

Questions to consider:

Can those women and men who today non-cooperate with evil for the sake of the child in the womb join hands with those who non-cooperate with evil for the sake of the born child?

What would such a politically incorrect, consistent-life movement look like?

Would the modern-day pharaohs who control us all then realize their most ingenious strategy had failed?

—Jim Douglass

Transformation at the Cross

*H*ow *shall we live as disciples of Jesus the Christ? The readings for these winding-down weeks of the year all address that question.*

These scriptures raise painful inner and outer questions of nonviolence. Many of them deal with gospel economics, the economics of the heart and the economics of the purse. The gospel is neither solely personal nor solely political. It embraces and transforms both—at the cross.

—Jim and Shelley Douglass

Sunday Between August 28 and September 3

Exodus From Violence

PSALM 105:1-6, 23-26 • EXODUS 3:1-15 • ROMANS 12:9-21 • MATTHEW 16:21-28

DOES GOD FREE ONE PEOPLE by enabling them to conquer another? The question arises from our first reading, taken from the Exodus story on which our whole Bible is based.

From the burning bush God tells Moses, "I have come down to deliver [the Israelites] from the Egyptians, and to bring them up out of that land to a good and broad land, a land flowing with milk and honey, to the country of the Canaanites, the Hittites, the Amorites, the Perizzites, the Hivites, and the Jebusites."

This is good news for the Israelites who will be divinely liberated from their oppressors in Egypt. But what about the Canaanites, the Hittites, the Amorites, the Perizzites, the Hivites, and the Jebusites who already live in that promised "land flowing with milk and honey"?

Is a vision of genocide implicit in the story on which our Bible is founded?

Biblical scholars say the 13th-century B.C. events narrated in the book of Exodus reached their current form eight centuries later. One school of interpretation claims the promise of the conquest of Canaan corresponds to a revolution by an alliance of peasant tribes (including an immigrant tribe from Egypt led through the wilderness by Moses) against the kings of the cities of Canaan who demanded submission and tribute.

But whether revolution from within or conquest from without, the end of the Exodus story by any reading identifies God with the winning side in a war for "a land flowing with milk and honey." Is Exodus a mythic celebration of an unending cycle in which every oppressed people is eventually blessed by God with a promised land but at the expense of new victims?

In our gospel from Matthew, Jesus breaks the cycle by making a different kind of promise: "If any want to become my followers, let them deny themselves and take up their cross and follow me. For those who want to save their life will lose it, and those who lose their life for my sake will find it."

Jesus breaks the cycle of violence in the Exodus myth by choosing the cross instead of the sword. He invites his followers to make the same nonviolent choice. The Promised Land is voluntary suffering. Our milk and honey is love of enemies. The Good News is an Exodus from violence itself.

—Jim Douglass

Sunday Between September 4 and 10

Bound and Free

PSALM 149 • EXODUS 12:1-14 • ROMANS 13:8-14 • MATTHEW 18:15-20

AGAIN WE MEDITATE on this saying of Jesus: "Whatever you shall bind shall be bound; what you loose shall be set free."

A triumphant, risen Jesus spoke this at Pentecost in John's gospel. Today we see that Matthew has used the same saying, putting it in the context of Jesus giving rules for the conduct of the church.

Matthew's community must be in conflict: trying to understand how to deal lovingly with breaks and tears in its own fabric as time passes and Jesus hasn't returned. How do we live when we hurt and anger each other? How do we live the gospel daily?

These readings answer that question: We maintain our common meal, our sign of unity and redemption. We love each other and follow God's commands. When relationships break down, we do our best to resolve conflicts in love: We talk to our opponent. We invite others to join in the dialogue. If all else fails, we resort not to blood-letting but to silence.

Church structure and discipline are always hard. How can we judge others? Especially when we've seen judgment so misused? How can we submit ourselves to judgment? We are reminded here that as community we are not only to nurture and affirm each other, but also to guide, teach, and remonstrate. Behind every action, however, must always be the rule of love. Love is the measure, even of our discipline.

—Shelley Douglass

Sunday Between September 11 and 17
Parable of the Unmerciful Nation

EXODUS 15:1-11, 20-21 • EXODUS 14:19-31 • ROMANS 14:1-12 • MATTHEW 18:21-35

TRANSPOSING TODAY'S GOSPEL into our time produces the following reading:

Compare the reign of God to a financial lord who wished to settle accounts with his debtor nations. When he began the reckoning, they brought to him one who was the president of a nation that owed him $5 trillion, the United States. And as the nation could not pay, the lord ordered that austerity measures be adopted by its government. Henceforth, all government services were to be canceled, millions of employees were to be dismissed, and all health, welfare, and social security payments were to be suspended until the United States' debt was paid. Every available resource was to go toward mounting debt-service payments.

So the president of the United States fell on his knees before the financial lord, imploring him, "Lord, have patience with us, and we will pay you everything." And out of pity for him and his people, the lord of that president released him and forgave the debt.

But that same president, as he went out, came upon the president of a small African country that owed the United States $100 million. Seizing him by the lapel, he said, "Pay what you owe." So his fellow president fell to his knees and besought him, "Have patience with us, and we will pay you everything." He refused and his economic advisers forced austerity measures on the African country, whose people died of malnutrition while their own resources were used up to service the debt.

When the presidents of other debtor countries saw what had taken place, because of their great distress they were moved to solidarity. And they went and reported to the financial lord all that had happened and their resolve to stand together. "We shall not pay our foreign debt with the hunger of our people."

Then the lord summoned the United States president and said to him, "You stupid man, I forgave you and your people all that debt because you besought me. And should not you have had mercy on your fellow president, as I had mercy on you? And look what you have done now! Those nations are in solidarity, and all of us who have held them in debt will be ruined!"

And in anger his lord delivered him and his nation to austerity measures and a great depression, and both president and lord then fell from wealth and power.

—Jim Douglass

Sunday Between September 18 and 24

God's Economy

PSALM 105:1-6, 37-45 • EXODUS 16:2-15 • PHILIPPIANS 1:21-30 • MATTHEW 20:1-16

GOD'S ECONOMY IS not like ours. We hoard and stockpile; we measure out the day's pay according to hours worked. God, however, simply sees that there is enough for everyone. Enough manna—but no more. A day's wages—no less.

In God's economy there is enough. In our world, which is God's, there is enough—but not if we take more than our share. What do I have that is more than my share?

In the human psyche, there is a bias against injustice. It amazes me to see how often my bias gets biased—I resent someone else's "enough" because they've worked less for it, come later, not fulfilled my expectations. Yet my sensitivity to injustice is remarkably tolerant when *I'm* the beneficiary of that injustice.

God in God's mercy forgives not only my greed but also my resentment and blindness. In God's economy, there is even enough forgiveness.

—Shelley Douglass

Sunday Between September 25 and October 1

Faith and Terror

PSALM 78:1-4, 12-16 • EXODUS 17:1-7 • PHILIPPIANS 2:1-13 • MATTHEW 21:23-32

EMPIRES CONTROL their subjects by fear of death. The Roman Empire terrorized its colonized peoples by threatening their leaders with crucifixion should they be tempted to rebel.

To those first-century peoples who lived under the empire's terror of the cross, what Paul says in today's epistle is a shocker: Jesus, though he was in the form of God, emptied himself, took the form of a slave, and became obedient to the point of death—even death on a cross. And God exalted him.

The Roman Empire's means of terror became the Christian's symbol of faith. Terror was overcome by the cross on which Jesus died—and lives. Jesus' resurrection and that of all who follow him "taking up their cross" nullified the coercive power of the empire. A faith in the cross means that the power of imperial violence is over.

So why isn't it?

In our ostensibly more democratic U.S. empire, the colonized of the two-thirds world are terrorized by the sudden "disappearance" of organizers. But people of faith who have analyzed their situation understand this modern equivalent of the cross and Jesus' command of resurrection, "Be not afraid." Their faith in the transforming cross of Jesus continues.

In the United States itself, the equivalent of the imperial rule of the cross may be the politics of assassination. Since the assassinations of John F. Kennedy, Malcolm X, Martin Luther King Jr., and Robert F. Kennedy, a deep politics of terror has ruled the country. This politics controlled by covert intelligence groups is supreme among those in power, and recognized by those who seriously challenge that power with truth. But because our empire's power of terror covers its tracks, stays behind the scenes, and remains unchallenged by the transforming cross of Jesus, it has not only continued but has seeped down into every American neighborhood.

Can we believe that Jesus became obedient to the point of death—even death by a hail of bullets? Can we believe that God exalted him—in Dallas, New York, Memphis, and Los Angeles?

—Jim Douglass

Sunday Between October 2 and 8

Seeing Ourselves

PSALM 19 • EXODUS 20:1-4, 7-9, 12-20 • PHILIPPIANS 3:4-14 • MATTHEW 21:33-46

MATTHEW'S GOSPEL TRIES to explain the destruction of Jerusalem in terms of the faithlessness of the Hebrew people to Yahweh. It's important to remember that when this gospel was written, Jerusalem had already been destroyed. The question for everyone, Jew and Christian alike, was: How had God allowed God's city, God's temple, to be destroyed?

The classic answer for the Hebrew people was that destruction was the fruit of disobedience. Therefore, Matthew says, contemporary Jewish people were punished for what? For not accepting Jesus.

We need to be careful here. It was the wealthy, the rulers, who collaborated with the Roman occupation in killing Jesus, a revolutionary prophet. Jesus was himself a Jew from the long and strong prophetic tradition; he was not rejected by the people, who followed him in crowds. That's why he was such a threat!

Later Christian readers have used this passage to justify their own persecution of Jesus' own people, so it must be handled with care. The care with which we handle it should be care to direct its criticism at ourselves. What was threatening about Jesus? His love for the poor; his love for enemies. His passion for justice; his mercy and forgiveness. His simple call to sharing and serving each other. His new gospel economics. His nonviolence.

What is threatening about Jesus today? The same things. To whom? To us. Perhaps most threatening is Jesus' radical commitment to nonviolence. What would have happened if the early community that heard Jesus had accepted his counsel to revolutionary nonviolence? What would happen if we accepted it today?

If we see ourselves in this Matthew reading, we can see our own idolatry, and read our own future.

—Shelley Douglass

Sunday Between October 9 and 15

Who's Coming to Dinner?

PSALM 106:1-6, 19-23 • EXODUS 32:1-14 • PHILIPPIANS 4:1-9 • MATTHEW 22:1-14

WHAT ARE WE TO MAKE of the jarring details in Matthew's version of Jesus' parable of the banquet? Is God represented by a king who burns a city for killing his slaves, holds his banquet in the same city, and then has his servants "cast into the outer darkness" a late-invited street guest for not wearing a wedding garment that no street person would possess?

Matthew has made the first part of the parable into a morality tale, taking the destruction of Jerusalem in 70 A.D. as God's punishment upon those Judeans who "refused their invitation" to the messianic banquet. In the second part, he has added a symbolic dress code for the finally invited Gentiles, that they put on the garment of Christian life if they want to remain at the messianic celebration.

Luke's version of the same parable offers a picture more consistent with Jesus' teaching on forgiveness and love of enemies. In his banquet (Luke 14:16-24), invitations are simply extended to "the poor, the crippled, the blind, and the lame" after others better off have made their excuses for not coming.

What is my response to Jesus' ongoing invitation to God's banquet table?

Am I too proud or busy to be with the poor, the crippled, the blind, and the lame who eat with Jesus?

—Jim Douglass

Sunday Between October 16 and 22

God's Hindquarters

PSALM 99 • EXODUS 33:12-23 • 1 THESSALONIANS 1:1-10 • MATTHEW 22:15-22

THIS EXODUS READING is one of my favorites: Moses' presumption, God's patience, God's humor, God's care and gentleness. What kind of wild glory is this, that to look upon it directly is to die? What kind of wild, glorious, funny God would think of sidling by with only (his) hindquarters exposed, so that Moses could see (his) glory and not die?

How could we possibly hope to understand such a being, to capture God's image, to confine God in rules? What could we possibly do except to laugh, to rejoice, to adore this totally foreign and amazingly intimate lover of humankind?

"Whose head is this, and whose title?" asks the tested Jesus. "Caesar's," they answer. Certainly not God's! God's image could never be imprisoned. Render to God the things that are God's. What is God's? The earth. Humanity. Creation. Love, justice, truth, righteousness. Render these things to God.

And what about taxes? A pertinent question today as political promises (and threats) fly, funds are distributed, weapons are bought. What about taxes? When taxes are used to enhance human life and creation, we can pay them. When they are used to destroy it, we must seriously question. Is it right to pay for weapons systems that destroy God's image in us? Right to pay for guns? Carry guns?

If we contemplate even God's hindquarters, I think that we can learn to honor that unknowable One, and in doing so to live so that without God, our lives make no sense. Then we'll know where praise and worship are due, and render our hearts (and our money) to the right ruler.

—Shelley Douglass

Sunday Between October 23 and 29

On the Way of the Cross

PSALM 90:1-6, 13-17 • DEUTERONOMY 34:1-12 • 1 THESSALONIANS 2:1-8 • MATTHEW 22:34-46

IN TODAY'S GOSPEL, Jesus joins the greatest commandment of the law in Deuteronomy 6:4-5 (loving God with all one's heart, soul, and mind) with a second like it from Leviticus 19:18 (loving one's neighbor as oneself). But the crux of his teaching is not this conjunction of the two, but his scandalous interpretation of the second.

The verse in Leviticus is a national creed. It limits the love of "neighbor" to one's own people: "You shall not take vengeance or bear a grudge against any of your people, but you shall love your neighbor as yourself."

It is when Jesus extends love of neighbor to include the enemy (Matthew 5:43-45) that he identifies himself as the traitor to every nationalism and imperialism. He is thereby on his way to the cross, as are his followers in the Roman Empire and our own.

In our reading from Deuteronomy, just before he dies, Moses goes up the mountain. And God shows him the promised land. Moses looks northward to Galilee, westward to the Mediterranean, and south to the wilderness of the Negeb. "But you shall not cross over there," God tells the prophet of the people who will cross over.

On the night before he died in Memphis, our greatest modern prophet also had a view of the promised land. He saw it in the midst of striking sanitation workers. He saw that land of freedom not in terms of a nation but rather a transformed, global people, most of them poorer than the sanitation workers and some of them his enemies. Following Jesus, he saw the way to freedom for their whole people as the cross he was about to experience from his enemies:

...it doesn't matter with me now. Because I've been to the mountaintop. And I don't mind. Like anybody, I would like to live a long life. Longevity has its place. But I'm not concerned about that now. I just want to do God's will. And [God's] allowed me to go up to the mountain. And I've looked over. And I've seen the promised land. I may not get there with you. But I want you to know tonight, that we, as a people, will get to the promised land. And I'm happy tonight. I'm not worried about anything. I'm not fearing any man. Mine eyes have seen the glory of the coming of the Lord.

—Martin Luther King Jr.

Amen. I believe.

—Jim Douglass

Reformation Day

In some traditions, Reformation Day is celebrated the last Sunday in October. See Appendix 1, "Reformation and All Saints' Days."

All Saints' Sunday

All Saints' Day (November 1) may be celebrated the first Sunday in November.

What's in a Name?

PSALM 34:1-10, 22 • REVELATION 7:9-17 • 1 JOHN 3:1-3 • MATTHEW 5:1-12

MY EARLY CHILDHOOD was spent in Toronto, Ontario, next to a Russian Orthodox church in a neighborhood populated by newly arrived immigrants. The children on my block spoke Greek and Spanish, Russian and Italian, and ate strong-smelling food in houses full of parents, siblings, cousins, and grandparents.

Each summer the church next door held a carnival, which I observed from my sidewalk and bedroom window. Unable to sleep through the music and laughter, I would lay awake and imagine that I was anything other than I was—a relocated, fifth-generation Dutch American, living off tuna casserole and, on a good day, Jell-O salad.

Our search for identity begins young, and never stops. If we are blessed, we have good guides who direct us to the right sources and teach us well.

But we live in a broken world, and are fallen, fearful people. When things become unstable, we despair over losing ground to someone whose race, taste, gender, or nationality does not resemble our own. Wars are fought, riots break out, and souls shatter—from the fields of Bosnia to the hearts of abused children. Most of my friends, though they'd be embarrassed to see it on paper, think of themselves as thoughtful, progressive, sensitive activists. Our greatest temptation is to write "other" people off as racist, sexist, nationalistic, and homophobic, playing God by separating them out as the goats.

Yet in the face of all of the name-calling in our world, God maintains the final say over who we are. The descriptions of God's children given in today's passages challenge all other claims on our lives. The beatitudes are the promise of all we are meant to be; they drown out all of the other labels we have for ourselves, substituting God's foolishness for our wisdom. This rule of life is not given to make our lives more difficult, but to set us free to lead truly good lives.

Psalm 34 describes us as people who are free from all of our fears, who have faces that are never covered with shame, who are saved from all of our troubles, who lack nothing.

The words of John's first epistle convey sheer delight about God's great love, lavished upon us; we are renamed as children of God. Another promise is given—that everything will be made clear and we will know ourselves to be like God. In other words, we will finally, really know who we are.

Some survivors of incest rename themselves to declare themselves reborn from their violent families. To a certain extent, we all need to be renamed. Some to leave behind the names of the fathers who lied to us about who we were, and who we could become. Some because disease or age have rendered us less able than we once were. Some because we have played the games of our world, found the successes offered hollow, and so wonder if there are other ways to be.

The answers come, slowly and in their time, from God, our author and perfecter, who at every moment is making all things new.

Turn your eyes upon Jesus, look full in his wonderful face, and the things of earth will grow strangely clear, in the light of his glory and grace. Amen.

—**Kari Jo Verhulst**

Sunday Between October 30 and November 5

Dumping Rank

PSALM 107:1-7, 33-37 • JOSHUA 3:7-17 • 1 THESSALONIANS 2:9-13
• MATTHEW 23:1-12

IN THE READING from the Hebrew scriptures, Joshua (following God's direct instructions) sends the priests bearing the ark of the covenant ahead as the Israelites prepare to cross the river Jordan. When the priests' feet touch the water, the river is held back and the people cross. How could they doubt that God was among them, and that their priests and leaders were truly holy?

In stark contrast, in the passage from the gospel of Matthew, Jesus harshly denounces the scribes and the Pharisees. He gives clear instructions to do as they teach, but not as they do, for they are hypocrites; not, Jesus says, meeting the standard they set for others.

Both passages are affected by their context. The book of Joshua is a part of Israel's telling of its story. Autobiographies often give the most glowing account of events.

The gospel of Matthew, on the other hand, was written by someone with a paradoxical attitude toward Judaism. On the one hand, the writer shows deep respect for the Law and its moral demands; on the other, the writer spares no scathing spin on Jesus' words about the Jews.

Some scholars speculate that the author of Matthew was a Jewish convert to Christianity who still deeply loved the institutions of Judaism, but was troubled by their failure to accept Jesus—and deeply hurt by persecution coming from the synagogues. Considering Christianity's troubling history of anti-Semitism, it is most important to remember that this was a quarrel between different factions within the same religious and ethnic context.

Were all scribes and Pharisees hypocrites? Probably not. Were some of them carried away by the trappings of honor and power? Since they were human, probably. Jesus counters the dangers that an emphasis on rank and prestige can cause to souls and to a community of faith by presenting a radically different and egalitarian way of living: "He who is greatest among you shall be your servant; whoever exalts herself will be humbled, and whoever humbles herself will be exalted."

—**Julie Polter**

Sunday Between November 6 and 12

Ready and Waiting

PSALM 78:1-7 • JOSHUA 24:1-3, 14-25 • 1 THESSALONIANS 4:13-18 • MATTHEW 25:1-13

WHEN JOSHUA GATHERS all the tribes of Israel in order to renew their covenant, he speaks for God, who wants to remind the people of their story. God sought out their father Abraham from beyond the river and has been with them ever since.

Then Joshua reminds them that the covenant is not just something that they inherit passively, like a story; it is a living thing, a story that they continue to create by their actions, by their faithfulness or lack of faith. To be in covenant with God is a choice that the people of Israel need to make actively. As the saying goes, when you choose not to choose, you still have made a choice. Not just their words, but their worship, their hearts, and their lives need to incline toward God.

For us too a statement of faith requires fulfillment in actions and integrity. We need to know the history of "how we got over," how God has been faithful to those who have gone before us and how they were faithful to God. But we also need to know that our faith history has a call and pull on our life *this* day.

In the parable of the 10 maidens in Matthew, the lesson isn't that faith means you will see God coming. (God specializes in coming in the guise of an unexpected person, or at an inopportune time.) But we do need to prepare for God's coming, to be expectant, to live as if our God may drop in at any time. If we want our lamps to be lit by holy fire, we need to have them filled and ready, stoked with prayer and scripture, Sabbath and worship, service and being served.

—Julie Polter

Sunday Between November 13 and 19

Buried Treasure

PSALM 123 • JUDGES 4:1-7 • 1 THESSALONIANS 5:1-11 • MATTHEW 25:14-30

THIS PASSAGE FROM 1 Thessalonians begins with a terrifying warning:

...The day of the Lord will come like a thief in the night. When they say, "There is peace and security," then sudden destruction will come upon them, as labor pains come upon a pregnant woman, and there will be no escape!

When I was a child, I took such descriptions as long-range weather forecasts—lacking just enough precision to seem inevitable, like the change of seasons. My fear often overwhelmed the vacation Bible school teachings about God's rainbow promise and Jesus being a loving man who liked to call children to his side and bless them.

Likewise, the parable of the talents made me nervous. I was raised to consider a good credit rating as bringing a person even closer to godliness than cleanliness. An investment riskier than a passbook savings account was viewed with suspicion. Making money through any method other than sweat and thrift was reckless wheeling and dealing. By those standards, the servant who buried her one talent was wisely cautious, doing her job and doing it well—certainly not deserving of casting into "outer darkness."

This heading-toward-final-judgment part of the liturgical calendar just made it hard for me to sleep at night.

The stated dramatic consequences of "living wrong" in these passages shouldn't be ignored. But we shouldn't lose the positive lessons that are also being given about our call to a different way of living in relation to God who isn't just in the End, or the Beginning, but is along for the ride through the long, bumpy Middle, too.

The choice about such things is left up to us. We can live like God is ineffectual or non-existent, meaningless to our days and nights. We can live like God is important and utterly brittle, so that we don't dare risk making a mistake—like our lives are fine china on loan from Grandma, and her rage about a broken plate would destroy us.

But there is yet another way, too. We can live like what we have—existence, talent, gifts of wit or welding—came from Someone who loves us, and a new day is a gift too, calling us out to take chances and plant seeds, to see what grows.

How is the world distressed and battered, even threatened with ending, through the belief that God isn't there or doesn't matter? What outer darkness do we create for ourselves and others out of our fear and the burying of gifts?

Paul follows the words of warning quoted above with words of instruction to the young, struggling, but faithful community at Thessalonica, words of power not of fear: Don't worry about thieves in the night if you are being children of the light. Keep awake; make faith, love, and salvation your defense. Most of all, encourage one another and build one another up.

—Julie Polter

Sunday Between November 20 and 26

Tagged by Mercy

PSALM 100 • EZEKIEL 34:11-16, 20-24 • EPHESIANS 1:15-23 • MATTHEW 25:31-46

THE SCENE PRESENTED in Matthew of the king presiding over the great judgment is kind of like a college student's nightmare: sitting down for a final exam and finding out that you read the wrong books all semester.

By the prevailing standards of human society, it's not at all predictable that the royal and holy child of God would come to visit in the way that this passage describes. According to this, the Christ is coming every day: a hungry child, an imprisoned rapist, the woman that turns tricks on the corner who's knocking on the door and asking for a sip of cold water on a hot afternoon.

On the other hand, the passage from Ezekiel turns this around, presenting the familiar image of God as a shepherd. This is still about as far from royalty as a person can get, but it does not show God as one of the broken, but rather as seeking them:

As shepherds seek out their flocks when they are among their scattered sheep, so I will seek out my sheep. I will rescue them from all the places to which they have been scattered on a day of clouds and thick darkness. I will seek the lost, and I will bring back the strayed, and I will bind up the injured and I will strengthen the weak, but the fat and the strong I will destroy. I will feed them with justice. —Ezekiel 34:12, 16

The images of final judgment focus on a distribution of justice, but this is not arbitrary. Ultimately, God's justice is measured out according to what we've been looking for. God is coming in the broken body, the broken heart, the broken spirit. And God is seeking us like scattered sheep. We are seeking and being sought. How do we find one another?

Unlike sheep, we don't have ear tags to identify us, and the Christ is not wearing a red carnation in his lapel. The meeting point, the place where we will know that we have found and been found, is mercy, the mercy we give and the mercy we accept.

—Julie Polter

CYCLE B

A Countercultural Season

Advent couldn't be more out of step with the doings of the dominant culture. Against the inflation and distortion of the commercial powers hyping their seasonal wares, it sets a spirit of barebones simplicity: John the Baptist, in domicile, diet, dress, putting an axe to their bloody roots.

Against the manufactured and well-targeted desire for things, Advent invokes that single-minded hunger—a yearning truly for God alone. Against the awful clamor and din that silences all contenders, this season sets that Word irrepressible. Against the grandiose and pretentious pose that goes with empire, it posits the hidden and unexpected. Over against despair that has become the emblem of political rule in our day, it utters a hope that thereby becomes freedom. Against dissipation and distraction, by which we are also controlled, Advent commends spiritual alertness. As the readings from Isaiah will suggest, Advent reminds us that we are exiles and resident aliens in a strange, strange land.

For all that, it is a season to make the heart sit up and take notice. In fact and practice, Advent exemplifies the characteristic attitude of believers approaching scripture itself: an urgent expectancy, a patient watching, and attentive listening for the coming of the Word.

—Bill Wylie-Kellermann

First Sunday of Advent

Pray for Disruption

PSALM 80:1-7, 17-19 • ISAIAH 64:1-9 • 1 CORINTHIANS 1:3-9 • MARK 13:24-37

TO BEGIN, IN ADVENT we pray for the end. Isaiah's prayer has the smell of exile all over it: a sanctuary ruined, a dream too long deferred, and a people trying to remember who in hell they are. Is God absent or are they absent-minded? Who has abandoned whom? Overwhelmed by the culture, they confess becoming like those whom God has never ruled (63:19).

The confession is, however (as all confessions are), virtually an act of faith. It is a wake-up call. Against amnesia, they recollect themselves as children belonging to God. So the prayer ends and begins (63:16, 64:8). Hope awakens in memory and its choices.

Such prayer is the prophet's work, or at least half of it. Bonhoeffer writes that to intercede is to feel another's need so deeply that you simply pray their prayer. The need of the people is in the prophet's heart and bones; Isaiah prays in the first person plural.

At the center of the prayer (64:1-4) is a plea for a tearing of the heavens, a break in history, an intervention that shakes the foundations of the world: a prayer for the big disruption. Business as usual has become intolerable. In prayer the fault line is imagined and foreseen. Such is an act of hope.

In the apocalyptic parable from Mark 13, God is similarly experienced as absent. Memory and fidelity are marked here by being awake and awatch. And the coming at time unknown is also connected to the collapse of a social world: "not one stone left upon another" (13:2). Even Paul's prayer, in its thanksgiving for the Corinthian congregation, invokes the end (1:8), the very coming of the One who is the end and the beginning.

—Bill Wylie-Kellermann

Second Sunday of Advent

Making a Way Out of No Way

PSALM 85:1-2, 8-13 • ISAIAH 40:1-11 • 2 PETER 3:8-15 • MARK 1:1-8

WITH THE WORD "COMFORT," the book of Isaiah begins a distinct collection of writings (chapters 40-55) commonly called Second Isaiah, which stems from the period in which Cyrus the Persian was piling up victories against Babylon. History was shifting; the empire trembled. Might it indeed collapse? Could the mighty arm of God be moving?

The poet in Babylon is discerning and alert. Isaiah is repatriated in the spirit, transported to Jerusalem with a living word of comfort and with hot news. To speak in the voice of God, after all, is the work of the prophet, or at least half of it.

The Hebrew behind "good tidings" (40:9) and the Greek behind "gospel" or "good news" (Mark 1:1) mean essentially the same thing. The Word travels and with effect, yet it feels as though Isaiah speaks tenderly to Jerusalem, for the sake of those still captive in Babylon. Remember home. Imagine the good news there.

Hence this famous "way" that seems to be something of a two-way street. On it God comes, a sovereign processing royally into the captured city. But it is for the exiles also a way out, the way home, the route of a new exodus straight through the wilderness, every obstacle overcome.

Now the first obstacle is neither distance nor rough place, it is the captive mind and heart that cannot imagine the way. Look! the prophet shouts: A highway! If you can't see it, you can't walk it.

There are elements of a prophetic call in this passage, so it's no wonder that John the Baptist should find a "vocation" here, living into it as his signature text. John, however, faces a similar problem in an opposite form: The people are home in Judea and Jerusalem, but they think like captive exiles. Could Jerusalem become Babylon?

John thinks like Second Isaiah. He shouts. Imagine a way and come out. In Mark we shall see "way" become a synonym for discipleship, a metaphor for the movement. John's marginal life and renegade ritual provoke the imagination: They summon and prepare that movement for the One who comes.

—Bill Wylie-Kellermann

Third Sunday of Advent

A Troublesome Joy

PSALM 126 • ISAIAH 61:1-4, 8-11 • 1 THESSALONIANS 5:16-24
• JOHN 1:6-8, 19-28

IN LITURGICAL TRADITION, this is a Sunday associated with joy. However, we are not talking about the ersatz variety hawked by our own culture like a marketing device attached ephemerally to things. That joy, so called, proves itself empty and without substance, a commercial fiction. If these readings are any clue, however, Advent joy has content about which we may be scandalously concrete.

The Canticle from Luke (1:47-55), a psalm not of David but of Mary, is the most revolutionary anthem in the Bible. Here is joy, in expectation of Jesus' birth, whose substance is a world turned upside-down. No mincing words: It sings a complete transformation of political and economic order.

The "good news" of the Isaiah reading is a joy from beginning to end. It is like the very oil of gladness that blesses those who mourn in lonely exile here (61:3). Or like the smiles of prisoners who circle their outdate and see it now closely come. It is a joy outrageously specific in content.

For the exiles this litany of liberation is about homecoming. Hence, for example, the repair and rebuilding of ruined cities (61:4). It is the joy so concrete you purchase a hammer and a saw. Imagine this good news in Gaza or Sarajevo, south central Los Angeles or southwest Detroit.

It might be recalled that when Jesus preached on this text to inaugurate his ministry (Luke 4:16ff), he was driven not only out of the pulpit, but out of town. The plan was to stone him. We ought thereby to be mindful that not everyone shares this joy. The captors and binders and debtholders, the rich and the ruiners of cities, the mighty on thrones and the proud in the imagination of their hearts—in short, all those invested in the present order—find this joy to be a trouble.

Just so, the priests and Levites are sent out by the Jerusalem authorities to scrutinize and size up John (1:19). His vocational reply must surely mystify them, like a claim to be the voice of prophesy itself. And his troubling conviction, that the one who comes stands already in their midst, must drive them up a wall. Yet for us it remains a present and abiding joy.

—Bill Wylie-Kellermann

Fourth Sunday of Advent

A Ready Faith

LUKE 1:47-55 • 2 SAMUEL 7:1-11, 16 • ROMANS 16:25-27 • LUKE 1:26-38

THERE IS WONDERFUL IRONY in the Davidic covenant of 2 Samuel 7. The king, having built himself a sumptuous palace, has decided that God ought to have a "house" as well. The prophet Nathan concurs, but then can't sleep well. His fitful night yields God's all but sarcastic reply: Do I need a house? Haven't I lived without one since I brought you out of Egypt? I am the God who walks in tents. And not only that, but I will make David (that peasant shepherd boy) a house that will last forever. Now this, of course, is not house as in self-constructed palace of cedar, but house as in "the house and lineage of David," a human chain of generations through which God's faithfulness is enacted.

On the promise of a prophet's midnight dream the faith of a nation has hinged. In this text are rooted generations of theological and political reflection. In times of exile or occupation, when the line appears broken or forced underground, such reflection tends toward the subversive.

As such a time it was, the conversation between the angel and the peasant woman in Luke is politically loaded. To speak of the Davidic line is to incite sedition. But then Mary is the sort who can as easily sing the Magnificat as say hello.

Given the weight of social realities, exalting those of low degree or raising up a peasant child to the throne of David might seem as impossible as a virgin bearing child. Given the risks and the costs, we could be understanding if she thought better and declined. Mary, nevertheless, believes that God is able and her readiness to join the chain bodily and become the house is the epitome of Advent faith.

—Bill Wylie-Kellermann

Christmas Day

Dress Rehearsal for Heaven

PSALM 98 • ISAIAH 52:7-10 • HEBREWS 1:1-12 • JOHN 1:1-14

A KEY FOCUS OF the "Christmas story" is the manger scene: the teen-age mother, the child who is born into poverty yet heralded by angels. In the rough, sparse, impoverished, and unlikely details of the birth of the King of Kings, we are concretely reminded that God's reign will not mimic our human understandings of majesty and might and justice. Instead all conventions will be turned on their heads or brought into a fullness that we can but barely imagine.

These readings for Christmas day seem far removed from that manger scene. Words of poetry paint scenes that encompass the universe, the full sweep of creation. Passages of theological discourse argue the very meaning of all that is, of the nature of Christ (and of God), of redemption.

But though they come from a very different direction, these readings, like the story of a peasant birth, also push us to break open and flip around our understanding of who Jesus is and what God wants for creation. The meaning and mystery of Christmas reside somewhere in the way the concrete details of the story meet these poetic songs and these theological arguments straining to express the inexpressible.

"And the Word became flesh and dwelt among us, full of grace and truth; we have beheld his glory...." A newborn lets out a tiny cat's mew in his sleep, swaddled against the cold, oblivious to the smell of manure suffusing the air. On any day we might struggle to hold together these two views of what scripture assures us is the same reality. But today is a day to sing to the Lord a new song, and let that song carry us, to feast and celebrate that the mystery is true.

Isaiah 52:7-10 proclaims the good news of God's victory over death and despair—news of peace, salvation, joy, comfort, redemption, and God's reign clearly visible to all. The prophet's words are not yet newspaper headlines; but today, try to live as if. Today we hold a dress rehearsal for heaven: Share the sweet bread of life with family and with strangers; fill your home with light. Pray for the grace in the new year to walk in mercy, to work for justice—and to expect the unexpected.

—Julie Polter

First Sunday After Christmas

Public Facts and Freedom

PSALM 148 • ISAIAH 61:10-62:3 • GALATIANS 4:4-7 • LUKE 2:22-40

THIS IS A DAY FOR PRAISE, though if Isaiah has his way that joyous sound will be openly linked with justice. Righteousness and praise (61:11)—too seldom wed in our theological factionalisms—are declared to be shoots from a single root. They spring forth before the nations.

This text echoes and overlaps the lection of the third Sunday of Advent, as if we ought to say it again in a new light. The anticipated joy of homecoming now turns into a full-tilt party. And a public one at that, in the face of kings. The prophet proclaims a festival of God's sovereignty in history.

In Luke, Mary—along with her husband Joseph—takes the child up to Jerusalem. The babe becomes a public fact. Under the law, she dedicates him by a sacrifice—the two turtledoves—which is the special provision for those who are poor (Leviticus 12:8). And Jesus is there confirmed in praise by the prophet Anna. She is a widow, the first of many in Luke/Acts (4:25; 7:12; 18:3; 20:47; 21:2; 6:1; 9:39) who exemplify the vulnerability of poverty hand in hand with the intransigence of faith.

She and Simeon are the first ones to affirm publicly the incarnation as a mighty act of God, done in the sight of all the nations, but as yet recognized only with the eyes of faith. It seems unlikely they were waiting and watching for a baby, probably something much greater that would in truth be much less. And yet they have both the gift and the freedom to discern in this child that everything has changed.

For Simeon the public fact gives personal assurance. In praise he declares his freedom now to die. I hear his canticle in evening prayer or as sung by the monastics in Gregorian chant at compline just before bed. It is a faith in which one may both risk and rest. That personal assurance is what John Wesley so earnestly desired and what he named as the very distinction between the faith of the servant and the faith of the son or daughter (Galatians 4:7): an inheritance of true freedom.

—Bill Wylie-Kellermann

Called by the Light

Epiphany season be-gins and ends in light. From the heavenly star to the radi-ant robes of transfigura-tion, Epiphany is about revelation, the kind of sud-den brightness that lights up the landscape of a mind or a community or a whole social order. The light reveals, but not pas-sively; it summons and sends.

These readings are rich in callings. Exiles, altar boys, prophets, and disci-ples—all are bidden. Come home, come and see, come follow. When Jesus appears, things get set in motion. Though we may not see where it all leads, we al-ready have our marching orders. This is a light that moves.

—Bill Wylie-Kellermann

Epiphany Sunday

Feast of Racial Reconciliation

PSALM 72:1-14 • ISAIAH 60:1-6 • EPHESIANS 3:1-12 • MATTHEW 2:1-12

SO ABRUPTLY DOES Isaiah of the exile announce a dawning of light in history that the scholars are prone to doubt this is the same voice as in the preceding chapters.

Surely the one who recites that drumbeat litany of transgression and judgment, whose promises sound more like threats, cannot be the same person who turns around to testify the dawn of return. A new writer must have stepped into the breach. The light of hope could not break so suddenly in heart or history. Only an incrementally pro-gressive hope, something more akin to a studied optimism, is realistic. Judgment and true hope ought not be so closely pressed, or the one arise from the other.

Well, surprise. There it is (one may wager) in the prophet's single voice.

The homecoming envisioned is so overwhelming that the whole world seems swept along in its movement. Universal, as they say, and bordering on cosmic. A pil-grimage, general and complete, is in motion. It is not merely exiles who make for Jerusalem, but peoples and rulers, nations and authorities all. The scattering of exile is healed in a global accompaniment. Its theft is reversed by gift.

The Magi, in Matthew's telling, act the very embodiment of Isaiah 60. Are they strangers in the land? They stand for all nations and peoples outside of Israel. Are they kings? They kneel on behalf of all authority. Do they bear gifts? Thoughtfully packed from the ancient text. Then Matthew adds his ironies, bitter as myrrh: The Jerusalem king remains in the dark (wherein he schemes); the foreigners are directed farther on.

The concrete mystery of "all peoples and nations" also preoccupies Ephesians. St. Paul's voice, set in the dark of prison, attests a hidden truth come suddenly to light: Jews and Gentiles are both "partakers" in the promise. By "partaking," a meal is im-plied. They sit at common table. In light of Christ, the "dividing wall of hostility" (2:14) no longer comes between. To this degree, Epiphany is a feast of racial recon-ciliation.

The "principalities and powers" of racism and nationalism seem ignorant of the truth. They revive the hostility and rebuild the wall. That is why we, as the church, are admonished to make known to them the wisdom of God (3:10). Arise, dear friends, and shine.

—Bill Wylie-Kellermann

First Sunday After Epiphany

Baptism: An Authority of Freedom

PSALM 29 • GENESIS 1:1-5 • ACTS 19:1-7 • MARK 1:4-11

THESE TEXTS BEAR the voice of God: It is in the air and on the wind, it makes the oaks whirl and splits heaven. But above all, as attested in the baptism of Jesus, it con-firms identity and vocation in the Word. From voice, vocation.

It is not incidental that when Jesus later initiates his confrontation with the tem-ple-system in Jerusalem, and the chief priests, scribes, and elders challenge him, "By what authority do you do these things?" (Mark 11:28), he takes recourse to John's bap-tism. In a way politically loaded, he thereby recalls the movement with which he'd identified in the Jordan, and the troublesome prophet arrested and executed by Herod.

Was that baptism, he asks them, from heaven or not (11:29)? If there is a trick in his own clever question back to the temple rulers, it is that he actually gives something of an answer to their challenge while saying he will not. He cites the renegade and charismatic authority of his baptism.

It is reported that when Martin Luther was assailed by temptation or suffered self-doubt in his struggle with church authorities, he used to sit in his study and recite, almost as a mantra, "I am baptized. I am baptized."

Need it be said unequivocally that baptism is the base authority for *all* Christian ministry? Not ordination. Baptism authorizes our freedom to be who we are uttered in the Word of God to be. And it authorizes our freedom to speak and act and witness in whatever situation we may find ourselves.

Is there any doubt that Jesus, a lay person himself, would return now and again to the beginning of his ministry, to the experience accounted at the beginning of Mark's gospel? In those waters he heard the Voice. On those waters he saw the Spirit hover. There his authority, and ours in him, deep and ancient as day one of creation, is voiced.

—Bill Wylie-Kellermann

Second Sunday After Epiphany

In Body and Name

PSALM 139:1-6, 13-18 • 1 SAMUEL 3:1-20 • 1 CORINTHIANS 6:12-20 • JOHN 1:43-51

THE WORD OF GOD, says our first reading, was rare in those days. (Needless to say, we too know such times in life and history.) But then the Word comes calling. It sounds suddenly in the night, taking an unlikely form: the name of a Shiloh temple altar boy. The name and the summons are the Word at that moment. Imagine your own name uttered as the Word of God. Therein is your calling.

There is something wonderfully palpable about words in the Hebraic view. God speaks a new thing, at which "the two ears of everyone that hears it will tingle" (1 Samuel 3:11). The Word itself is something almost physical. In ancient Semitic culture, people would actually duck to avoid the path of a curse being uttered.

Further on in this text (3:19), to indicate the authenticity of Samuel's vocation, it is said that never were God's words allowed to fall to the ground! (They went, presumably, straight to their mark.) Little danger of that in our culture. Words are so eviscerated of substance and meaning they float away into thin air like so much pollution.

The Word is heard by Samuel and acknowledged by his mentor Eli. It effects a transition of authority from one to the other, setting in motion a whole new period in Israel's life.

The gospel lection is also about a transition: from the Baptist, a mentor of sorts himself, to Jesus. John's disciples take the clue and make the move. But talk about your palpable, bodily words: here the very Word incarnate.

Likewise, in 1 Corinthians, a momentous shift is implied in the phrase, "your [plural] body is a temple of the Holy Spirit" (6:19). It is a notion in line with the gospel idea: Destroy this temple and I'll build another in three days...but he spoke of his body (John 2:19-21). The community has supplanted the temple-system in a whole new era for Israel and the church. The body is the temple. And ethics, as Paul suggests, are become literally incarnational. The Word ought seldom be rare if so palpably present.

—Bill Wylie-Kellermann

Third Sunday After Epiphany

The Scandalous Freedom to Follow

PSALM 62:5-12 • JONAH 3:1-5, 10 • 1 CORINTHIANS 7:29-31 • MARK 1:14-20

IT SEEMS IMPOSSIBLE to read this minimalist edition, this matter of fact kernel of the Jonah story, without recalling the drama that surrounds it in the person of the prophet himself. Jonah, let it be said, is more of an anti-prophet: The sum total of his prophetic utterances (speaking of minimalist) come down to five Hebrew words (3:4). And these from a guy who begins by refusing his call (1:3) and ends pleading for death in a self-righteous pout (4:9).

Who is the witness of faith in this tale? Why, the city of Nineveh—imperial capital of Assyria, enemy and oppressor of ancient Israel. Who exercises the freedom of repentance? An entire city of mythic proportion, a collective totality taking in great and small, government and king, even flocks and herds. They match the solidarity of sin in violence with the solidarity of freedom in repentance. Here is an ironic tale bigger than the whale. Of course the final freedom is God's—who also repents of anger in judgment.

But Jonah? He clings to his fear, to his bitterness, to his prophetic dignity and repute, to hatred of his enemies, the damned imperialists. From beginning to end, he can't let it go.

He is to that degree the countersign of discipleship.

When Jesus calls the four in Mark, they drop everything and follow. His summons is minimal and direct. The text, as Bonhoeffer puts it, is "ruthlessly silent" about any fuller information or their previous knowledge of him. They simply let go their nets, their "worldly" affairs, the security of a family business, and come.

This is the same scandalous freedom enjoined in Corinthians. Not any particular prescription, but the grace of "as though," which disentangles women and men from the order of the present system that is passing away. When Gandhi commended it to the truth warriors, he called it non-attachment. In it they were freed for radical commitment to personal and social transformation. Freed for risk and service.

Paul knew it and practiced it in his way. But its emblem and source, for us, is Christ. The gospel lection begins with John's arrest. That, in the logic of the world-system, ought to be Jesus' clue to lay low or head the other way. Instead, like a zen slap on the cheek, it signals for him the decisive moment, ironically the very opening of freedom. He walks in and through, inviting those who'd follow.

—Bill Wylie-Kellermann

Fourth Sunday After Epiphany

The Sunday before Ash Wednesday is Transfiguration Sunday. If Ash Wednesday falls in this week, skip to the readings for Transfiguration Sunday, page 55.

True in a Din of False

PSALM 111 • DEUTERONOMY 18:15-20 • 1 CORINTHIANS 8:1-13 • MARK 1:21-28

THE BOOK OF DEUTERONOMY is cast as a farewell message from Moses, a last will and testament from a prophet who's been to the mountain top and looked over into the land of promise, toward the future of Israel and Judah. In the present text, a successor prophet is foreseen, though more is implied. It's almost as though the prophetic "office" were being sanctioned. Eventually this text would bear the weight of messianic expectation: the hope of "one like Moses." Jesus will be portrayed as filling the bill.

However, there are warnings here as well: a solemn charge to those who hear the prophet's message, and a warning against prophets who presume to speak a word not commanded by God. (They give themselves over to death.) The compunction to speak, it seems, carries more than one risk. And a people for whom the Word full force seemed too much to bear are now left with the ambiguities of discerning the true from the false. There lies the rub.

Such a din may have been raised in Galilee. When Jesus appears he calls out more than disciples; his presence summons antagonistic powers into the public arena. A conflict is provoked. When he teaches in the Capernaum synagogue, people recognize and acclaim the genuineness of his authority as distinct from the scribes. But immediately a voice cries out from their midst, "What have you to do with us Jesus of Nazareth? Have you come to destroy us?" (Mark 1:24). On whose behalf does the voice speak? In whose spirit?

Ched Myers suggests that in Mark's gospel this encounter initiates a continuing public clash between the authority of Jesus and the authority of the scribal elite. (See *Binding the Strong Man*, Orbis, 1988. Hey, for that matter, keep it close at hand for *all* the gospel lections of year B.) In Mark much of the discipleship teaching is played out against this conflict, even within it. The disciples struggle to learn true from false authority.

Would that this were only an ancient dilemma. Instead it is as biblical as the present moment. False prophecy has become the order of our day. From the justifications of imperial aggression to the assurances of technocratic fixers, from urgings of Madison Avenue hucksters to the piety of media-wise religious marketeers, the mimicry of the Word and the presumption of divine authority are rife.

We pray to discern the true in a din of the false.

—Bill Wylie-Kellermann

Fifth Sunday After Epiphany

The Sunday before Ash Wednesday is Transfiguration Sunday. If Ash Wednesday falls in this week, skip to the readings for Transfiguration Sunday, page 55.

Rise Up as Eagles!

PSALM 147:1-11, 20 • ISAIAH 40:21-31 • 1 CORINTHIANS 9:16-23 • MARK 1:29-39

THE GOSPEL PASSAGE CONTAINS an odd little scene, ignored by most commentators, that strikes modern sensibilities as slightly amiss, or at least incomplete. Jesus goes to Simon's home, where Simon's mother-in-law is ill. (Opponents of married priests take note: Simon Peter, the first pope, the rock upon which the church is built, was married.) Jesus touches her, heals her, and—here's the part that doesn't go down easy—she gets up and serves them.

This is the first reference to women in the first gospel written; and, though only three verses long, it's filled with significance. By touching her, Jesus takes a stand against ritual impurity. And her action shouldn't be misunderstood: Mark's word for "serve" (*diakonein*) was a term used to describe the ministry of Christians—ministry that evolved into the formal deaconate. For Mark, to serve is to be a true disciple. Indeed, it is the mark of Jesus, the suffering servant, to which Matthew's gospel refers in his telling of this story (8:14-17).

Isaiah's words (and all of chapters 40-55) are foundational for anyone who seeks to understand our relationship with temporal power. The people of Israel have been conquered, taken away from their ancestral home to exile in Babylon. Their hope for salvation, what little remains, is fading fast. How could they ever hope to overcome the power of Babylon, mighty Babylon, which appeared well nigh invincible—especially to those it had conquered. For almost a century the dynasty of Nebuchadrezzar had ruled the Near East, and (especially to its victims) didn't appear to be going away anytime soon.

Into this bleak picture blow the comforting words of the author of Second Isaiah. Isaiah's tone, however, is far from comforting: You can almost feel his sarcasm, his mockery, in the face of Israel's faithlessness. Don't you know? Haven't you heard since the beginning? Haven't you been paying attention? Who led you out of Egypt? Is God some puny, insignificant runt, quaking in fear at the "mighty" Babylonians?

On the contrary. These supposedly "invincible" powers are as nothing to God, as ephemeral as grass. God has only to breathe, and they wither and fade away. But God, Isaiah reminds his readers, is eternal, enthroned forever, does not faint or grow weary.

Isaiah's purpose here, of course, is to restore perspective. He's not telling them anything they don't know, as much as reminding them what they've forgotten. Remember who you are! Remember who made you! In that remembering, they too will rise up as eagles.

—Jim Rice

Sixth Sunday After Epiphany

The Sunday before Ash Wednesday is Transfiguration Sunday. If Ash Wednesday falls in this week, skip to the readings for Transfiguration Sunday, page 55.

Bathing in the Waters

PSALM 30 • 2 KINGS 5:1-14 • 1 CORINTHIANS 9:24-27 • MARK 1:40-45

JESUS' PUBLIC MINISTRY has hardly begun and already the seeds of conflict with the authorities have been sown. There's more to the healing of this leper than meets the eye! Beyond the simple compassion and pity that he showed, Jesus' act was a symbolic gesture, a proclamation of his power and authority, a message to the ruling class that couldn't be missed.

Several significant religio-cultural mores were breached in this interaction. The violation of accepted practices begins with the leper's approach to Jesus. We don't hear the required calls of "Unclean! Unclean!" This sick man, this "unclean" one, doesn't keep the distance that his status requires.

Being unclean, of course, was as much a spiritual and social condition as a physical one. The moral connotation was of impurity, unholiness—the implication being that the disease had its roots in iniquity. The priests, following the Levitical code (see Leviticus 13:2-14:57), had the authority to pronounce persons ceremonially unclean, and with that effectively to shun them, to ban them from the community.

But the leper in Mark's story seems to appeal that decision to a higher authority— he takes his case to Jesus: "If you wish, you can make me clean." This leper somehow knew that Jesus' authority overrode that of even the highest religious figures in the land. At his words, Jesus is moved with pity and compassion. Or is it something else? Some ancient manuscripts say that Jesus is "moved to anger" (*orgistheis*). Why would the leprosy make him angry? In *Binding the Strong Man*, Ched Myers argues that Jesus' anger is directed "against the symbolic order of purity of which this man is the victim." And Jesus' response—he "touched him"—made Jesus himself ceremonially unclean.

After the physical healing of the leprosy, the job was incomplete. Spiritual and social purification was still needed. (The man probably wished he could just wash seven times in the Jordan, like Naaman, and be done with it!)

So Jesus sent him back to the temple officials, as a living testimony of what he had done. Since their power rested on the authority granted them by the Law, the fact that Jesus "could make me clean" took away their exclusive claim. Thus this story stands as a proper introduction to the next section of Mark (2:1-3:6), with its five stories of conflict between Jesus and the Jewish authorities—which leads, ultimately, to the cross.

—Jim Rice

Seventh Sunday After Epiphany

The Sunday before Ash Wednesday is Transfiguration Sunday. If Ash Wednesday falls in this week, skip to the readings for Transfiguration Sunday, page 55.

A New Authority

PSALM 41 • ISAIAH 43:18-25 • 2 CORINTHIANS 1:18-22 • MARK 2:1-12

JESUS HERE BEGINS TO REVEAL his true nature and authority. His actions described in the previous chapter have spread his fame, so that on his return to Capernaum the crowds are so great that a major home "improvement" has to take place to enable the paralytic to get close to him. He understands these out-of-the-ordinary efforts as a sign of faith, and responds accordingly.

That's when the trouble starts. For Jesus, the spiritual and the physical are inseparable. When he heals, it has more to do with redemption than mere cure. But it has a fundamental social and political aspect as well, a very explicit message to the religious authorities.

The scribes, representing Jewish officialdom, are very much participants in this little drama. When the paralytic is laid before him, Jesus knows his deepest needs, and responds to them: He forgives the sick man's sins. The scribes are conspicuously unhappy about this; they grumble to themselves that he has usurped authority that doesn't belong to him—not just theirs, but God's!

Jesus clearly expects such a reaction, and he's ready. His next action is directed to them: "So that you may know..." (2:10). The healing is done for their benefit, as a witness to them. (It's safe to assume the former paralytic appreciated it as well.) They had declared, "Only God has the authority to forgive sins." Jesus' response is immediate, direct, and unmistakable—a proclamation of who he is. They're beginning to understand—if they only have the eyes to see—that he's more than just an itinerant preacher and faith healer. This guy has power and authority far beyond their own, beyond even the structures and institutions they administer, which pale in comparison.

No wonder they begin to see him as a threat! It wasn't just that he preached justice for the poor and downtrodden; it was that he embodied the new order of things. In his person was the manifestation and the seed of God's upside-down kingdom. To that beloved community, there was no automatic admission by birth or position; only the free ticket gained by grace and by the cross. Before that miracle, we all can "be amazed and glorify God"!

—**Jim Rice**

Eighth Sunday After Epiphany

The Sunday before Ash Wednesday is Transfiguration Sunday. If Ash Wednesday falls in this week, skip to the readings for Transfiguration Sunday, page 55.

The Nature of Love

PSALM 103:1-13, 22 • HOSEA 2:14-20 • 2 CORINTHIANS 3:1-6 • MARK 2:13-22

HOSEA, THE FIRST BOOK of the minor prophets, here gives us some of the most intimate and passionate images for Israel's relationship with God. The previous chapter contains perhaps the Old Testament's most distressing words of condemnation and rebuke, as Yahweh tells the unfaithful Israel, "You are not my people and I am not your God" (1:9). Israel's unfaithfulness has threatened to destroy the covenant established when God brought them out of Egypt (see Jeremiah 31:31-34). But God's steadfast love prevails, and merciful forgiveness—not righteous judgment—is the order of the day. As the psalmist says, God "nurses no lasting anger," and deals with us "not as our sins merit" (103:8-10).

The prophet's understanding of our relationship with God goes even deeper. Israel's sin is that of an unfaithful spouse (Hosea 2:15), and God's anger is likened to that of a jealous lover. God's response to the shameful infidelity is not to reject or spurn the philanderer, but instead to "allure her" (2:16), to entice her, back to faithfulness, back to the honeymoon period when Israel first came out of Egypt.

And again, deeper. Whereas human lovers may separate, God's faithfulness is forever, towering over us as the heavens over the earth, yet as intimate and personal as a compassionate father (Psalm 103:13).

And finally, even deeper yet. Despite our undeservedness, we are not just God's children, but God's beloved. Just so we are not confused, Hosea spells out the nature of that love (2:18): It is not that of a master (*baal*) with dominion over another, but that of a husband (*iysh*), a lover, who crowns us with tenderness and mercy (Psalm 103:4).

What a transformation! The passage begins with threats of vines and fig trees being laid waste and devoured, of punishment and rejection. It ends with the covenant renewed, strengthened, affirmed. Bless the Lord, my soul!　　　**—Jim Rice**

Transfiguration Sunday

(Sunday before Ash Wednesday)

A Place to Come Down From

PSALM 50:1-6 • 2 KINGS 2:1-12 • 2 CORINTHIANS 4:3-6 • MARK 9:2-9

AT THE END OF EPIPHANY and the threshold of Lent, there is no better vantage point than the mount of transfiguration. A commanding view looks back to the Jordan valley baptism and the Galilean ministry; before us the road to Jerusalem and beyond. In Mark it represents, along with Caesarea Philippi, something of a continental divide. A direction and intent are now manifest. Momentum gathers inexorably. The way of the cross has been invoked.

To a certain extent that way begins in mountain solitude, in a conversation with Moses and Elijah. Yes, the scene is iconic—a triptych of law, prophet, and new covenant; there is much for meditation. But the imagination runs to this conversation (unheard) in the light of glory. What did they talk about? What counsel did the ancients offer? These two had been to some pretty famous mountain tops.

But, more to the moment, they had each faced off with some high-powered authorities, empty-handed but for the promise of God. Do they utter encouragement? We only know his garments go white as a martyr's robe (Revelation 7:13-14).

The disciples, granted the glimpse, remain in a fog. The god of this world, the spirit of the age, the myth of messianic might will not permit them to comprehend at least until the resurrection. Their minds are blinded.

As if to underscore his confusion, Peter blurts out the proposal to construct dwellings. He doesn't get it, but clings to the experience. The moment is not for the sake of frieze or tableau, but for strength to come down the mountain toward confrontation and its cost. It is one thing to see Jerusalem from afar, another to walk there.

We think readily of Martin King as one who had been to the mountain top. He was granted the vision that frees and sustains. But he never imagined the mountain top was his dwelling place. He came down to the streets, to walk with the sanitation workers in Memphis. He came to meet the powers. He knew the movement, at least since Birmingham: A church is a place you go out from. Just so, a mountain is a place you come down from.

Listen. See. Come down. Go out.　　　**—Bill Wylie-Kellermann**

God's Downward Mobility

*P*rior to Constantine, when the church was outlawed and, with some regularity, systematically persecuted, the reception of members was a rigorous and risky proposition. Those wishing to become "hearers" (catechumens) were brought by sponsors who could vouch for them. Thereupon began a three-year period of prayerful instruction that concluded with intensive examination, with exorcism and fasting.

In an act of solidarity, others would join this fast anticipating the Easter Vigil. From these fasts, accounted variously in different places, the Lenten season of 40 days (echoing Jesus' struggle with the powers of death in the wilderness) was developed.

Lent arose from the confessional rigors of baptismal preparation. In that respect, it's fitting that the Hebrew Bible readings for this year should trace the history of covenant in Israel. Here they inform our own repentance and baptismal covenant. And they serve as a powerful subtext for Jesus' question on the road to Jerusalem: "Are you able to drink the cup that I drink and be baptized with the baptism that I am baptized with?'

—Bill Wylie-Kellermann

First Sunday of Lent

A Sign for All

PSALM 25:1-10 • GENESIS 9:8-17 • 1 PETER 3:18-22 • MARK 1:9-15

BIBLICALLY ORIGINAL AND most ancient, the rainbow covenant is with all humanity—indeed with all creation. But first recall that the flood that precedes is God's way of setting a limit to violence (Genesis 6:11) and beginning again. The opening chapters of Genesis are simply an escalating history of human violence: From the blood of Abel crying out from earth to Lemech's pledge of exponential revenge "seventy-sevenfold" (4:24), a mushrooming of violence is set in motion.

So the judgment fits the sin, or is an extension of it: God fights chaos with chaos, the floodwaters rolling in. God's sovereignty restored, the weapon (Lamentations 2:4; Habakkuk 3:9) is hung up for all time. The bow is set aside in glorious plain sight and by its sign all creation is drawn into covenant.

Our own experience, from cruise missiles to the multiplication of handguns (200 million in our country), surpasses, it seems, even the brutality of primordial history. (In the United States, every 14 minutes someone dies from gunfire.) I suppose we ought to cling to the rainbow sign.

Even more so, 1 Peter suggests the baptismal covenant. This, in a letter to a community facing a campaign of state terrorism and its spin-off mob violence. The hymn line, "by the light of burning martyrs," refers specifically to Nero's practice, then current, of lighting his garden parties with human torches—Christians bound aloft. New horrors were being invented.

Hold to your baptism, 1 Peter urges, like a raft in the storm, a passage through chaos. Hold to the knowledge that God in Christ is sovereign over the powers. They have been faced in the wilderness testing, and finally in the cross and resurrection. They are overcome not by further chaos but by nonviolent love.

More is implied. Since Christ overcame all powers, and died for all, baptism signifies not only the unity of the church, but of all humanity. Indeed, this is the sacramental covenant in which all alienation is overcome, where right relationship to the creation itself is restored. Christians live in that reconciliation—a true beginning again. An ancient sign fulfilled.

—Bill Wylie-Kellermann

Second Sunday of Lent

Walking in the Presence

PSALM 22:23-31 • GENESIS 17:1-7, 15-16 • ROMANS 4:13-25 • MARK 8:31-38

THE COVENANT WITH Sarah and Abraham is shamelessly particular. In the mystifying concreteness of God's initiative, they are chosen so that "all the families of the earth shall be blessed" (12:3). And apart from the ritual particulars, their part of the deal, according to God, is mainly to "walk in my presence and be blameless" or as the New English Bible translates, to "live always in my presence." The phrase calls to mind the contemplative exercise of a 16th-century monastic: "the practice of the presence of God."

This is a kind of synonym for faith. It is what precedes the law and, in a way, supplants it. To live every moment before God is to be free to stand at any moment before the judgment of God. It is thereby the freedom to die. That is the plain meaning of justification—trusting God and not our own righteousness (which is to say even our own work for justice).

There is, nonetheless, direction to all this. For the disciples to "practice the presence" means sticking with Jesus on the way to Jerusalem. They don't like the sound of what's to come (and their fears give voice to his own temptations; see Mark 8:33).

Ched Myers argues cogently that saving or losing one's life has to do with courtroom solidarity under pressure of threat. To be ashamed of Jesus and renounce him may save one's skin, but lose one's life—as it dawns on Peter in the high priest's courtyard. In any event, the topic remains the freedom to die. And trusting God's judgment above all others.

What goes unnoticed, as though Jesus had trailed his sentence off in an afterthought, is the first mention of resurrection in the gospel (8:31). It's like a half-smile breaking through the heavy talk. The presence of God in spite of our practice.

Walk in my presence and I'll show you the impossible, says God. Or at least the ridiculous, Abraham laughs. So does Sarah (18:12). Paul mentions everything but the "laughter." He should have remembered. It's the name of their first descendent, "Isaac."

—Bill Wylie-Kellermann

Third Sunday of Lent

Overturning Ideology

PSALM 19 • EXODUS 20:1-17 • 1 CORINTHIANS 1:18-25 • JOHN 2:13-22

IN THE ORTHODOX JEWISH accounting of the decalogue, the first commandment is, "I am Yahweh your God, who brought you out of the land of Egypt, out of the house of bondage" (Exodus 20:2). This is a command? Yes, in the manner of "Hear, O Israel...." In this case: Know, O Israel, that before your covenantal obligations were ever uttered, God had already acted unilaterally and unconditionally on your behalf, making you a free people. Know that whose you are precedes what you do. Know that grace precedes law.

By that simple preface or commandment, the remainder becomes a sign of faith. And the very form of justice for a community living in freedom.

That form begins with God alone, and with the prohibition against idolatry. I'm reminded of the discipline for the Vietnamese Buddhist order founded by Thich Nhat Hanh during the Vietnam War. It began with a similar impulse: "Do not be idolatrous about or bound to any doctrine, any theory, any ideology, including Buddhist ones." Including this discipline? Yes. Put it another way: Even the law?

In the history of covenantal faith, there have been contenders aplenty for confusion, seduction, false worship—yet the most subtle has been the law and all its trappings. Certain prophets railed against the legal misdirections of cult. Jeremiah, like Stephen to follow, preached against the idolatry of the temple itself. They paid a price for that.

In John's gospel the temple action by Jesus happens up front—though still at Passover time. The feast of liberation had been all but lost in a bondage of confusion. Jesus overturns the idol of the temple system. He pays a price for that. On the cross he trusts in God alone.

Paul preaches, the letter says, Christ crucified. That remains the final undoing of every idolatry. It is an affront to the intellectual wisdom of Greeks and the expectations of Jews. It is foolishness to every ideology: capitalist and nationalist, Marxist and Jungian, deconstructionist and post-modern—all. It exposes New Age syncretism, liberalism, and of course fundamentalism. But what about radical Christianity? By the cross even its pretensions are overturned.

—Bill Wylie-Kellermann

Fourth Sunday of Lent

Lift Jesus Up!

PSALM 107:1-3, 17-22 • NUMBERS 21:4-9 • EPHESIANS 2:1-10 • JOHN 3:14-21

THE COMMON ASSUMPTION TODAY is that young people want to be gratified instantly, and so are less willing to put up with hardships than their parents or grandparents were. However, the passage from Numbers is one of many that shows that grumbling isn't a specialty of Generation X...or any other modern generation. Neither, in fact, is challenging authority. The ancient Israelites got to be pretty good at both during their sojourn in the wilderness.

It is not that they didn't have reason to "murmur," as our church elders called it. Dust, dirt, wind, 40 years of wandering in the desert sun: You might get a little cranky too.

Yet if we allow ourselves to dwell too long on our misfortunes, we will soon find that we have been consumed by them. This happened to the Israelites who interpreted the poisonous snakes, people-swallowing earth, and other plagues that struck them during their years in the wilderness as the fruit of their negative attitudes and actions.

Much like the Hebrews in the desert, modern Christians also spend much of their energy bemoaning their lives—sometimes with cause, sometimes without. While nobody can deny the difficulty, pain, and injustices that we do our best to face day after day, our lives also contain moments of great beauty and joy that we often overlook.

This Sunday's readings offer a perspective of reality so positive and powerful that it fuels the entire message of the gospel: "For God so loved the world..." (John 3:16). "For by grace are ye saved;...it is the gift of God" (Ephesians 2:8). "God's steadfast love endures forever" (Psalm 107:1). These are God's assurances to us that, as Martin Luther King Jr. would say, the arc of the universe is long, but it bends toward justice. And though the struggle is long and arduous, we know that, in the eternal realm, the battle has been won.

Focusing on the positive end of our faith means more than skipping around with a glib "don't worry, be happy" attitude. A perspective that is grounded in the truth of God's promises should radically shape our lives and work in the here and now, making it possible for us to "keep on keeping on" in our efforts to incarnate the love of Christ and reconcile the world to God.

"Just as Moses lifted up the snake in the desert, so the Son must be lifted up, that everyone who believes in him may have eternal life" (John 3:14-15). What a strange twist that transforms the tragic image of Christ crucified into the triumphant object of our praise.

—Aaron Gallegos

Fifth Sunday of Lent

More Real by Heart

PSALM 51:1-12 • JEREMIAH 31:31-34 • HEBREWS 5:5-10 • JOHN 12:20-33

JEREMIAH'S MOST STUNNING contribution to covenant history and theology is in this word to the community of exiles, a people without access to the trappings of temple and state. It will be different, he says, from the Sinai pact (another time they possessed neither) because it will be "written on their hearts."

One implication is that legal sanctions would become unnecessary, the practice of the covenant being simply inseparable from who they are. This is good news indeed to a people suffering the biggest historical sanction they could imagine. The transforming importance of forgiveness (31:34) is precisely the love which ends that sanction.

The prophet commends something radically incarnational: covenant come in the flesh. And radically egalitarian. This is a covenant fully accessible to all. By heart. It's known and remembered even without the apparatus of instruction, mediated by neither king nor priest. It is in fact the same covenant—"I will be their God and they will be my people"—but pressed to a new level of reality.

The book of Hebrews quotes this text in full (8:8-13) and then cites it yet again in the course of an argument that the new covenant of Christ has replaced the old of temple, cult, and law. There is far more here than some spurious superseding of Jewish by Christian. And it goes in the direction of Jeremiah's offering to the exiles: deeper into life and reality. Today's epistle reading suggests that Jesus is qualified for high priesthood not by levitical genealogy, but by loud cries and tears. By Gethsemane and by the cross. Official priestly authority is subverted and supplanted by life and death, by flesh and blood.

I think of Oscar Romero (who died March 24, 1980). He fulfilled his vocation as priest and bishop not by the trappings of office, but by heart, with loud cries and tears. He followed his episcopal call deeper into reality. Really, really, I say to you, unless a grain of wheat falls into the earth and dies, it remains alone; but if it dies, it bears much fruit.

—Bill Wylie-Kellermann

Palm Sunday

Have This Mind

PSALM 31:9-16 • ISAIAH 50:4-9 • PHILIPPIANS 2:5-11 • MARK 14:1-15:47

THE THIRD SERVANT SONG of Isaiah is always the Hebrew Bible reading for this last Sunday of Lent that begins Holy Week. Thoroughly apt. It bespeaks a fusion of vulnerability and utter intransigence in a way that evokes (and perhaps nourished) the spirit of Jesus in his passage through city and week. Here is one who listens, encourages the weary, who suffers abuse and takes the heat but whose face is set like flint, challenging adversaries. The details of the gospel could be marshaled example by example.

What gives pause is the repeated use of disciple (Isaiah 50:4) in the passage, as in "those who are taught." Are we listening? And the nagging ambiguity of the Servant's identity doesn't help. Cyrus, the scholars say. Or Israel. The prophet or the prophetic community. An eschatological figure. Or, perhaps, the lection coming far too close to home...some nondescript disciple.

Oh, we sigh, that this vulnerable intransigence were not so impossible to generate. Except that it is Yahweh who gives, who wakens, who opens the ear. It is Yahweh who helps and vindicates—before whom we stand.

A disciple named Paul writes a letter from prison. "Have this mind..." he says, quoting a hymn that could rattle some walls. (This too is the lection each year.) It describes the downward mobility of God in Christ. A refusal of every grasping claim to power and domination. A faithfulness in the face of torture and death itself. Have this mind, he says, suggesting that all the qualities of communal solidarity (Philippians 2:1-4) may be predicated upon it.

Today, the Passion account is read in its entirety. Listen as those who are taught. The leper's house and the woman remembered. A plot with an agent at an underground meal. A hymn and a night of prayer. Arrest, assorted hearings, and trials. Abandonment and denial. The torture room and the executioner's technique. Mockery and humiliation. The women with the guts to watch. The awful silence of God.

But above all, or in it all, listen for a certain presence of grace with an edge, of vulnerability and steel intransigence. Dare we have this mind?

—Bill Wylie-Kellermann

An Easter Cliffhanger

There is no more brilliant literary surprise, I think, in all of scripture than the shocking cliffhanger abruptness of Mark's resurrection account. Literally inspired. Its stark brevity leaves the remainder of Year B Eastertide Sundays scrambling for resurrection narratives from Luke and John. But its pointed question hangs over them all, as it hangs over our own narratives: What will you do with the resurrection news?

In a sense, the Book of Acts is the early community's answer to that very question. These Sunday readings therefore work out some Easter implications pastorally, socially, economically, and politically. The answers we glimpse are as stunning as the question.

—Bill Wylie-Kellermann

Easter Sunday

The Opening Door

PSALM 118:1-2, 14-24 • ACTS 10:34-43 • 1 CORINTHIANS 15:1-11 • MARK 16:1-8

THE WOMEN DISCIPLES who have the nerve to stand by, eyes and hearts open at the foot of the cross, are also the ones with the nerve to attend the grave when the Sabbath is over. The legal unreliability of women as witnesses (so the culture had it) is often noted for its irony. (And ironically as evidence of historical veracity, on the premise that no church concocting testimony would begin with women witnesses: Notice, indeed, that Paul and Peter omit them utterly in today's lections.)

The degree of their courage, however, is generally unaccounted. This movement has been targeted and ostensibly crushed. The shepherd has been struck so that the sheep will scatter. But the women hang in. They refuse to go quietly away. Their act of memory and mourning and the freedom of their continuing open association has been compared to the Mothers of the Disappeared in South America standing watch in one plaza or another.

Isn't the irony that in the stark reversal of Mark's abrupt ending (verse 8) their fear should punctuate the entire narrative as a question mark? They fear neither men nor powers, but an empty tomb? The women fear God alone. Their knees buckle to imagine the transforming power that is here and now being unleashed. What next? A door opens before them at the end.

Thank God, even unacknowledged, Peter and Paul followed the women through that door. Moreover, as these texts have it, they recollect and recite the resurrection in moments of transformation, personal and social: Peter, in his monumental breakthrough to community with Gentiles; Paul, in a letter that summons the healing freedom required by a beloved community fracturing to bits. A door, they both testify, has opened....

The question remains: Will we now, in fear and trembling (not to mention utter joy), walk through?

—Bill Wylie-Kellermann

Second Sunday of Easter

Touching the Word

PSALM 133 • ACTS 4:32-35 • 1 JOHN 1:1-2:2 • JOHN 20:19-31

THE DOORS WERE SHUT for fear of the authorities (John 20:19). The disciples have entombed themselves. The One who has broken out of death must now break in to bear them peace.

Thomas I like—perhaps because I know him too well, this twin of us all. Absent and wary. Does he hold shut the heart's door for fear? For tough-mindedness? For the doubt that is his fame? What he does know is worth a stack of sermons: how to recognize Jesus. By his wounds, of course. As if to say again, you can't see the Risen One unless you can see the Crucified. To look for, to touch the one is to touch the other—one and the same.

By conventional logic you would think the 1 John text would find a home in the Christmas lections, celebrating the feast of the incarnation. Thomas, no doubt, has beckoned it here. That which we have seen and heard and touched with our hands concerning the Word of Life....What have we touched to which we now testify in joy complete? Wounds of the Crucified? One another in the loving circle of community? Eucharist passed hand to hand? All this and more—reality itself transfigured?

The resurrection testimony of Acts 4 is not an incidental inclusion in a laundry list of communal acts. It is at the heart of a fundamental restructuring of the community's commonlife. As though the core assumptions of how we now live and organize our lives had enjoyed a seismic or even cosmic shift. And the material reorganization is a testimony too. A resurrection economy. Something the poorest among them could sink their teeth into, or pass hand to hand around the circle, touching the Word of Life.

—Bill Wylie-Kellermann

Third Sunday of Easter

Recognizing Resurrection

PSALM 4 • ACTS 3:12-19 • 1 JOHN 3:1-7 • LUKE 24:36-48

THE RECOGNITION of the resurrected Jesus is once again at issue in Luke 24. The whole of the Emmaus road story is invoked in the opening line (verse 35), how he was known to them in the breaking of the bread. Then, as if the wounds on his hands and feet were not enough, he eats a piece of fish.

A friend says if you can read the gospels without getting hungry you're not paying attention. Jesus comes eating and drinking: So many feasts and feedings, table teachings and banquet parables, last suppers and Easter barbecues—one gets the feeling the kingdom was convened as a gigantic floating potluck, the poor being seated first. In the resurrection he can walk and talk with them, speak in their midst, but they're not quite sure 'til, Look! He has bread or fish in his hand—it's the Lord!

1 John offers the ominous comfort that the world doesn't recognize us because it never recognized Christ (verse 1). It gives pause to imagine the form of resurrection recognizable in our own lives. What wounds? What bread? What freedom?

Peter says, Why do you stare at us? This healing is not by our piety or power (verse 12). Yes. True. But even so I might stare. Resurrection is here. Well, of course, Peter preaches it, a no-holds-barred accusation that this crowd didn't know what they were looking at in Christ Jesus. But more than that, it's in the freedom to preach in a place the authorities will quickly forbid. Temple cops are on the way. This is not the same Peter slinking away in fear at cockcrow. These are not the same disciples huddling in the dark behind closed doors. Well, they are the same and more. The Risen One is here. Has claimed them. Has brought them out from death.

It does not yet appear what we shall be, but you can bet your life it'll look like Christ.

—Bill Wylie-Kellermann

Fourth Sunday of Easter

Wolves in the Window

PSALM 23 • ACTS 4:5-12 • 1 JOHN 3:16-24 • JOHN 10:11-18

IF TODAY'S GOSPEL calls up for you images of a familiar stained-glass window, the good shepherd with a lamb cuddled over the shoulder, then it's probably best to envision it with a brick being thrown through. The tension of this reading is between the literally "pastoral" character—the tenderness of love for the flock—and the predatory violence of the beast. The stillness of waters and the rushing of the wolves.

The power of death (or as the famous Psalm puts it, the shadow of death) hovers just beyond the window's frame. The work of the pastor (whose Latin root means shepherd or feeder as in pasturer) is to love, nourish, stand by, and lead, but finally to die for the flock. (Oughtn't this come up at services of commissioning or ordination?) The hireling may "love in word and speech," but the shepherd loves in "deed and truth" (1 John 3:18).

The basis of pastoral work is here portrayed as love, but coupled with the freedom to die. No one takes my life, I lay it down of my own accord (John 10:18).

Peter's testimony in Acts is a straightforward witness to the resurrection. Well enough as it stands. But, like a brick through the window, we realize this is courtroom testimony after a night in jail. The disciples will be threatened and sent away under injunction no longer to preach or teach in this name. They have the resurrection moxie to declare their freedom before going: "Whether it is right in God's sight to listen to you rather than God, you must judge; for we cannot keep from speaking about what we have seen and heard" (4:19-20). Indeed, they will be back shortly in this courtroom.

It is probably best to recall the whole story of chapters 3 and 4, brick by brick (see "The Politics of Healing" in my *Seasons of Faith and Conscience*). Perhaps the most amazing element is the story of the one lame from birth. He is alluded present at trial. How? Also arrested, spending the night at hymns and prayers with Peter and John in jail? Subpoenaed by the authorities? I think not. They don't want him there. He is the living evidence, a testimony they wish suppressed. They'd prefer him lame again.

Apparently he has simply walked in and presented himself, come to stand beside the disciples. This is a nervy witness: The real miracle is not just that he's standing, but that he's standing there. This new congregant in Peter's pastoral care has caught his own case of resurrection freedom.

How the wolves must howl.

—Bill Wylie-Kellermann

Fifth Sunday of Easter
Roots of Nonviolence

PSALM 22:25-31 • ACTS 8:26-40 • 1 JOHN 4:7-21 • JOHN 15:1-12

ON THE ONE HAND, it's no surprise in Acts: A high government official is intrigued and perplexed by a classic biblical text of nonviolence. And yet his questions are lucid ones (indeed the scholars still ask them of the servant songs in Isaiah): Of whom does the passage speak? The prophet? Someone else, perhaps a messianic figure? Or is this a more collective image, of a remnant or even Israel as a whole?

Philip seizes the question as an opening. He begins where the Ethiopian official is. He tells the story of Jesus as though its form and outline were there to be seen on the page with the suffering servant, or as though gospel nonviolence and the way of the cross could trace it roots to this very text.

Nonviolence is of the moment in these chapters. Stephen's fiery and forgiving martyrdom is accomplished and a full tilt persecution is abroad (chapter 7). Saul, still breathing threats, will be stopped dead in his tracks in the next (chapter 9). Between Stephen and Paul is Philip, crossing barriers first to the hated Samaritans, now to a black African (a Gentile even?) from beyond the imperial borders. The conversation concerning the servant song is a still point around which much is swirling.

In Luke-Acts, love of enemies is the acid test of the gospel. In the letters and gospel of John, the acid test is to love one another in community. (I won't presume to judge which is the tougher.) The commandment to love is connected to the vine (another image that goes back to Isaiah, 5:1-7). In fact, the vine in John is essentially an equivalent for what St. Paul calls "the body." You can't bear the fruits if you don't have the roots. The branches stay connected. They abide in love.

Philip, for his part, speaks as though the roots were nourished in the servant songs.

He acts as though the vine could sprawl across the map. As though its branches needn't stop for barriers or border guards. As though love of strangers or even enemies and love of community were not so different as we like to imagine.

—Bill Wylie-Kellermann

Sixth Sunday of Easter

The Politics of Friendship

PSALM 98 • ACTS 10:44-48 • 1 JOHN 5:1-6 • JOHN 15:9-17

ALLOW US TO CONSIDER another well-known text, from a letter of Thomas Merton to a young activist: "Concentrate not on the results but on the value, the rightness, the truth of the work itself. And there too a great deal has to be gone through, as gradually you struggle less and less for an idea and more and more for specific people. The range tends to narrow down, but it gets more real. In the end, it is the reality of personal relationships that saves everything."

Apart from the Society of Friends, who have made it an emblem and a practice, friendship is too little honored in the church. When Jesus names the disciples his friends he changes the shape of things—the community is not to be a pyramid but a circle. The notion of friendship supplants hierarchy with a certain mutuality and equality. Above all friendship implies freedom. Not to mention delight in one another's presence, that love which is "joy complete."

And yet. When discipleship becomes friendship, the way of the cross is borne along in the bargain to lay down one's life for one's friends. A deeper version of the same freedom. A deeper version even of the same joy.

In a community, like John's, under persecution of one variety or another, friendship entailed a clear choice. Richard Cassidy *(John's Gospel in New Perspective)* points out the contrast implied in being a "friend of Caesar" as coveted brutally by Pilate (19:12), and being a friend of Jesus. To "abide" in Jesus, to "remain" with him, meant a durable friendship. One that could endure the heat.

We stand by Jesus (he stood by us first). We stand by our friends. Love one another as I have loved you. The range narrows, but it gets more real.

—Bill Wylie-Kellermann

Ascension Sunday

In some traditions, the Ascension Sunday texts are used in place of the Seventh Sunday of Easter.

The Ultimate Drama

PSALM 47 • ACTS 1:1-11 • EPHESIANS 1:15-23 • LUKE 24:44-53

LUKE, THE DRAMATIST of dramatists! The Greek who can out-Greek the Greeks when it comes to theater! Luke sets us up in the first chapter of Acts: "When we last left our hearty band of disciples, Theophilus..." (assuming that we have read his previous cliffhanger—see Luke 24:44-53). Before we get to the second verse of Acts 1, our hero-protagonist, Jesus, has been "taken up to heaven," after leaving a cryptic set of instructions through the Holy Spirit to his crew.

Now, a brief flashback through post-resurrection appearances—gleaming angels at the tomb, the stranger on the Emmaus road, Jesus popping in on the disciples for a fish dinner—is offered as context. Fade out narrator Luke, up audio on the dialogue:

"Lord, are you now going to restore the kingdom to Israel?" Note how this question fits so tightly with the dialogue in Luke 24:44-49. We are swept right up in the drama toward Acts 1:9, where Jesus is "taken up before their very eyes, and a cloud hid him from their sight."

Ascensions are not an everyday occurrence. In the Greek pantheon, Heracles is deified through ascension and Ganymede became immortal when Zeus lifted him to heaven. In the Hebrew scriptures, ascension is more associated with mystical visions rather than death, as in the cases of Enoch and Elijah.

The ascension of Christ, however, is unique because of its eschatological significance in the early church. In the resurrection Jesus exerts power over all earthly life, conquering death and becoming in every essence the Human One. In his ascension, Jesus displays his reign over all heavenly powers as well; all minor deities and those plaguing demonic powers are subdued through the ascension of Christ. Luke gives a sharp rebuke to the Gnostic movement which would stand staring into the sky and promoting the heresy that the baptized Christians were now themselves divine through Christ's ascension.

Luke's point is to prepare us for the outpouring of the Holy Spirit, which was promised through history by the prophets and by Jesus. Jesus instructs the disciples to stay in Jerusalem so that this coming divine revolution can happen on the Feast of Shavu'ot (Moses' receiving of the Law), when the most amount of people will be in the biggest town. John Calvin put it this way, "As the Law was given to the people 50 days after Passover, written by the hand of God on tablets of stone, so the Holy Spirit, whose work is to write the Law on our hearts, the same number of days after the resurrection of Christ, who is the true Passover, fulfilled what had been prefigured in the giving of the Law."

Pentecost: It's coming soon to a frightened little band of faithful near you!

—**Rose Marie Berger**

Seventh Sunday of Easter

In some traditions, the Ascension Sunday texts are used in place of the Seventh Sunday of Easter.

A Prayer Upon Us All

PSALM 1 • ACTS 1:15-17, 21-26 • 1 JOHN 5:9-13 • JOHN 17:6-19

THE REPLACEMENT OF JUDAS with Mathias in the first chapter of Acts is not administrative busywork for the idle days between ascension and Pentecost. Something more poignant feels at work. In the absence of the Lord, Judas' empty place at the table must be an ache too much to bear, like a branch lopped from the vine, or an open wound in the body. Judas was "numbered" among them. Now their number is incomplete.

Lots are cast to replace him. With credentials only that he was with them from the beginning, Mathias fills an ache and a place and a ministry—an opposite number of austere anonymity—never to be mentioned again in scripture. But the prayer of election falls upon him.

Let us venture to suggest that the prayer of Jesus in John 17 falls upon him as well. It is certain that, even at a distance of time, those in the community of the beloved disciple (see verse 20) experienced this as an intercession for themselves in a dark hour. In the same way, in the mystery of time, we know ourselves prayed for in this passage. The words of Jesus wash over us in love and also in sober warning: The world will hate them as it has hated me.

Scholars agree that *kosmos* here is not so much the universe or the planet, but the "world" of human social existence and especially that world as fallen, a realm of alienation estranged from God. Walter Wink has suggested "system" as a translation for this special meaning, as in, "My kingdom is not of this system," or, as in the present case, "The world system has hated them because they are not of the system, even as I am not."

Judas is alluded to in the prayer as one lost. His place is already empty. The infiltrator at the table, the agent of the authorities, representative of this world system, has already fled to his work. But the prayer avails nonetheless. Even now we pray it washes over us, pray to know its power.

—Bill Wylie-Kellermann

Pentecost Sunday

A Spirit Exceeding Promise

PSALM 104:24-35 • ACTS 2:1-21 • ROMANS 8:22-27 • JOHN 15:26-27, 16:4-15

IN THE SYNOPTIC GOSPELS, the promise of the Holy Spirit is regularly associated with the ability to speak boldly and coherently in court or before the authorities (Mark 13:9-10, Luke 12:11-12, Matthew 10:17-20). Likewise, the promise in John is connected with the trials of persecution (15:18-25, 16:1-4) and the Spirit is named with a courtroom term. The paraclete is one "called alongside" to stand with disciples in court, a counselor in the manner, say, of a defense attorney. (Susan Thistlethwaite has sometimes translated it as "resistance counselor.") The Advocate is one who will prove the world system wrong about judgment, because the ruler of this old world order is the one who is truly condemned (16:8, 11).

In these readings, however, the life of the Spirit far exceeds such a promise. For Paul in Romans, the Spirit knows our hearts. It stands with us, faithful at our very depths. Its advocacy is intercession before God, articulating the groans of our hearts (which resonate as one with the groans of creation itself). We know, it seems, neither how to speak nor pray. The Spirit's utterance names that hope which is both our own transformation and the transformation of all creation, freeing it from bondage to death (Romans 8:18-22). The groans are as a woman in childbirth—a new world being born.

Come the day of Pentecost, it is certainly that new world which is glimpsed in the dreams and visions identified in ancient texts (Acts 2:17). And talk about the Spirit giving utterance! Talk about boldness and freedom! Not only in court or at prayer, but in the streets. The old order is thoroughly transcended. The binding constraints of nation and culture and tongue, of age and race and sex (of even more by dint and hint) are broken in overpowering exuberance. The new world is here anticipated, here born.

The disciples themselves are made new. Who they are in the renewal of the Spirit stands them in pretty good stead when, soon enough, they appear in the dock.

—Bill Wylie-Kellermann

Trinity Sunday

Calls and Responses

PSALM 29 • ISAIAH 6:1-8 • ROMANS 8:12-17 • JOHN 3:1-17

ISAIAH'S CALL, coming as it does in the midst of a worship service, is a rarity in scripture. Apparently his stunning vision is granted in the course of a temple liturgy—one of the very few biblical altar calls. It's as if the Sanctus at a Communion were suddenly joined by seraphim (or angels, archangels, and all the company of heaven!) crying, Holy Holy Holy.

The transcendent clarity of such a vision constitutes a call; but it also exposes a fearsome guilt, both personal and collective (6:5), which constrains Isaiah. Woe is me. But then that coal from the altar. In its white-hot ministration is release, a freedom loosed. Here am I; send me.

Nicodemus is being called too. It's drawn him out of the temple precincts under cover of night. He comes already constrained by a fear at once personal and collective. Jesus names his need, but Nicodemus can't afford to get it. He knows too much to understand the change required of breaking into that light which newborns see.

Romans speaks to the difference between the two—living according to the flesh or led by the Spirit. Walter Wink translates "flesh" as the "alienated self" externalized and subjugated to the opinion of others, self socialized into a world of unauthentic values. Does Nicodemus not qualify? He encounters Jesus bound in a "spirit of slavery, falling back into fear" (8:15). Yet he yearns (you can hear it beneath his questions) for adoption as a child of God, for birth from above, for freedom. He yearns (as John's readers would hear it) for that baptism, for the inner grace and the outer public sign, water and spirit.

May that be upon us all in the name of the Creator to whom our cries (holy, glory, *abba*) arise; in the name of the One Sent in whom this world is so loved; and in the name of the Spirit who stands by us in freedom. Amen.

—**Bill Wylie-Kellermann**

Seeking the New Vision

*T*he scriptures for our meditations come from 1 and 2 Samuel, the Psalms, the gospel according to Mark, and Paul's second letter to the Corinthians. The meditations follow a pattern of tracing the Story from its beginning in the Hebrew scriptures to its climax in the memories of the early church as reflected in the gospels, and then on to what sense the first Christians made of the connection between the two, as worked out in the epistles. At each step along the way, the effort is made to glean what the scripture passage may say to us today, either individually or corporately.

The Story continues with us. In our meditations we step into a flowing stream.

—**Verna J. Dozier**

Sunday Between May 29 and June 4

(if after Trinity Sunday)

An Intimate Union

PSALM 139:1-6, 13-18 • 1 SAMUEL 3:1-20 • 2 CORINTHIANS 4:5-12 • MARK 2:23-3:6

SAMUEL'S CHILDHOOD—when "the word of the Lord was rare and visions were not widespread"—certainly doesn't sound like it was a time of spiritual fireworks. Rather, Israel's human energy was being consumed by ill-fated and imperialistic military campaigns against the Philistines (1 Samuel 4), while their spiritual energy was being eaten up—quite literally—by corrupt and self-serving priests (1 Samuel 2).

Women and men of profound devotion and persistent faith—like Samuel's mother Hannah—were hard to find. Then, in the midst of this spiritual desert, God intervened, pouring upon a little boy the thirst-quenching rain of direct revelation.

Today, many have a hard time believing that God actually speaks to people, and that the Supreme Creator of the universe is truly "acquainted with all of our ways," as Psalm 139 says. Finding words to describe these instances of divine revelation—which vary throughout the Bible and from person to person—is a little like trying to fit the ocean into a bottle. This knowledge of God's intimacy with us is "too wonderful," though it is perhaps never harder to attain than in times of tragedy or when the presence of evil causes us to question its reality.

Yet God, who "knit us together in our mother's womb" (Psalm 139:13), never expects us to become super-saints or angelic beings through the experience of heaven-sent revelations. God never forgets that we carry the treasure of Christ in hearts that are frail as "earthen vessels" (2 Corinthians 4:7).

Rather, these grace-filled moments at the edge of the divine sea deepen our understanding of God's intimate union with our lives and strengthen us in times of trial and affliction. Indeed, as the scripture alludes to, when we embrace the reality that Christ has been broken with us in our pain, then the life of Jesus is truly revealed in and through us (2 Corinthians 4:10-11).

—**Aaron Gallegos**

Sunday Between June 5 and 11

(if after Trinity Sunday)

A Different Vision

PSALM 138 • 1 SAMUEL 8:4-20 • 2 CORINTHIANS 4:13-5:1 • MARK 3:20-35

SOMETIMES A LIGHT SURPRISES. "The Christian when he sings..." went Cowper's old hymn. That can also be the experience of one reading the disparate texts of a lectionary. Each one is a part of the same great Story, but what single message do they all have for me today?

In the Hebrew scripture, the people of God confront God's prophet Samuel about their anxiety for the stability of their system of government. They ask for a king "like other nations."

The psalm is one of thanksgiving and joy, secure in the knowledge that "God will fulfill God's purpose for us."

The gospel presents Jesus' radical ministry, which causes his family so much concern that they come after him to bring him back to the safety of his home. They can't get close because of the crowds so they send word: "Your mother and your brothers and sisters are outside, asking for you."

He makes the astounding reply, "Who are my mother and my brothers? Here are my mother and my brothers! Whoever does the will of God is my brother and sister and mother."

The biblical record ends with the epistle and the great apostle Paul assuring his little flock, "We look not at what can be seen but at what cannot be seen."

The message for the week: A different vision.

The caution for the week: Let's not absolutize the different vision.

Sometimes the different vision can be as cautious as deserting the new thing to be like everybody else. Sometimes it can be as bold and imaginative as Jesus' new definition of family. We can remember the faith of the psalmist. God will fulfill God's purpose for us. We can remember the faith of Paul. Look not at what can be seen but at what cannot be seen.

—Verna J. Dozier

Sunday Between June 12 and 18

(if after Trinity Sunday)

The Old Order Changes

PSALM 20 • 1 SAMUEL 15:34-16:13 • 2 CORINTHIANS 5:6-17 • MARK 4:26-34

LAST WEEK THE SCRIPTURES invited us to contemplate the new—a different possibility. This week we begin to live into that new possibility: first in the Hebrew scripture, a new king; a prayer for that new king in the psalm; parables about the mystery of growth and change in the gospel; and in the epistle, a salute to the new creation.

The selection of the unlikely David has overtones of the selection of great David's greater son, "the stone that the builders rejected." The question is asked, "Can any good thing come out of Nazareth?" But we remember the different vision. "We look not at what can be seen but at what cannot be seen."

Looking not at what can be seen but at what cannot be seen may illumine an often overlooked parable. Two parables are put here close together; the second one about the mustard seed has eclipsed the first one in familiarity. However, the first one, about the process of growth, speaks to our different vision. Someone scatters the seed. That is all she or he does. The earth produces of itself! Jesus was talking about the inevitability of the coming of the kingdom. That is the assurance with which we work.

It was also the assurance with which St. Paul worked: "If anyone is in Christ, there is a new creation: Everything old has passed away; see, everything has become new."

—Verna J. Dozier

Sunday Between June 19 and 25

(if after Trinity Sunday)

Power of God

PSALM 9:9-20 • 1 SAMUEL 17:1, 4-11, 19-23, 32-49 • 2 CORINTHIANS 6:1-13 • MARK 4:35-41

AFTER LAST WEEK'S SURGE of optimism, even with our deepest wishing that it were so, we find ourselves sinning against the Holy Spirit, doubting the power of God.

We need this week's scriptures.

We begin with the ancient and beloved tale of David and Goliath. It is an ill-matched battle, as you can imagine. The contest begins with the usual exchange of compliments from the warriors. Goliath promises to give David's flesh to the birds of the air and to the wild animals of the field.

David replies, "You come to me with sword and spear and javelin, but I come to you in the name of the Lord of hosts, the God of the armies of Israel whom you have defied." David continues, "so that all the Earth may know that there is a God in Israel."

David, a shepherd lad, prevailed over an awesome warrior.

By the power of God.

The psalm celebrates that power. "The Lord is a stronghold for the oppressed." But the psalm, with the realism of Hebrew religion, acknowledges that the events may not always bear this out. While the psalmist sings his faith that God will not forget the cry of the afflicted, this is no Pollyanna refusal to look at the affliction. There is trouble in the world. But it is not the last word.

The gospel underscores this. The last word is God's. "Peace, be still."

This is a beloved story. Does its attraction for us suggest we sense the words are addressed to us? "Lord, do you not care?" we cry. It is an act of faith. We are in frightening circumstances. We have no resources to help ourselves. We cry out to the only One who can. Has it not been said human extremity is God's opportunity? Can it be that in the most desperate of circumstances, we are reminded that the last word is God's? Peace, be still.

The power of God is demonstrated most gloriously in changed human lives, and what better example than Paul of Tarsus. Our New Testament scripture is an excerpt from one of Paul's letters to a group of people called by his work among them to be saints. As we read the account of what is meant for Paul to continue in his ministry, we have no other explanation for his power to continue than the power of God.

—Verna J. Dozier

Sunday Between June 26 and July 2

Out of the Depths

PSALM 130 • 2 SAMUEL 1:1, 17-27 • 2 CORINTHIANS 8:7-15 • MARK 5:21-43

FOR THE LAST WEEK OF JUNE, the days of which the poet sings, "O what is so rare...?," our lectionary takes us to the somber halls of death.

We begin with the superb dirge for Saul and Jonathan, believed to be an authentic composition of David, a poem to secure his place among the poets of the world. It is marked by moving repetition and simplicity of language. No trace of bitterness for the man who tried to kill him mars the poem, and the grief David felt at the loss of his "brother" Jonathan is effective in its restraint. "How the mighty have fallen" speaks to many times and occasions.

The mood of sorrow and sadness is deepened by Psalm 130, a masterpiece of a lament for personal sins. Because there are no specifics about the cause of the experience of the depths, the psalm has a universality that speaks to the lost condition of the human race and the grace and mercy of God. What humility and wisdom are in the lines,

If you, O Lord, should mark iniquities,
Lord, who could stand?

And what trust! "There is forgiveness with you."

As we watch for the morning, this psalm is a good companion—whether it is the morning of the next day or of our life!

There is so much gold in the gospel story that one day's meditation or one week's or one's lifetime is not sufficient to mine it. In one story Mark gives us a vivid picture of Jesus the healer and Jesus the teacher.

Jesus responds equally to calls from the high and from the lowly. His healing ministry reaches out beyond the ancient taboos of a religious system. He knows who he is and what he can do and knows when he has accomplished the task. His very being heals. He incarnates the ritual.

Can you imagine the emotions that surged through the leader of the synagogue who saw and heard it all? But then the final word comes. The synagogue leader's child is dead. There is no more you can do. The depths. But this teacher lives out that there is always something else you can do. Do not pay attention to the counsels of despair.

After this high gospel drama, the epistle seems to plunge to mundane issues of institutional survival. Do what you can, counsels Paul. Your offering is acceptable according to what you have, not according to what you have not. Quoting a later Paul, "You are accepted." Out of the depths.

—Verna J. Dozier

Where Will God Dwell?

We trace the Story—our story—from its beginnings in the Hebrew scriptures, through its climax in the memories of the early church as reflected in the gospels, and then on to what sense the first Christians made of the connections between the two as reflected in St. Paul's letters.

At each step along the way, as inheritors of that Story, we participate today by reflecting on what it says to us corporately as that continuing community of faith, or as individual members of the continuing community. Scripture cannot fully be grasped either as a historical or literary enterprise. It speaks, as one scripture student said, "from faith to faith."

—Verna J. Dozier

Sunday Between July 3 and 9

The Old Order Must Change

PSALM 48 • 2 SAMUEL 5:1-5, 9-10 • 2 CORINTHIANS 12:2-10 • MARK 6:1-13

SAMUEL AND MARK are almost like contrapuntal music. We can only judge what is abnormal by having experienced the normal. David goes from glory to glory. "All the tribes of Israel" come to him, citing his great works and his evident acceptance by the Lord. The old order is rejected. David "became greater and greater, for the Lord, the God of hosts, was with him."

The psalm carries forward this triumphal note: "Thy right hand is filled with victory." The pilgrim is bidden, "Walk about Zion, go all around it. Count its towers, consider well its ramparts; go through its citadel that you may tell the next generation that this is God."

Whether the ruler is Saul or David or the president of the United States, the old order changes but remains distressingly the same.

Then great David's greater Son strides into history. To read Mark 6:1-13 against 2 Samuel 5:1-5, 9-10, is to realize something new has entered history. Like David, he came of bone and flesh. "Is not this the carpenter, the son of Mary?" A later teller of the Story than Mark was to say, "He came unto his own, and his own received him not."

Sometimes we don't want the old order to change. We have become very comfortable with it—or we have come to hallow it. Notice that Mark sets Jesus' rejection at Nazareth in the religious place.

The disciples were to go without providing for the morrow, proclaiming that all should repent. All? They looked different from the old order, and their message was different. Gone was the proud boast of the towers, the ramparts, and the citadels.

Small wonder they took offense at Jesus. If the new does not offend, it may be we have not truly heard, or we have quickly absorbed it into what we already understand.

The new order has its temptations, too, as Paul so eloquently and agonizingly illustrates. Jesus taught by word and example that there is power in weakness, but such is the deviousness of the old order that the citizens of the New Order can take pride in their lack of pride.

But Paul hears the marching order of the new order: "Power [God's power] is made perfect in weakness [human weakness]." The promise: Behold, I make all things new.

All things.

—Verna J. Dozier

Sunday Between July 10 and 16

Two Kings and Two Dancers

PSALM 24 • 2 SAMUEL 6:1-5, 12-19 • EPHESIANS 1:3-14 • MARK 6:14-29

THE WORDS "David danced before the Lord" richly evoke the young king's enthusiastic response to the holy charge to bring the ark of the Lord home to Jerusalem. The psalm can be read as an affirmation of David's act:

Who shall ascend the hill of the Lord and who shall stand in his holy place?
Those who have clean hands and pure hearts.

Michal, David's wife, did not see it this way. When she looked out of the window and saw the king leaping and dancing before the Lord, the text says, "she despised him in her heart."

David is the hero of this story—it is Michal who fares badly. But who has clean hands and a pure heart? Even to think we have is a sign we haven't. The confidence of Psalm 24 gives way to the reality of Psalm 51:

Create in me a clean heart, O God,
And put a new and right spirit within me.

The gospel brings us to an encounter with another dancer, another king, and a fiery prophet who made life very uncomfortable for those who didn't follow the law, even if they were kings. John's public denunciation of Herod for marrying his brother's wife, Herodias, aroused her wrath. Imprisoning John did not satisfy her. Her daughter danced for the king on his birthday and he promised her whatever she wanted as a reward. Coached by her mother, she asked for John's head.

Even though John said of Jesus, "He must increase and I must decrease," the effect of this powerful desert figure remained with the people. Many thought the young rabbi Jesus was a reincarnation of John the Baptist. Even Herod, in guilty terror, thought so. He must have felt a dance had cost him too much.

There is no dancer in the epistle, but the majestic rhythms of the prose lift our spirits so we can dance. The passage begins with lofty thanksgiving to God for "every spiritual blessing in the heavenly places." We have been chosen before the foundation of the world, destined for adoption as God's children, our sins forgiven, and to ourselves made known the mystery of God's plan. The words tumble over each other and defy the sober mind to organize them into coherence. If the heart has reasons of which reason has no knowledge, as Pascal said, here the spirit has order of which order has no knowledge.

—Verna J. Dozier

Sunday Between July 17 and 23

The Holy Temple

PSALM 89:20-37 • 2 SAMUEL 7:1-14 • EPHESIANS 2:11-22 • MARK 6:30-34, 53-56

"DESTROY THIS TEMPLE," Jesus said, "and in three days, I will raise it up." The Jewish worshipers were amazed, as the evangelist John reports it. "This temple has been under construction for 46 years," they said, "and will you raise it up in three days?" (John 2:19-20).

The language of metaphor and poetry always confuses those who are bound by the language of fact and prose. It isn't a matter of one being right and the other wrong. Those very terms belong to an understanding of reality that always has to have the other reality explained, and so the evangelist explains Jesus "was speaking of the temple of his body."

Our scriptures this week lead us to meditate on that temple.

David assumes God wants what David wants. He feels uncomfortable living in a house of cedar while God still lives in a tent. Nathan the prophet agrees with David's wish to change the situation, but that night the Lord sends Nathan a different message. "I've lived in a tent all these years," God said. "Have I ever given anybody the idea I was dissatisfied with the arrangement?"

David's job is to solidify God's work, to give God's people a safe and secure place. When that is accomplished, then God will see about God's house, which will be the work of David's son.

Mark shows us the work of David's greater Son. He heals the sick; he feeds the 5,000; he walks on the water. He is the new thing in the world that makes a difference in the world. This is the test of worship.

Ephesians differs from the other letters ascribed to Paul in that it does not deal with the trials and tribulations of one little community of faith, but lifts up a vision of what all the communities, the church, should be. Some believe it was a cover letter for a collection of the individual letters.

This week's passage stresses the unity of Jews and Gentiles. In Christ, "those who were far off have been brought near by the blood of Christ. He is our peace, having broken down the dividing wall, the hostility between us. Jew and Gentile are citizens with the saints and also members of the household of God, built upon the foundation of the apostles and prophets, with Christ himself as the cornerstone."

In him the whole structure is joined together and grows into a holy temple in the Lord, a dwelling place for God.

—Verna J. Dozier

Sunday Between July 24 and 30

The Heart of a Fool

PSALM 14 • 2 SAMUEL 11:1-15 • EPHESIANS 3:14-21 • JOHN 6:1-21

SOMETIMES IN THE THEATER, when an awful thing is about to happen, the stage lights go dim and the music wails. Such would be appropriate for the 11th chapter of 2 Samuel, David's use of Bathsheba and his unscrupulous efforts to cover up the violation.

The music might well wail the opening line of Psalm 14: Fools say in their hearts, "There is no God."

Though it was time for the spring military campaigns, "David remained at Jerusalem"—an ominous beginning. Why wasn't he with his soldiers? An idle hand is the devil's workshop, the old proverb goes.

David is walking on the roof of his house and sees the beautiful Bathsheba, wife of Uriah, bathing. He has her brought to him and lies with her. When she sends word that she is pregnant, David immediately becomes frantic and tries scheme after scheme to cover up the sin.

He arranges for Uriah to have a vacation from the war, but Uriah, the blunt and honest soldier, will not enjoy the pleasures of peacetime while his comrades are in the fields. (A telling contrast to David!) The next stratagem is to wine and dine Uriah royally, so that in a drunken stupor the soldier will stumble into his wife's bed. But Uriah, the innocent, maintains enough of a clear head not to return to his own house.

Theologian Walter Brueggemann's comment on Psalm 14 is enlightening: The fool does not announce atheism. It is only in his heart, i.e. he thinks and decides that way. The outcome is that such a person's action is corrupt, without discernment, and exploitative of other people. "They eat up my people," says the psalmist, "as they eat bread." Uriah is consumed.

Continuing the contrast between David and David's greater Son, our scriptures for this week give us the miracles we had last week: Jesus healing the sick, feeding the multitude, and walking on the water. Of course the stories differ in details because we are dealing with powerful memories, not computer reports.

Ephesians closes our meditations with a timely prayer that Christ may dwell in our hearts through faith.

—Verna J. Dozier

Living Bread

In the language of "left brain, right brain" constructs, the scriptures for the weeks of August call upon our right-brain gifts. We leave the world of what we can see and touch and document and enter a world of imagination and creativity, a world of poetry and emotion.

We pass from the last vestiges of the wilderness and the prophet of the wilderness, Samuel, to the courtly chronicler and the beginning of the record of the Kings. We had begun such a transition last month with the movement from the swift action and immediacy of Mark to the leisurely contemplation of the meaning of it all in John.

There is a world of human experiences in the scriptures and many ways in which those experiences are shared. Let us be open to them all. This is our Story. These are our spiritual ancestors who are speaking to us. What can we hear from the Hebrew record, from the gospel, from the epistle that will speak to us today so that we can, in our own voice, pass the Story on?

—Verna J. Dozier

Sunday Between July 31 and August 6

Grace to Grow By

PSALM 51:1-12 • 2 SAMUEL 11:26-12:13 • EPHESIANS 4:1-16 • JOHN 6:24-35

IT IS HARD TO IMAGINE it getting worse than this. King David's abuse of power to fulfill his lust for Bathsheba and Ammon's rape of his sister Tamar in 2 Samuel are two of the most infamous sins committed in the history of Israel.

These incidents illustrate quite clearly the unequal status between men and women during this time—an inequality that continues throughout much of the Bible. In these two chapters, we hear much about the desires, deviousness, and anguish of the father and son violators. Little, however, is mentioned about what the violated women experience, except that Bathsheba "mourned for her husband" (11:26) and Tamar futilely attempted to resist her brother (12:12-13).

The injustice of this unequal gender stratification is made worse by men who take advantage of the system to fulfill what Tamar rightly names as foolishness (12:13). David and Ammon take the social sins of the society they were born into and make them their own, contributing to the cycle that oppresses women by committing sins for which they are personally responsible. And though we may not all be adulterers, murderers, or rapists, there are few men among us who can truly claim not to have played a part in this cycle in one way or another. As the prophet Nathan condemns David, "You are the man!" (12:7).

Similarly, both men and women have contributed in some way to the tyrannical system of sin that has oppressed all of humanity since the Garden of Eden. "For all have sinned, and come short of the glory of God" (Romans 3:23). Yet this Sunday's collection of lectionary readings—and the very gospel itself!—points to the grace and healing that is offered to sinners who approach God humbly and with true intentions to work for change.

The adage "You can lead a horse to water, but you can't make it drink" has no more tragic implications than when applied to humans' response to God's free gift of grace. For some it seems like it takes more work to keep sinning—more knaving, sneaking, and hiding—than it would to keep our hands clean and remain with a pure conscience. Like those who followed Jesus across the Sea of Galilee, we are attempting to fill our inner hunger with "food that perishes" and not "the food that endures for eternal life" (John 6:27).

But as long as we continue to consume what Dietrich Bonhoeffer called "cheap grace," we remain "children tossed to and fro" (Ephesians 4:14) and never able to grow into the maturity in Christ which is our true vocation.

David, when he realized the seriousness of what he had done, lowered himself to the dust and composed one of the most heartfelt confessions ever known (Psalm 51). Isn't it time for us—personally and as church—to call ourselves to a similar response?

—Aaron Gallegos

Sunday Between August 7 and 13

Between Heaven and Earth

PSALM 130 • 2 SAMUEL 18:5-9, 15, 31-33 • EPHESIANS 4:25-5:2 • JOHN 6:35, 41-51

"THE SINS OF THE FATHERS are visited upon the children." No more graphic example of that proverb is given than the household of David the King. David, the winsome, fearless, gifted shepherd boy grew up to be a powerful leader who could rule kingdoms but not his sons or himself.

David did nothing to prevent the rape of his daughter Tamar by one of his sons. But her brother, Absalom, the half brother of the rapist, took his wretchedly violated sister into his household and for years plotted revenge. With revenge accomplished, he then conspired against his father, making it necessary for David to flee for his life. In pursuit, Absalom's glorious hair was caught in a tree, and he died as he had lived, hanging between heaven and earth.

Our lectionary gives us the matchless Psalm 130 to express David's grief for his son, paralleling his grief for Saul and Jonathan. But the words in the book of Samuel have entered history as an eloquent expression of a father's grief: "O my son Absalom, my son, my son Absalom! Would I had died instead of you, O Absalom, my son, my son."

From that dark, tragic scene, it is a relief to turn to the sixth chapter of John, where we will stay for the rest of the month to meditate on one of John's great "I am" passages. John has Jesus identify himself as the bread of life while speaking in a synagogue. He reminded the gathered learners that their mothers and fathers had eaten manna in the wilderness and had died. He offers them himself, which they can eat of and not die. Understandably, they were confused. "How can this man give us himself to eat?" they asked.

The epistle for the week describes the new life of the eucharistic community, that, week by week, eats the bread and drinks the wine and experiences the bread as flesh indeed and the wine as blood indeed.

—Verna J. Dozier

Sunday Between August 14 and 20

The Beginning of Wisdom

PSALM 111 • 1 KINGS 2:10-12, 3:3-14 • EPHESIANS 5:15-20 • JOHN 6:51-58

THE KING IS DEAD. Long live the king. We move to a new king and a new court reporter. "So Solomon sat on the throne of his father David, and his kingdom was firmly established."

Near the beginning of his reign, Solomon had a dream that God had appeared to him and asked what Solomon should be given. Solomon replied, "Give your servant an understanding mind to govern your people" (New Revised Standard Version); "an understanding heart" (King James); "a heart with skill to listen" (New English Bible); "a hearing heart" (American Standard Version).

What rich implications for the word wisdom! It's not just piles and piles of facts. It recalls, "The heart has reasons of which reason has no knowledge."

There was a time in ancient Israel when this kind of wisdom—a union of heart and head and will—was highly valued. The responsive psalm chosen for this passage is Psalm 111, which contains the verse: "The fear of the Lord is the beginning of wisdom." The word "fear" means the attitude of worship that takes a first measure of who I am, that I am creature not Creator. Walter Brueggemann, in his commentary on the psalms, sees that fact as an occasion for doxology.

An easy transition this time to the Johannine Jesus and Ephesians' guidance for the new community of the Eucharist. There is much repetition in the John passage; it has mesmerizing effect. Prose cannot do it justice. The spirit longs to sing the music that is so present there. Brian Wren has given us the words, and an American folk melody has given us the tune:

I come with joy to meet my Lord/Forgiven, loved, and free/In awe and wonder to recall/His life laid down for me.

I come with Christians far and near/To find as all are fed/The new community of love/In Christ's Communion bread.

As Christ breaks bread/And bids us share/Each proud division ends/That love that made us makes us one/And strangers now are friends.

And thus with joy we meet our Lord/His presence always near/Is in such friend-ship better known!/We see and praise him here?

Together met, together bound/We'll go our different ways/And as his people in the world/We'll live and speak his praise.

—Verna J. Dozier

Sunday Between August 21 and 27

An Army of Equals

PSALM 84 • 1 KINGS 8:1, 6, 10-11, 22-30, 41-43 • EPHESIANS 6:10-20 • JOHN 6:56-69

THESE MEDITATIONS MAY be difficult for us who are weary of impressive mon-uments of stone and precious jewels built by slave labor; who grow utterly weary of wars and rumors of wars, so that even the armor of God may have little appeal. Then we hear a wistful Jesus saying, "Will you also go away?" And we hear Jesus in the garden, "Can you not watch one little hour?" And we return to find what, in our haste to judge, we may have missed.

All the elaborate work for the building of the temple is finished and now all is made ready for the ceremony of dedication. The temple had been made so that it was more beautiful as you approached the place where the ark would rest. Now it rested there in a place of thick darkness. And then the amazing prayer of dedication—a house of prayer for all people. Not only the prayer of the Israelite will be heard, but "like-wise the foreigner." The king prays that his prayer will be heard "that all the peoples of the earth may know your name." Such is the vision of this house.

"How lovely is your dwelling place, O Lord of Hosts!" (Psalm 84:1). The Johannine meditation on the living bread goes on, but it becomes too much for many and the report is that because of it, many of his disciples turned back and no longer went about with him. Jesus asked the Twelve, "Do you also wish to go away?"

Peter, the spokesperson for us all, replies, "Lord, to whom shall we go?"

Those who stayed are provided with the whole armor of God. The talk of shields and swords and breastplates and helmets may not be appealing to us who prefer the image of beating swords into plowshares and spears into pruning hooks. But Marcus Barth, who spent years working on the Anchor Bible commentary on Ephesians, re-searched every item of equipment mentioned here and found that every item was the equipment of an officer. There is no one of low rank in God's army. All God's soldiers are equal!

—Verna J. Dozier

Sunday Between August 28 and September 3

Springtime Rhapsody!

PSALM 45:1-2, 6-9 • SONG OF SOLOMON 2:8-13 • JAMES 1:17-27
• MARK 7:1-8, 14-15, 21-23

THE HEADING FOR this week's meditation is from the New Revised Standard Version's Hebrew scripture passage.

The voice of my beloved!/Look, he comes/leaping upon the mountains/bounding over the hills.

Look, there he stands/behind our wall/gazing in at window/looking through the lattice. —Song of Solomon 2:8, 9

It's wonderful and exciting poetry, pulsating with youth and vigor. One wonders what form of denial was operating that made the old King James version caption these exuberant frolics of young love as "Church's Love for Christ" and "The Love of Christ and His Church." That Christ and that church were hardly a part of human experience when these wedding songs were written. The ancient Hebrews knew what they were about when they acknowledged sexuality—the full range of the body as worthy to be celebrated, a fit offering for God.

Perhaps a pale glimpse of this experience lingers in the Havergal hymn we sang in Sunday school:

Take my hands and let them move
At the impulse of thy love:
Take my heart, it is thine own
It shall be thy royal throne.

The responsive psalm is an ode for a royal wedding. The colors and the odors excite.

The gospel passage shows the evangelist in a strangely didactic mode that, though not intended, can give us food for reflecting on how we have been reluctant to enjoy our bodies. Jesus is calling into question the scrupulous tradition about washing before eating. "Listen to me, all of you and understand: There is nothing outside a person that by going in can defile, but the things that come out are what defile."

The Bard of Avon remembered that. There is "nothing either good or bad, but thinking makes it so."

—Verna J. Dozier

Turned Upside-down

*I*n September the or-
dered world of
Proverbs and James is
read against the cross of
Mark's world. Walter
Brueggemann reminds us
of Karl Marx's dictum,
"The ruling ideas of each
age have ever been the
ideas of its ruling class."

*Who benefited by our
pious simplistic characteri-
zations of the Hebrew scriptures as law and the New
Testament as grace? How
did reading Proverbs and
not the Prophets prepare us
so easily to turn the symbol
of the authorities' answer to
those who defied them into
a symbol of the devotional
life that posed no threat to
the authorities? Septem-
ber's meditations will bring
a chill to "whatever is, is
right."*

*Likewise, October's
Bible passages may enlarge
and disturb our image of
God. We meet a God who
asks us questions. We meet
a God who balances the
scales in the marital relationship and puts children
at the center of what God is
about, and a woman who
models what it means to be
faithful in a relationship.*

New world a-coming.

*Disturbing world a-
coming.*

—Verna J. Dozier

Sunday Between September 4 and 10

Who Are God's People?

PSALM 125 • PROVERBS 22:1-2, 8-9, 22-23 • JAMES 2:1-17 • MARK 7:24-37

EARLIER TRANSLATIONS render the second verse of today's proverb as "The rich and poor meet together," but the New Revised Standard Version specifies the basis of the meeting: "The rich and poor have this in common: The Lord is the maker of them all."

These proverbs assigned to a royal author do not question the fact that there are rich and poor people in the world. He is only concerned with how they are to be treat-ed. He who has a "bountiful eye" will be blessed.

The responsive psalm assures us the Lord protects the people. The nagging ques-tion stays with us: Who are the Lord's people?

The gospel begins to break through with unexpected answers to that question. In the first place, Jesus is in Gentile territory—no longer in the land of the chosen peo-ple. In the second place, he has an encounter with a woman—a feisty woman at that. He is tired. He wants his whereabouts to be unknown, but a woman, a Gentile with an urgent mission—her daughter is ill—finds out he is there and comes for help. His reply to her has troubled the commentators on this passage for hundreds of years.

God-made-man responds in all his humanness. He is tired, weary, a Jew encoun-tering a Gentile. "Let the children be fed first, for it is not fair to take the children's food and throw it to the dogs." The woman is undaunted. She takes the worst he can throw at her and tosses it back at him. "Sir, even the dogs under the table eat the chil-dren's crumbs."

Too little attention has been given to this, one of the great encounters in the New Testament. It doesn't fit with our pious picture of Jesus. Did he laugh? She had turned the tables on him. Did he say, "Lady, you win"? The record doesn't say. We can only imagine. The record does say that "for saying that, you may go—the demon has left your daughter."

The people of God have been enlarged.

—Verna J. Dozier

Sunday Between September 11 and 17

How Long Will You Love Being Simple?

PSALM 19 • PROVERBS 1:20-33 • JAMES 3:1-12 • MARK 8:27-38

THE MYSTERIOUS AND ATTRACTIVE figure of Wisdom enters our meditations. She cries aloud in the streets, asking a poignant question: "How long, O simple ones, will you love being simple?"

How long, O Lord, how long?

How long will we refuse to understand?

Psalm 19 tells us of the wonders of God. "The heavens are telling the glory of God, and the firmament proclaims God's handiwork." Image is piled on image: The sun comes out like the bridegroom and, like a strong man, runs its course with joy. The law is as much a wondrous creation as the heavens, "sweeter also than honey."

Wisdom's question remains with us. How long, O simple ones, will you love being simple? How long will we refuse to understand?

Within the joy and beauty of Psalm 19, we are reminded that the law is as much a wondrous creation as the heavens. To the nature worshipers comes he who fulfilled the law and paid the price of a cross.

The gospel brings us to that moment on the road to Caesarea Philippi when Jesus was trying to make the disciples understand. "Who do people say that I am?" he asked them. He got a variety of answers—all good possibilities but none reflecting the new thing God was about to do. Finally Peter said Jesus was the Messiah ("Christ" in Greek), he by whom the kingdom of God would be made known.

In parable after parable, Jesus had told them what the kingdom of God was like, but a world turned upside-down was outside the realm of the possible for them. A suffering and dying Messiah? A crucified Messiah?

Too complicated for us. We love our sweet little Jesus who died for our sins—not because of our sin, the choice against God's way.

Is it possible we love being simple? It is safer that way. If we don't understand, we don't have to be challenged, confronted, disturbed. If we don't understand, we can keep our religion personal and private. Wisdom was right. We love being simple.

—Verna J. Dozier

Sunday Between September 18 and 24

Week of the Law

PSALM 1 • PROVERBS 31:10-31 • JAMES 3:13-4:3, 7-8 • MARK 9:30-37

THIS WEEK WE ARE BACK to simplicity—and a rude awakening. The reading from Proverbs presents us with the well-known image of the good wife. Today, it is almost impossible for many women to take this image of the biblical paragon seriously. We live in an age of comic strip figures—Hi and Lois where Hi is left to placate the children with a makeshift dinner while Lois dashes off breathlessly, attache case in hand, to close out a real-estate deal (surprisingly, not unlike the good wife of Proverbs who "considers a field and buys it"). Today's woman will surely note that missing from this is the husband who only appears to praise.

What can we learn from this passage? Is it wishful thinking? An apology for all the harsh images of women elsewhere in Proverbs?

The responsive psalm is Psalm 1, the epitome of the well-ordered world of Torah life. Into that well-ordered world crashed the Prophets with a new message—"I abhor the pride of Jacob." And then the last and greatest of the Prophets, who, as Ched Myers says in his commentary on our passage from Mark, constructs a new social order.

It may seem strange to us that immediately after hearing Jesus talk about his impending death, the disciples would argue about who is the greatest. Not so at all. These young men had risked everything to embark on a great adventure, following a leader who would change the world. They didn't understand what he was about any more than the church 2,000 years later understands.

They saw the adventure coming to a glorious conclusion. There would be a struggle with the powers in Jerusalem, he would win, and they would reap the spoils of victory. They had better get the pecking order assured now. The rude awakening was that there would be no place for that kind of thinking in the new order Jesus would bring in. The new order would turn the old order upside-down.

—Verna J. Dozier

Sunday Between September 25 and October 1

Radical Trust

PSALM 124 • ESTHER 7:1-6, 9-10, 9:20-22 • JAMES 5:13-20 • MARK 9:38-50

THE LESSON FROM the Hebrew scripture is the story of Esther, one of the beloved heroines of the Bible. (It is not a part of our lectionary, but take a peek at the story of Vashti [1:10-23], also a remarkable woman and definitely not "a good wife"!) But Esther claims our attention now—a young woman, dutiful, loyal, courageous, and very beautiful. She didn't hesitate to use all of her feminine charms to save her people. She, too, might say, "For this was I born, and for this I was brought to this place."

With the success of her stratagem, she might have given thanks with Psalm 124, a psalm of thanksgiving for a communal deliverance. Let Esther sing, "If it had not been the Lord who was on our side, when our enemies attacked us, then they would have swallowed us up alive."

The ninth chapter of Mark closes with a collection of quotations from the tradition that are not necessarily connected. The original context is lost. Together, however, they make some radical statements about the nature of Christian discipleship.

The community does not have to worry about tests of membership: "Whoever is not against us is for us." A good deed done by anybody rebounds to the glory of God and makes the kingdom of God more visible—"Oh, that's what it's like!" It's a sobering discipline to practice. God is everywhere, and God is always working. Watch for God's footsteps.

The next batch of quotations suggests in what high regard we should hold our relationship with God. If any part of us gets in the way of that relationship, don't hesitate to get rid of it.

This may be one of the times when a personal application of the tradition may be more helpful than a community application. It is more difficult to discipline oneself than to see the offending member as one of the community. The church has a sorry history of judging and excluding. "Go and sin no more" is an example of the radical trust our Lord gave.

—Verna J. Dozier

Sunday Between October 2 and 8

Pressed Down and Overflowing

PSALM 26 • JOB 1:1; 2:1-10 • HEBREWS 1:1-4, 2:5-12 • MARK 10:2-16

THESE SCRIPTURE PASSAGES are too varied in their content even to be touched on in one devotional period, but too important to be passed over with just a cursory reading.

The drama of the book of Job is precipitated by one of the great religious questions: Does Job worship God for nothing? The beginning is an extravagant picture of Job's wealth and piety. He is so scrupulous in his religious observances that he even makes sacrifices for the sins his children may have committed in their hearts.

God offers Job as exhibit A to a skeptical Satan, who promptly throws down a gauntlet. Doesn't Job's piety benefit him greatly? God is sure Satan's cynicism misreads the situation and so gives Satan freedom to destroy all Job's comforts.

The searing question remains with us. Why do we worship God? For benefits in this life—or in the life to come?

The responsive psalm is well-chosen. "Vindicate me, O Lord, for I have walked in my integrity." The Special Providence of America's founding religion; the automatic whine, Why did this happen to me? The smug acceptance of all the good things that happen.

In the gospel we meet the radical Prophet who turned that thinking upside-down. In this week's scripture, he is disturbing a more specific detail of the status quo and calling for a new reimaging of relationships.

To the crowds he rooted the marital relationship in the very purposes of God in creation. Any alteration in that relationship was a human accommodation to a human hardness of heart. With his disciples he went on to an even more radical understanding. Men and women have equal rights and equal responsibilities in the marital relationship. The implications of the radical new thing were being spelled out.

The disciples still living in the old order wanted to protect him from the children, but Jesus welcomed them. "This is what I am about," he said. How do children manifest the kingdom? Their lack of status? Their willingness to trust? Their openness to new possibilities?

—Verna J. Dozier

Sunday Between October 9 and 15

What is God Like?

PSALM 22:1-15 • JOB 23:1-9, 16-17 • HEBREWS 4:12-16 • MARK 10:17-31

JOB, AFFLICTED BY GOD and harassed by his friends, is still laboring under the old delusion that God is reasonable: "Oh, that I knew where I might find him." Job would come to God's dwelling and lay his case before God. He is certain an upright person could reason with God and be acquitted.

God is like an honest judge.

Job's agony is fittingly reflected in Psalm 22, mirror of the woes of the rejected and engraved on our hearts as the cry from the cross.

But in Mark's gospel Jesus adds another dimension to the right way to respond to this all-powerful God. A rich man offered his credentials for finding favor with God. He had kept all the commandments from the days of his youth. Jesus told him he lacked one thing. Sell all he has, give the money to the poor, and come and follow him. The man was shocked, as indeed Job would have been, as indeed all of us who strive to impress God on our own terms would be.

Jesus responded to his shocked disciples with a venture into humor, which, if the Twelve got it, the church has missed almost completely because we have been unwilling to see a love of money excluding a love for God. What kind of God demands that we choose between them?

Hebrews presents us with a God whose word is fearsome, "sharper than a two-edged sword, piercing until it divides soul from spirit, joints from marrow...before him no creature is hidden...to [this One] we all must render an account."

Perhaps we need to live into that image of God before we can fully appreciate the vision of the great high priest of Hebrews. We do not have a high priest who is unable to sympathize with our weaknesses. The old gospel hymn well expressed the feeling:

Can we find a friend so faithful/Who will all our sorrows share?/Jesus knows our every weakness/Take it to the Lord in prayer.

—Verna J. Dozier

Sunday Between October 16 and 22

The Secret Messiah

PSALM 104:1-9, 24, 35 • JOB 38:1-7, 34-41 • HEBREWS 5:1-10 • MARK 10:35-45

GEORGE CROLY, a popular 19th-century English divine, wrote prolifically during his lifetime, but only one hymn outlives him. It contains a line pertinent to our reflection on this great poetic passage of the voice from the whirlwind, the Hebrew scripture for our meditation this week: "Stoop to my weakness, mighty as thou art/and make me love thee as I ought to love."

God answers Job's questions with questions of God's own. The modern mind tends to resist this image of the Almighty God roaring out of the heavens at God's pitiful creature and flees for its religious comfort from the God of the Old Testament to the sweet and gentle Jesus of the New. Hear, O people of God, the Lord thy God is one.

And the God of the whirlwind hears and heeds and responds in the most beautiful poetry.

What more do you want God to do? What do you think God wants you to do?

Job would understand the responsive psalm. God is the creator and sustainer of all things, but there is a right way to respond to this all-powerful God, and woe to those who don't.

The gospel is the story of the disciples' amazing response to Jesus' announcement of his forthcoming passion and Jesus' even more amazing description of the way of the new order.

For the third time, Jesus had told them what was going to happen to him in Jerusalem. In response, the two with Peter, the inner circle, the ones closest to him, make an audacious request for place and privileges. They were still very much into old order thinking.

The messianic secret that runs through Mark—Jesus constantly telling his followers not to reveal who he is—was the effort not to build on the old expectations that would be aroused by the use of the term "Messiah." The Messiah was the one who would restore the Davidic kingdom and make the Jews once more a world power. Jesus is still misunderstood today. We hear, "My kingdom is not of this world" as a designation of geography, not of a way of life.

Jesus called the disciples together and patiently explained what life would be like in the new order, the kingdom he would bring in. There is little evidence that the church—the churches—that the disciples left behind got it. There is little evidence that the church today has got it.

—Verna J. Dozier

Sunday Between October 23 and 29

What Do You Want Me to Do for You?

PSALM 34:1-8, 19-22 • JOB 42:1-6, 10-17 • HEBREWS 7:23-28 • MARK 10:46-52

THE GOD OF THE WHIRLWIND has made the case. Job's surrender is unconditional. He even uses God's words of judgment. He admits to speaking about things too wonderful for him to understand. He repents in dust and ashes. The friends are rebuked by God because they had not spoken of God as God is.

If only the compilers had left the poem there! The mystery of God is too great for us. There is no reward deserved for comprehending that elementary fact. The only right relationship between creature and creator is faith.

We might have wished for Psalm 139 as the responsive psalm: "Such knowledge is too wonderful for me/It is so high that I can not attain it." But our lectionary chose Psalm 34, a praise for deliverance from trouble. Like the ending of Job, it makes no place for the non-deliverance in life. "And they all lived happily ever after" is the stuff of fairy tales. We need the prophetic faith that affirms that the creating Word of God will accomplish that which it intends.

The gospel is the dramatic story of the healing of blind Bartimaeus. Jesus of Nazareth is passing by. With the audacity of the desperate, Bartimaeus calls out, "Jesus, Son of David, have mercy on me!" Son of David? Is that a recognition of royal lineage? Are the powers of Earth and hell being put on notice? The minions of the status quo order him to be quiet, but he is already moving in another world.

He calls out even more loudly, "Son of David, have mercy on me!" Jesus stops, saying, "Call him here." The blind man with reckless abandon throws off his cloak— the mark of his way of life—springs up, and comes to Jesus. Those first young fishermen he had called had not responded more readily.

And then Jesus' startling question: "What do you want me to do for you?" The obvious answer is, of course, I want to see. But is it? What you don't see you don't have to take responsibility for. A queen, told her subjects had no bread, replied, probably as much out of ignorance as callousness, "Let them eat cake." A president of the United States, sponsoring a trickle-down theory of economics, propounded, "A rising tide lifts all boats."

Blindness protects us from harsh realities. Blindness also means someone else will take care of us. Think, Bartimaeus. There is cost as well as promise to the new life that will open up for you. "What do you want me to do for you?"

"I want to see."

He regained his sight, and the record is that he follows Jesus on the way. The way to the cross.

—Verna J. Dozier

Reformation Day

In some traditions, Reformation Day is celebrated the last Sunday in October. See Appendix 1, "Reformation and All Saints' Days."

All Saints' Sunday

All Saints' Day (November 1) may be celebrated the first Sunday in November.

Who Are You Calling a Saint?

PSALM 24 • ISAIAH 25:6-9 • REVELATION 21:1-6 • JOHN 11:32-44

"WHO SHALL ASCEND the hill of the Lord? And who shall stand in God's holy place? Those who have clean hands and pure hearts, who do not lift up their souls to what is false, and do not swear deceitfully" (Psalm 24:3-4).

Perhaps the constructors of the Revised Common Lectionary included this psalm with the readings for All Saints' Sunday to help us clarify who might be a saint. This question—which often brings with it political overtones and ecclesial intrigue—has been controversial almost since the establishment of the church.

The New Testament uses the same word (*hagios*) for both "holy" and "saint," and the Romance languages continue to do so. However, while many in the church think of saints exclusively as those who have ascended to a nearly superhuman level of spiritual perfection, the New Testament often used the term to refer to all believers. While the canonization process was established to recognize officially the unusually gifted in the history of the church, we sometimes forget that "the saints" are all those who had been made holy by Jesus Christ and consecrated for God's service.

One sign of the holy among us are those who are "living as if." Maybe they are the visionaries who live as if the New Jerusalem—a place where God wipes away all of our tears, and where there shall be no more death, sorrow, or pain (Rev. 21:4)—is a distinct possibility. Perhaps they are the doers whose actions make sense only if we "fix our eyes not on what is seen, but on what is unseen" (2 Corinthians 4:18). The 11th chapter of Hebrews contains an impressive list of the "cloud of witnesses," who the writer of the epistle regarded as saints because of their unquenchable passion for "a better country, that is, a heavenly one" (verse 16).

To many, the quest for "a new heaven and a new earth" doesn't seem very realistic. Yet, there are innumerable people who "seek a better country" by working to heal victims of abuse, feed the hungry in soup kitchens, stop the cycle of violence with gang members, and visit those in prisons, as well as through many other ministries. And though those who look for results will find much of this work impractical—it will never fully solve the root cause of these problems—these believers expand our understanding of what is possible, and perhaps foreshadow what the reign of God looks like. As Jesus told Martha, the woman who has become almost an archetype of level-minded practicality, "Did I not tell you that if you believed, you would see the glory of God?" (John 11:40).

What do your saints make possible? **—Aaron Gallegos**

Sunday Between October 30 and November 5

Toward New Possibilities

PSALM 146 • RUTH 1:1-18 • HEBREWS 9:11-14 • MARK 12:28-34

THE HEBREW SCRIPTURE for the week begins the story of another remarkable woman of the tradition, Ruth the Moabite. A famine in the land of Judah caused a certain man of Bethlehem to go to Moab to live with his wife, Naomi, and two sons. The sons took Moabite wives, Orpah and Ruth. He died, and the two sons died, leaving Naomi alone in a country strange to her. Hearing that the famine was over in her homeland she decided to return.

Following the custom of their land, her daughters-in-law went with her, but she released them from any obligation to her, and Orpah turned back to her native land.

Not so Ruth. Despite Naomi's protest, Ruth clung to her with the memorable words of Ruth 1:16:

Entreat me not to leave thee, or to return from following after thee, for whither thou goest, I will go; and where thou lodgest, I will lodge; thy people shall be my people, and thy God, my God.

Surely it recalls the Word of the Lord to Abram: "Get thee out of thy country, and from thy kindred, and from thy father's house, unto a land that I will show thee." This woman did no less than the father of our faith.

The responsive psalm appeals to Israel's memory of the acts of God on behalf of the powerless. The Lord upholds the orphan and the widow.

The gospel passage shows Jesus on the other side of the questioning process—and doing very well. In fact so well that our pericope shows a scribe, impressed by Jesus' answers, trying out on him the favorite issue of the disputers. "Which commandment is the first of all?" Jesus answered, "You shall love the Lord your God with all your heart and soul and mind and strength," and he added, "The second is you shall love your neighbor as yourself."

The scribe was so delighted with the response he elaborated with a little homily of his own and caused Jesus to commend him with the words, "You are not far from the kingdom of God."

Hebrews continues with its excitement about the new possibilities of the new priesthood. Again an old gospel hymn rings through our meditation:

Not all the blood of beasts/On Jewish altars slain/Could give the guilty conscience peace/Or take away the stain/But Christ the heavenly lamb/Takes all our sins away/A sacrifice of nobler name/And richer blood than they.

So sang the old folks.

The question for us is what difference does it all make? For what new possibilities for the world are we cleansed and made new? **—Verna J. Dozier**

Fulfilling the Time

God is working God's pur-
pose out
As year succeeds to year
God is working God's pur-
pose out
And the time is drawing
near
Nearer and nearer draws the
time
The time that shall surely
be
When the earth shall be
filled with the glory of
God
As the waters cover the sea.

So runs a triumphant hymn of the last cen-tury—edited with a touch of inclusive lan-guage! It strikes a fitting note for our last reflec-tions before Advent, the season of watching and waiting and expecting.

"Lord, will you at this time restore the kingdom?" Somehow we human beings have never got the point. God has done God's work. Created a good creation. Created human beings with freedom to choose. Lived out before us the Way. Still we come to the end of each liturgical year gazing up into heaven.

The patient God still waits.

These scriptures call us to ponder how God acts, the God whose coming we await at Advent.

—Verna J. Dozier

Sunday Between November 6 and 12

From This World to the Next

PSALM 42 • RUTH 3:1-5; 4:13-17 • HEBREWS 9:24-28 • MARK 12:38-44

THE HEBREW SCRIPTURES for this week deal with this world—living and dying and all the problems caused by living and dying, leaving one's home and returning to it, the ties that bind, and new possibilities for life. It is this world to which they attend; in this world God works God's purposes out with faithful people.

The lesson from the Hebrew scriptures is the lovely story of two remarkable women—Ruth and Naomi. These two brief excerpts set the stage of Naomi's misfor-tunes and the birth of her grandson, Obed, the father of Jesse, the father of David.

The story should be read in its entirety. Two women in the face of devastating odds work out their salvation with fear and trembling. Naomi, emptied of all promise, goes back to her home, and Ruth refuses to let her go alone. Naomi uses the traditions of her people to secure life for Ruth and herself. Ruth, trusting her in all things, wins a place in salvation history.

The psalm eloquently captures the sorrow and the faith triumphant of the women: "Why are you cast down, O my soul/and why are you disquieted within me?...Hope in God, for I shall again praise him/My help and my God."

—Verna J. Dozier

Sunday Between November 13 and 19

God Doing the New Thing

1 SAMUEL 2:1-10 • 1 SAMUEL 1:4-20 • HEBREWS 10:11-25 • MARK 13:1-8

THE PLEA OF HANNAH'S HUSBAND to his grieving wife, "Why is your heart so sad?" recalls last week's psalm, "Why are you cast down, O my soul?" And in the Hebrew scripture this week, as last week, God comes to the aid of a woman. The cul-ture saw childlessness as a curse, even though Hannah's husband obviously didn't. He favored her above the child-bearing Peninnah, and his pitiful plea, "Am I not more to you than 10 sons?" indicates that in Hannah's husband God was doing a new thing.

But this scripture is not Elkanah's story. It is Hannah's. Hannah bargains with God. The intensity of her prayers misleads the priest, but in the end she has a son, a major figure in Hebrew history, Samuel, priest and prophet and the last of the judges of Israel.

Keeping her vow, Hannah brings the child to the temple, and the song she sings is the psalm for this week. It is a song for the ages because it echoes richly in Mary's song of exaltation when she visits her aged relative, also surprisingly pregnant. Mary's song magnifies the Lord as did Hannah's.

Hannah sings: "He has brought down the powerful from their thrones/And lifted up the lowly." As Robert McAfee Brown says, "Reversal is the order of the day in the kingdom of God."

The strange 13th chapter of Mark is called a "little Apocalypse." It would seem to be Jesus explaining the last days to his disciples, but beyond our lesson in verse 14 is a parenthesis, "let the reader understand." Has Mark inserted a revolutionary broad-side into his gospel?

Our lesson begins with the disciples' awe. Ched Myers, in his political reading of Mark, sees the stage direction of Jesus taking a seat facing the temple as the dramatic action symbolizing Jesus' utter repudiation of the temple state, the entire socio-sym-bolic order of Judaism, and its exploitation of the poor. A word so timely it might have been spoken to our headline religion: "Beware that no one leads you astray."

The epistle picks up on the theological dimension of the new thing that God is doing with the destruction of the temple as seen through Christian eyes. We are back to the old gospel hymn:

Not all the blood of beasts
On Jewish altars slain
Could give the guilty conscience peace
Or wash away the stain
But Christ the heavenly Lamb
Takes all our sins away
A sacrifice of nobler name
And richer blood than they.

—Verna J. Dozier

Sunday Between November 20 and 26

A Glimpse of the King

PSALM 132:1-12 • 2 SAMUEL 23:1-7 • REVELATION 1:4-8 • JOHN 18:33-37

"A MAN'S REACH must exceed his grasp," the poet said, "else what's a heaven for?"

If the tradition can be trusted—and David was a poet, capable of expressing himself in the beautiful imagery of these lines—

A just king is like the light of morning
like the sun rising on a cloudless morning,
gleaming from the rain on the grassy land.
Is not my house like this with God?
For he has made with me an everlasting covenant.

Walter Brueggemann, commenting on this poem, says the three motifs of "God's sovereign power, God's moral expectation, and God's abiding fidelity provide the clues to the shape and significance of David's rule." Brueggemann concludes, "It is evident that the historical reality of David stands in considerable tension with this magisterial assertion."

But David had a greater Son—and for him in the coming days of Advent we wait.

The gospel is a disturbing reminder that our expectation may be a stumbling block to our perception of the reality. One of the most troubling moments in all history is the meeting of Jesus and Pilate. Pilate, in all the pomp and power of this world, obviously is disturbed by the calm young rabbi who is unimpressed by all the might of Rome, which held his life and the life of all his people in its wide-ranging rule.

"Are you a king?" Pilate expected a revolutionary, someone who would challenge the authority of Rome with arms. "What have you done?" Pilate expected a criminal, someone who had broken the cultic laws. "My kingdom is not from this world" is Jesus' reply. "I came to testify to the truth!"

What are your expectations of the One you are expecting? Will your expectations blind you to the reality of his coming?

The Revelation to John is all but meaningless to us who live in a "Christian nation" and sing triumphant songs—"Lift High the Cross." The reality of the situation that the Christians to whom John was writing faced is all but lost to us.

John writes grace and peace from Jesus Christ, the faithful witness, the first born of the dead. For John, "witness" and "the dead" were synonyms. To be a witness was to be a martyr. The choice was between God and Caesar. You could not have both.

Is that the One you will be expecting these next few weeks—a God who demands that there be no other God beside?

Prepare.

—Verna J. Dozier

CYCLE C

Receive the Mystery

The journey of weeks is like a treasure hunt, in which each clue reveals a truth and points us on to the next. God is the mystery behind the puzzle.

During Advent, we wait for God to reveal God's self in human form, as one of us. In the weeks that follow, we see God as Spirit, creator, light, judge, and giver of grace. This is a season of awe, a time to rest in the amazement of having been created, loved, and redeemed by a God who defies description, yet chooses to reveal the mystery to hearts that can receive it.

—Joyce Hollyday

First Sunday of Advent

Get Ready

PSALM 25:1-10 • JEREMIAH 33:14-26 • 1 THESSALONIANS 3:9-13 • LUKE 21:25-36

THE HUMMINGBIRDS DISAPPEARED a month ago. This morning a family of Canada geese, including six young ones that just a few months ago were tiny yellow balls of fluff, took off in a flurry of wings and honks. Goodbye for now. On to a warmer South.

The mountains are erupting in a blaze of color. The wind chimes dance with increased fervency. Fireflies that lit up the trees like sparkling magic last summer now flicker diffidently, scattered over the ground for their dying.

It is time. Time to dust the cobwebs out of the woodstove and split the pile of logs waiting under the beech tree. Time to replenish the supply of bird seed and get in hay for the horses, while their coats turn from shiny to shaggy. Time to prepare.

The signs are everywhere. It's in the air. Change is coming. A time of portent, disruption, newness. Get ready. Don't be left behind.

The first tinge of chill in the air always brings a rush of excitement. Can Christmas be far behind? And yet we wait. And while we wait to see the face of God, we get ready.

Do the work inside yourself that can't be done outdoors. Prepare a fallow heart to welcome mystery, water a dormant soul with springs of joy. Cultivate awe. Plant a seed of hope.

—Joyce Hollyday

Second Sunday of Advent

For What?

LUKE 1:68-79 • MALACHI 3:1-4 • PHILIPPIANS 1:3-11 • LUKE 3:1-6

IT'S THE SORT OF GOSPEL passage you always hoped not to have to read aloud in Sunday school. All those hard-to-pronounce names, like Ituraea and Lysanias. And what does it matter who was tetrarch of Abilene anyway?

It matters. Especially if you're someone who cares about power and authority and having things done right. Let's try it again. In the second year of the reign of Clinton, Jesse Helms being senator from North Carolina, Dan Quayle getting ready for 1996, and Pope John Paul II sitting on the throne in Rome, the Word of God appeared in a tenement in inner-city Chicago. Or a slum in Port-au-Prince. Or something like that.

You get the picture. It was a scandal. This Word overlooked the ruling powers, both secular and religious, and went straight to the edges of acceptability—to the wilderness. The lesson was, if you want to understand the reign of God, look in unexpected places. Go to the margins.

And watch out for this Word. It has the power to level the hills and fill in the valleys. It is like "a refiner's fire" and "a fuller's soap," according to Malachi. It will purify by the torch and rub you clean until it hurts.

You were expecting maybe just an innocent baby?

—Joyce Hollyday

Third Sunday of Advent

Take a Seat

ZEPHANIAH 3:14-20 • ISAIAH 12:2-6 • PHILIPPIANS 4:4-7 • LUKE 3:7-18

JOY, JOY, JOY! Our Zephaniah, Isaiah, and Philippians passages are brimming with invitations to rejoice in the God who brings justice.

On the last day of September 1981, I was walking on Capitol Hill in Washington, D.C. All the cafes were adorned with banners entreating patrons to "Ring in the New Year Here!" New Year? In September? Is our Congress three months ahead of the rest of us, I wondered, or miserably behind the times?—well, let's not go into that. The mystery became clear when I saw a banner that had added the word "Fiscal" in front of "New Year."

The next day, October 1, 1981, was the first day of the Reagan budget. I happened to be sitting in a cell in the D.C. jail as a result of a political protest. I will never forget the conversation with the other women there.

Most of them already felt pushed by desperation and despair into prostitution or selling illegal drugs. They spoke openly about the changes they feared were coming: severe cutbacks in education and job-training opportunities, in Food Stamps and drug rehabilitation programs. Whether or not fiscal year 1981 was something to celebrate had everything to do with whether you were sitting in a Capitol Hill cafe or the D.C. jail.

Perspective. That's what these passages are really about. So we have the ironic juxtaposition in Luke of axes being laid to the roots of trees, a winnowing hook clearing the threshing floor, and chaff being burned with unquenchable fire—followed by "So, with many other exhortations, John preached *good new*s to the people." Good news indeed! Cause for joy and celebration.

For some, that is. It depended on where you were sitting.

—Joyce Hollyday

Fourth Sunday of Advent

Vacant Thrones

LUKE 1:47-55 • MICAH 5:2-5 • HEBREWS 10:5-10 • LUKE 1:39-45

A THRONE WOULD NOT BE a particularly good choice of seat. Mary knew that. She knew, before anyone else, about the radical social upheaval that was about to be ushered in by the fruit of her womb. It had already begun.

You couldn't get much lower in those days than to be a woman in a patriarchal society, a Jew under Roman occupation, and a peasant in a land of plenty. A poor, Jewish woman in occupied Palestine was bearing the gift for which the world longed.

Mary was chosen to be the bearer of God's incarnation. God's promises had already become truth in her flesh. The poor were already being exalted. No end to the ironies.

At the news, she went "with haste" to see her cousin Elizabeth. It was a natural response. When afraid, go see a friend who will listen and make it all feel a little less lonely and overwhelming.

The account of their greeting is one of my favorite passages in all of scripture. What a blessed moment for womanhood when Mary, still trembling with the news of what was to be fulfilled in her, ran to the elderly Elizabeth and embraced her. At Mary's greeting, Elizabeth's womb came to life, and the child "leaped for joy" within her!

The Magnificat, Mary's song of praise and hope, flowed forth in this setting. And two miraculously pregnant women basked in the secret of the quiet revolution that was to be accomplished through them. Two women incarnated the truth that, with God, nothing is impossible.

I like to imagine what their days together were like. They must have been filled with shared secrets, laughter, a few tears, and dreams of a future unlike any they had conceived before. They watched their wombs swell, felt their sons growing within, probably rubbed each other's aching backs and sore feet at the end of the day.

Elizabeth, in her experience and wisdom, had much to share with her younger cousin. She understood the requirements of faith and the challenges of marriage. She knew that some would point with scorn at Mary, pregnant before her wedding, just as some had spoken of her own barrenness with reproach. She knew how to live proudly despite the whispers behind her back, and how to be grateful to God no matter what the circumstances. She understood what it meant to be a vessel of God's will.

Hearing of Mary's pregnancy, Joseph wanted at first to "dismiss her quietly." Zechariah was struck dumb for the duration of Elizabeth's pregnancy because of his doubt. Shepherds quaked, Herod raged. In the birth narratives, Mary and Elizabeth carried the faith—as well as the future.

Together they nurtured a revolution. The tables began turning. The thrones began crumbling. What joy! What HOPE!

—Joyce Hollyday

Christmas Day

Be a Light

PSALM 98 • ISAIAH 52:7-10 • HEBREWS 1:1-12 • JOHN 1:1-14

AN 11-YEAR-OLD BOY with cancer lost all his hair as a result of chemotherapy treatments. When it came time for him to return to school, he and his parents experimented with hats, wigs, and bandanas to try to conceal his baldness. They finally settled on a baseball cap, but the boy still feared the taunts he would receive for looking "different." Mustering up his courage, he went to school wearing his cap—and discovered that all of his friends had shaved their heads.

You can't hide the pain of the world. You can't cover it up. You can only share it. Make someone else's journey a little easier. Be willing to go to great lengths to help someone else carry their pain.

God did. God left whatever throne people had put him on in their imaginations and came to earth. And God made the absurd choice to arrive as a baby, vulnerable and dependent, subject to all the pains and fears and frustrations that plague the rest of us humans. A choice for incarnation.

John reminds us that we have all been given power to be the children of God. To be lights to the world. "The true light...enlightens everyone."

Whatever darkness may envelop the globe, whatever gloom may hang in our own lives—it isn't strong enough to suffocate the light. The smallest match will light up a room. The smallest gesture of kindness, act of compassion, or work of mercy will light up the globe. "The light shines in the darkness, and the darkness did not overcome it." Be a Christmas light today.

—Joyce Hollyday

First Sunday After Christmas

At One With the Human One

PSALM 148 • 1 SAMUEL 2:18-20, 26 • COLOSSIANS 3:12-17 • LUKE 2:41-52

OH, SWEET CHRISTMAS! Gerard Manley Hopkins catches the season: "In a flash, at a trumpet crash, I am all at once what Christ is, since he was what I am."

Smell the yeasty, triumphant, fragrance of Hannah's Song in First Samuel. "There is none as holy as the Lord, for there is none beside thee; neither is there any rock like our God." 1 and 2 Samuel are a gold mine for reading about women in ancient Israel: Hannah, the "medium of Endor," the "wise women of Tekoa and Beth-maacah," Abigail and Michal, Merab, and Tamar.

Hannah is the favored wife of Elkanah, and she is childless. Though Elkanah has other children and goes to great lengths to comfort Hannah, she feels her loss acutely, thinking it is a sign that God is against her. Hannah decides to take her case directly to God and deal. If God will return her fertility (thereby releasing her from power-lessness), she will give her first "fruit" back to God (with the assumption that she will be able to have more children later).

Contrary to the priest who suspects that Hannah is drunk, God thinks the deal is sound. Hannah gives birth to Samuel. At the first festival she takes him to the temple at Shiloh to live with the priest Eli (whose own sons are clearly temple scofflaws). Later, the Lord "visited" Hannah, and she gave birth to two daughters and three sons; "and the child Samuel grew on, and was in favor, both with the Lord, and with men." Samuel is the midwife of monarchy for Israel.

Like Hannah, Mary and Joseph go each year to the temple, not in Shiloh but in Jerusalem. When their son is eight days old they bring him to the temple for his naming and circumcision. They go again for Mary's purification and Jesus' redemption rituals. The prophet Anna and old Simeon meet them in the temple and shine the light on the hidden life of the young Jesus. Simeon shouts, "Now, I can die a happy man! For I have seen the salvation of my people!" Ancient Anna, who has not left the temple grounds since her husband died 84 years earlier, also raises her hands in praise to God and lights out into the city to tell anyone who will listen that "redemption has come to Jerusalem."

Jesus' hidden life resumes in Nazareth until he is 12 and goes back to Jerusalem for the Feast of Pesah, the Passover. Here he stays in the temple after the rest of the crowd has headed home; Mary and Joseph figure that he's riding with the neighbors. He is missing for three days. In the temple, Jesus is seeing to his own education. Debating, arguing, probing, listening, learning, delving into the scripture and traditions with his wise elders.

There is sufficient question in translations from the Aramaic into Greek as to whether Jesus actually labored as a carpenter who learned his trade from his father, or whether the phrase "carpenter" is a reference to the Aramaic noun used in the Talmud denoting carpenter or artisan as a scholar or "wise elder." Either way, Jesus started his education early, and continued to "grow on, and was in favor, both with the Lord, and with men."

Ring the bells! Crash the trumpet! We are what Christ is, since he was what we are!

—Rose Marie Berger

Senses and Sensibilities

Epiphany is here! God has made herself known to us. How? God, respecting our humanity, comes to us in the sights and sounds—the senses—of our world.

In the gifts of the Magi, our senses are overwhelmed: the glitter of gold, the fragrant aroma of the African-grown resin frankincense, and the East Asian gum myrrh. In the early stories of Jesus—recounted in the Epiphany season—we are asked to have ears to hear and taste buds for the wine at a wedding feast. The coming of God affects us where we live our lives—sights, sounds, sensations, smells, and tastes.

In God's coming, we need not rely on the gift of gold. Jesus points us toward realities that gold cannot touch. We are invited into a community, a new creation, that is both with us and yet to come. We are offered hope and light, a light much brighter than the glitter of gold.

All we must do to receive this free gift is to come to our senses. We can see that the God of the stable (with all its attendant sights and smells), who sides with the poor and outcast, offers us a place at the table. God graces us with the presence of God.

We must ask ourselves whether the joy we receive in this gift is something we can risk sharing, or must we keep it to ourselves? Is it abundant enough to share, or do we live with a fear of scarcity and hoard the grace? The readings for Epiphany challenge us to be light unto the world, and to share the God-with-us in fervent conviction.

—Bob Hulteen

Epiphany Sunday

The Longing of God

PSALM 72:1-14 • ISAIAH 60:1-6 • EPHESIANS 3:1-12 • MATTHEW 2:1-12

POETRY IS THE LANGUAGE of longing. When exposition fails us, conversation falters, and speeches fade, we turn to that expression which rivals "groanings too deep for words." The words of the psalms and the prophets are saturated with this type of language: hearts longing for something better—justice, provision, safety, home.

These verses are filled with that expression of longing, and it is common to hear and associate these voices in the context of our own desires. Who doesn't long for the defense of the afflicted, the salvation of needy children, rescue from oppression and violence? Who doesn't long to find the Savior who often seems hidden from our sight? Who doesn't long to see the light of peace and joy cover the earth, and all racial, cultural, and ethnic barriers transcended by the love of God? These verses, taken together, paint this very picture.

Yet within these verses there is a voice of longing even deeper than ours. It is a voice that dreams the same dreams we dream, a voice more empathic than even the most sensitive of us. It is the voice of the one who dreamed our dreams—the voice of God.

This longing for righteousness and prosperity, for "hearts throbbing and swelling with joy," for opening all the nations of the earth to God's nature, saturates these verses. It is God's yearning for the salvation of all the earth to come in fullness that fuels the heart of Epiphany. The longing we all feel for change is birthed in the heart of the one who created us.

When we wonder if there is any real hope for humanity, or if our small efforts will ever amount to anything of substance, we must remember the one who waited patiently in the manger for the Magi to arrive. He desired not their worship or their exotic gifts, but was eager to begin a journey that would offer hope to a dying world, not just the world of the Jews but to all the nations of the earth. It is the longing, the yearning of God that sustains us and drives the manifestation of God's reign in our world. It is a yearning that holds, never sleeping nor waning, and a longing that will not, ultimately, be denied.

—David A. Wade

First Sunday After Epiphany

Surprised by God

PSALM 29 • ISAIAH 43:1-7 • ACTS 8:14-17 • LUKE 3:15-17, 21-22

JUST WHEN WE THINK we have a grip on God, God surprises us. Loving creator, yes. Merciful redeemer, yes. The natural world and Jesus reveal parts of God's nature. But there is more.

We are familiar with the God of the still, small voice. But what of this God of Psalms whose voice thunders over mighty waters, breaking cedars and causing oaks to whirl, flashing forth flames of fire? If we have learned anything, we should have learned by now that God cannot be nicely wrapped up and contained by our limited views and finite minds.

God is Spirit, and Spirit rushes where it will—around and over and up, beyond our control. Beyond our hopes. For how could we have known that we needed this sustainer? This comforter?

Baptism by fire, by water, by Spirit. For each one of us, the heavens open, a dove descends, and God says, "You are my beloved, my precious one. I have called you by name. I have taken you by the hand. Do not be afraid."

A God so cosmic we cannot contain or comprehend the vast truth. A God so intimate we are never alone. What a revelation. Epiphany!

—Joyce Hollyday

Second Sunday After Epiphany

The Wedding Feast at Cana

PSALM 36:5-10 • ISAIAH 62:1-5 • 1 CORINTHIANS 12:1-11 • JOHN 2:1-11

THE WEDDING FEAST at Cana is an epiphany of the Lord, Jesus' first public miracle. The role of Mary rivets our attention: She notices the wine's short supply; she takes action; she overrides Jesus' appeal to the fact that his "hour has not yet come"; she directs the steward to "do whatever he tells you."

Furthermore, Jesus uses the title "woman" in addressing his mother to indicate her crucial place in salvation history. She is the woman whose offspring will crush the serpent's head (Genesis 3:15); she is the one to whom Jesus will entrust the church (John l9:26); she is the one to whom "great things have been done" (Luke l:49).

The Isaian reading for this Sunday uses the image of a wedding covenant to highlight God's care for the chosen people, even after their infidelity and exile to Babylon. "And as a bridegroom rejoices in his bride, so shall your God rejoice in you." The prophet prefigures the beginning of the messianic age that is pointed to in the wedding feast of Cana. There Jesus makes use of Jewish ritual objects—the stone water jars for purification—to make more wine for the celebration.

As is often the case in the lectionary, the middle reading offers a very different reflection from the first and third. Paul lifts up the challenging image of the variety of gifts with which the Spirit graces the church. All gifts are for "the common good." In an age where "me-ism" predominates, the reminder of gifts given for others comes as a healthy corrective, especially for church people.

—Joe Nangle, O.F.M.

Third Sunday After Epiphany

Anointed by the Spirit

PSALM 19 • NEHEMIAH 8:1-3, 5-6, 8-10 • 1 CORINTHIANS 12:12-31 • LUKE 4:14-21

THIS SPIRIT IS DISTURBING. Its gifts are for the upbuilding of the church, to be sure. But that is not enough. Jesus knew.

Luke 4 recounts his first public appearance in the synagogue in Nazareth. He was handed a scroll of the prophet Isaiah, and he knew just where to turn in it. The Spirit had anointed him for a mission: to bring good news to the poor, to heal the blind, to free the prisoners and the oppressed.

He came "to proclaim the year of the Lord's favor"—the year of Jubilee, in which debts were erased and slaves were freed. Every 50 years, everybody started over again with a clean slate. All were forgiven and received into the community of faith on equal footing.

With the words "Today this scripture has been fulfilled in your hearing," Jesus concluded his reading and launched his mission. It was a shrewd and stunning announcement of his purpose. The message had become political.

—Joyce Hollyday

Fourth Sunday After Epiphany

The Sunday before Ash Wednesday is Transfiguration Sunday. If Ash Wednesday falls in this week, skip to the readings for Transfiguration Sunday, page 96.

Called to Truth

PSALM 71:1-6 • JEREMIAH 1:4-10 • 1 CORINTHIANS 13:1-13 • LUKE 4:21-30

THIS SUNDAY'S HEBREW SCRIPTURE and the reading from Luke's gospel seem particularly appropriate for people of faith today in the United States. In both texts we find the phenomenon of prophetic vocation.

Jeremiah is called at a time when his nation has fallen into idolatry and faces the terrible prospect of exile. For some 40 years he exercises his ministry, through a time of hope (King Josiah's reform) and a time of despair (the Babylonian captivity). Jeremiah had the enormously unpopular vocation of warning the Jewish people of impending doom.

Similarly, in the reading from Luke's gospel, we have Jesus claiming that same prophetic calling, with a strong and unpopular message for the people. Having just made reference to the Jubilee time for restoring equity, he foretells the rejection he will experience in Nazareth: "No prophet gains acceptance in his native place."

Prophets in our society today experience similar rejection. Yet their message rings with the same clarity and urgency as in the days of Jeremiah and Jesus. "The world isn't working. The Earth is gasping for breath; the poor are dying; and the middle class is urged to keep shopping." Unless our nation listens and repents, can we escape the fate of ancient Israel? We are living pre-exilic times today in America.

Prophecy is an act of love. Paul's hymn of love in today's reading underscores the prophet's qualities: patience, kindness, selflessness, rejoicing with the truth, forbearance, trust, hope, and endurance. We pray for prophets and ask God to raise up yet greater ones in a country still mostly without ears to hear them.

—Joe Nangle, O.F.M.

Fifth Sunday After Epiphany

The Sunday before Ash Wednesday is Transfiguration Sunday. If Ash Wednesday falls in this week, skip to the readings for Transfiguration Sunday, page 96.

Transformed by Grace

PSALM 138 • ISAIAH 6:1-13 • 1 CORINTHIANS 15:1-11 • LUKE 5:1-11

FOR A BRIEF TIME, it was a solitary mission. Jesus went from Nazareth to Capernaum and on throughout Judea, casting out demons, healing the sick, and preaching the Word of God. The crowd pressed so near on the shore of Lake Gennesaret that he climbed into a boat and taught the people from there.

Then he told Simon Peter to move the boat into deep water and let down his nets. Peter protested briefly. He had hauled nets all night and caught nothing. But he did as Jesus asked.

So great was the haul of fish, the nets began to break with the weight of them! Peter had to summon the other fishermen. Bring out another boat. Too many fish to hold in one. And both the boats began to sink.

Peter's response was immediate. He was down on his knees, overwhelmed. He knew he was in the presence of an amazing man. Next to Jesus' greatness, Peter saw his own need and sin. "Go away, for I am sinful." But what he was really saying was, "Stay, for I need to be forgiven. I need to be near to this power you have."

And so nets and boats lay abandoned on the shore. Peter, James, and John forsook possessions, vocation, and family to follow a stranger with a power they had never before witnessed. They began a lifelong venture, the consequences of which they could never have imagined. They surrendered themselves to be changed completely.

The invitation is there for us as well. Let go and be willing to be transformed—by love and grace. Join Paul in the affirmation, "By the grace of God, I am what I am, and God's grace toward me was not in vain."

—Joyce Hollyday

Sixth Sunday After Epiphany

The Sunday before Ash Wednesday is Transfiguration Sunday. If Ash Wednesday falls in this week, skip to the readings for Transfiguration Sunday, page 96.

Take Root

PSALM 1 • JEREMIAH 17:5-10 • 1 CORINTHIANS 15:12-20 • LUKE 6:17-26

ECHOES OF HIS MOTHER'S SONG come to mind. Blessed are the poor, the hungry, the sad. It's an upside-down world in the eyes of God. Contrary to the overwhelming evidence, justice is real and hope is possible.

The only way to persevere is to put down deep roots of faith. Reach far below the surface of what appears to be truth. Then when you're buffeted by gales that speak anger, or drought times bring doubt, the roots will not let go.

Be tenacious in faith. Not like desert shrubs that take flight as tumbleweeds when the parched season comes, blown by winds of fear. Plant yourself where you will be fed by streams of faith and hope.

On the small mountain farm where I live, blackberry bushes ring the lake. Much to my dismay, the owner of the farm came one day last spring to tear them out. But within days, small shoots began to reappear. By late spring the thickets were providing a canopy of protection for a nesting goose and burrows of baby rabbits. By midsummer, a few of the bushes were putting out fruit—enough for a few days' worth of fresh berries on my cereal and several blackberry cobblers.

Next year there will be more. Whatever destruction came to the branches, the underground network of roots held, providing an anchor for rebirth. Roots that go deep can bear a lot and still survive.

"Blessed are those who trust in the Lord....They shall be like a tree planted by water, sending out its roots by the stream. It shall not fear when heat comes, and its leaves shall stay green; in the year of drought it is not anxious, and it does not cease to bear fruit."

—Joyce Hollyday

Seventh Sunday After Epiphany

The Sunday before Ash Wednesday is Transfiguration Sunday. If Ash Wednesday falls in this week, skip to the readings for Transfiguration Sunday, page 96.

The Courage to Forgive

PSALM 37:1-11, 39-40 • GENESIS 45:3-11, 15 • 1 CORINTHIANS 15:35-38, 42-50 • LUKE 6:27-38

LAST FALL, 25 members of Murder Victims' Families for Reconciliation toured Georgia on a "Journey of Hope," speaking throughout the state about their experience. All had lost a loved one to murder. And all had taken the long journey from grief through bitterness to forgiveness. They had discovered, as Don Mosley of Jubilee Partners, a sponsor of the tour, put it, "the power of compassion to heal their own wounds."

The community at Jubilee Partners gathered one evening to hear George White, one of the tour members, share his struggle to overcome the hatred that had poisoned his life for years after the murder of his wife.

"A man kills your wife, and you forgive that man?" responded an emotion-laden voice in the crowd. "I don't understand how it is possible!" The voice was that of a 16-year-old Bosnian who had recently arrived at Jubilee as a refugee from her war-torn land. "I hope..." she continued softly, her eyes brimming with tears, "I hope I can forgive the Serbs like that in 10 years."

Mr. White, who has a daughter about the same age as the young woman, crossed the room and gently placed his hands on her shoulders. "Honey," he said warmly, "you have to try. It's the only way to find healing from all this rotten mess."

From two very different situations, half a world apart, two hearts met and beat together with truth. It is a truth as ancient as the story of Joseph, brutally sold into slavery by his brothers, who wept and kissed them upon seeing them again. It is the truth of the psalmist who exhorts, "Do not fret because of the wicked."

It is the truth of Jesus, who went to the cross for the sins of others, uttering among his last words, "Father, forgive them...." His gospel command remains before us as a challenge, seeming like an impossibility: "Love your enemies." But it is attainable. Others have shown the way. God, give us the courage to follow them.

—Joyce Hollyday

Eighth Sunday After Epiphany

The Sunday before Ash Wednesday is Transfiguration Sunday. If Ash Wednesday falls in this week, skip to the readings for Transfiguration Sunday, page 96.

Be Doers of the Word

PSALM 92:1-4, 12-15 • ISAIAH 55:10-13 • 1 CORINTHIANS 15:51-58 • LUKE 6:39-49

OF THE SEVERAL THEMES highlighted in today's readings, that of God's effective Word stands out. Isaiah claims on behalf of Yahweh that the Word which goes forth from God's mouth shall not return void but shall do God's will, achieving the end for which it was sent. Reflection on this prophetic claim sets the stage for this Sunday's gospel text, the conclusion of Jesus' great discourse in Luke.

"Why do you call me 'Lord, Lord,' and not put into practice what I teach you?" Jesus asks. The Word must be operative, acted on, efficacious. We are called to be doers of the Word, as Paul says, and not hearers only.

This theme has received intense attention by liberation theologians. It is one of their principal gifts to the universal church. Orthopraxis—right action—ranks higher in importance than orthodoxy. Said another, more startling, way, it is more important to follow Jesus than to know him. We have heard it so often: Our call is to faithfulness.

The consequences of this biblical teaching are numerous. They can perhaps be summed up in that celebrated text from Matthew 25. Jesus rests the full weight of judgment on all human's lives upon how we responded to hunger, thirst, nakedness, loneliness, and imprisonment among our less fortunate sisters and brothers.

—Joe Nangle, O.F.M.

Transfiguration Sunday
(Sunday before Ash Wednesday)

Just Who is Transformed?

PSALM 99 • EXODUS 34:29-35 • 2 CORINTHIANS 3:12-4:2 • LUKE 9:28-43

JESUS, LIKE MOSES before him (as told in the Exodus passage), has the ultimate mountaintop experience. He goes up the mountain to pray, and there he meets God. That, of course, is the purpose of prayer. But for Jesus, the experience visibly transformed him. (In Matthew's [17:1-8] and Mark's [9:2-8] versions of this encounter, Jesus is "metamorphosed"; Luke uses the much less colorful phrase "was altered.")

We know that prayer is transforming. But who is really transformed here? Jesus has led for the most part a humble, ordinary human life. At the same time, he is the center of the divine event toward which all creation has been moving, and by which all creation is given the gift of salvation. His closest friends and disciples have heard hints of this extraordinary mystery—just a few verses before (9:22), Jesus foretold his death and resurrection—but this is their first glimpse of resurrection glory.

Peter's reaction to this miracle, in typical salt-of-the-earth Peter fashion, is very practical: He wants to set up tents for Jesus and the distinguished visitors. But Peter just doesn't get it—he did not know what he was saying, as Luke says. Some interpreters take this as a warning about the risk of trying to institutionalize a mountaintop experience, of trying to control and contain the mystical. Hiding away in tents, you might just miss the transfiguration!

Luke is the only one of the parallels that tells us what the three discuss: Jesus' imminent "departure" at Jerusalem (9:31). Some translations say they talked of Jesus' "passing" or his "decease." The Greek word (*exodus*) is so much richer! This journey to Jerusalem and the events that will transpire there aren't about death so much as life. The story isn't about the imprisonment and execution of one man as much as it's about the liberation and redemption of humanity. The Exodus of the people of God from captivity, commenced by Moses and Elijah—the Law and the Prophets—is finally in Jesus brought to fruition, to completion.

Jesus' ministry began with his baptismal anointing (Matthew 3:17). That blessing ("This is my Beloved Son") is now echoed on the mountain, and Jesus' story enters its culminating chapter as he begins the journey to Jerusalem.

—Jim Rice

Journey Toward Joy

*T*he landscape of Lent is often painted as a desert. These weeks before Easter can be a thirsty time, a lonely time. They invite us on a journey of examining our souls to see where we fall short, making our way between the oases that reveal God's mercy.

The journey may seem unending at times. We make it in the shadow of the cross. But we gently carry the knowledge that death doesn't have the final word. There is new life on the other side—and joy. So we are invited to enter the season boldly, knowing that we walk toward a promise.

—Joyce Hollyday

First Sunday of Lent

A God Who Delivers

PSALM 91:1-2, 9-16 • DEUTERONOMY 26:1-11 • ROMANS 10:8-13 • LUKE 4:1-13

TELLING THE GREAT STORIES builds up the faith of the people. And so the tale of the mighty deliverance from Egypt was recounted again and again among the people of God: the pillars of cloud and fire, the outstretched arm, the parted sea, all manner of signs and wonders by a steadfast and strong God.

Jesus would have participated in the ritual of remembrance at least 30 times before he stood on the edge of his own wilderness. He entered the lonely time of temptation confident of the God who is shelter and refuge, protection and deliverance.

Famished after 40 days without food, Jesus refused the invitation to satisfy his need with acts of magic. On the verge of launching his ministry, he rejected the offer of easy glory and power. About to reveal to the world his true identity, he refused to force God's hand.

Jesus rejected the showy, compromised power of the world and chose the power of the Holy Spirit. Some would say it was a mistake. You can wind up on a cross that way. But it was that compassionate emptying that turned the world upside-down.

As we venture through our own wilderness time this season, may we have the strength to embrace that power. And may we trust in a God who still delivers.

—Joyce Hollyday

Second Sunday of Lent

Vulnerable to the Powers

PSALM 27 • GENESIS 15:1-12, 17-18 • PHILIPPIANS 3:17-4:1 • LUKE 13:31-35

THE DELIVERER GOD of last week is contrasted this week with an intimate God who comes to us in comforting images of light and salvation. This God desires that we seek her face. She takes Abraham by the hand and shows him the stars, promising him countless descendants. She is like a mother hen, who desires to gather her brood protectively under her wings.

It is no coincidence that Jesus compares himself to a hen and calls Herod a fox. The threat is obvious. The children of God are vulnerable to the powers of the world.

Soon the strength of that power will be all too real. Jesus knows what waits in Jerusalem. The cross is already in view.

But the promise of victory is just as real. The day is also coming when the powers will know their limits. "Wait for the Lord; be strong, and let your heart take courage; wait for the Lord!"

—Joyce Hollyday

Third Sunday of Lent

Thirsting for God

PSALM 63:1-8 • ISAIAH 55:1-9 • 1 CORINTHIANS 10:1-13 • LUKE 13:1-9

IN OUR CULTURE, it's hard to understand thirsting. Most of us can have all the water we want at the turn of a faucet.

These scriptures bring to mind images of women I saw in South Africa several years ago. At dusk they lined up, with children at their sides and on their backs, containers balanced on their heads. Long after nightfall, they were still there, moving slowly toward the one spigot that served most of the black township outside Pretoria.

Those women had no choice. Patience and long-suffering were required to obtain water. And life could not go on without it. Water was necessary for cooking and washing. But it was also bedrock sustenance for people who often had little else.

In those days, the thirst for freedom was as strong as the thirst for water. People were willing to die for it. And then, in May 1994, rivers ran in the desert for the people of South Africa. One overwhelming thirst was quenched.

It is that sort of thirsting that our scriptures talk about. In the desert landscape of Lent, our souls long to know God, our flesh yearns to be refreshed by the promise of new life. The longing consumes us, superceding all else.

Therefore repent, and know God. Turn from sinful ways and be welcomed back to the springs of forgiveness. And be assured by this promise from today's epistle: "No testing has overtaken you that is not common to everyone. God is faithful and will not let you be tested beyond your strength."

—Joyce Hollyday

Fourth Sunday of Lent

The Passing of the Old

PSALM 32 • JOSHUA 5:9-12 • 2 CORINTHIANS 5:16-21 • LUKE 15:1-3, 11-32

SOME YEARS AGO sectors of the Catholic Church in Latin America asked permission from Rome to celebrate Lent and Easter in October and November, which is springtime in the Southern Hemisphere. Theirs was a clear understanding of what Paul tells us in his letter to the Corinthians today: "The old order has passed away; now all is new." Lent and Easter celebrate the fact that "all is new," and they are best observed when the Earth itself is in renewal.

The gospel today underlines this lesson with Luke's account of the prodigal son. It is indeed a new order when an ungrateful offspring, after squandering his inheritance, can return and be welcomed with open arms by the parent who images God. And if elder sons cannot understand such largess and forgiveness, neither are they/we rejected: "You are with me always, and everything I have is yours."

The new order is made possible by our brother "who was dead and has come back to life. He was lost and is found." We have here a wonder-filled identification between the wayward son and Jesus: "For our sakes God made him who did not know sin to be sin...."

We look forward this Sunday to the approaching springtime feast of humanity's renewal by Jesus. With his taking on evil itself at Calvary and conquering it on resurrection Sunday, nothing again will ever be the same. "The old order has passed away; now all is new!"

—Joe Nangle, O.F.M.

Fifth Sunday of Lent

A Torrent of Hope

PSALM 126 • ISAIAH 43:16-21 • PHILIPPIANS 3:4-14 • JOHN 12:1-8

THE PHILOSOPHER A. N. WHITEHEAD once remarked that it can take a thousand years for a really new idea to make its way, given human resistance. Exodus—now that was truly new: For the first time a divine being siding, not with the mighty, but the powerless, not with masters, but slaves (Isaiah 43:16-17). But now, 800 years after the exodus, Isaiah declares, God is about to do a new thing! It will be 600 years before that new thing is manifest in Jesus, and then it takes millennia just to begin to be heard. Write: What is the "new thing" God is still trying to do in our time? Why does humanity resist it so?

The "old thing" included Israel's nonviolence at the cost of Yahweh's violence at the Red Sea. The "new thing" involves, among other things, a restored creation, a peaceable ecosystem (Isaiah 43:19-20). Has Yahweh become nonviolent? Is such a vision as Isaiah's illusionary? Can human beings learn to live peaceably and ecologically responsible? Realistically, how much dare we hope for?

Isaiah provides the corrective vision. God gives us water to revive us in the wilderness. It wets our tongues for praise (43:21). Praise is the homeostatic principle by which humanity is kept in ecological balance with God and the universe. We cannot praise God and devastate God's creation. We cannot worship God and idolize our own power.

Do you find praise difficult? If so, why? Are you sure you thought big enough about what God is about to do?

—Walter Wink

Palm Sunday

Scandalous Love

PSALM 31:9-16 • ISAIAH 50:4-9 • PHILIPPIANS 2:5-11 • LUKE 22:14-23:56

THE EVENTS OF THE LAST WEEK of Jesus' life have a disconcerting familiarity: the Last Supper, the lonely agony in the garden, Judas' betrayal and Peter's denials, the humiliations before Pilate and Herod, the clamor of the crowd for his death. What often gets little attention is the dispute that broke out among his friends at the table.

They wanted to know which of them Jesus regarded as the greatest. That moment must have been among Jesus' loneliest—like his discovery of them sleeping in the garden, or the interchange around drawing swords. Facing the most anguished time of his life, Jesus was utterly alone. His closest friends still didn't understand.

It was a scandal, after all—this surrendering, emptying, going peacefully to the cross. What about insurrection? What about calling on God to do a miracle and save them from this terrible ending?

They never understood that to lead meant to serve; to save meant to let go; to live meant to be willing to die. It is a tough lesson for all of the followers of Jesus.

—Joyce Hollyday

Easter Sunday

Joyful Witness

PSALM 118:1-2, 14-24 • ACTS 10:34-43 • 1 CORINTHIANS 15:19-26 • JOHN 20:1-18

THE GOSPEL ACCOUNTS VARY as to which women stood by the cross and went to the tomb. But all agree that Mary Magdalene was there.

This devoted disciple was the first witness to the resurrection, an astounding truth considering that the testimony of women was not considered valid in a court of law at the time; women were deemed unreliable witnesses. In Luke's account, when the women went to tell the disciples about the empty tomb, they considered it "an idle tale" (Luke 24:11).

But in John's version, Peter and John ran straight for the tomb on Mary Magdalene's word. They saw the linen wrappings and believed that what was promised had come true. Then they went home.

For Mary Magdalene was reserved the special grace of seeing the risen Christ. The tender beauty of the garden scene was all hers. Jesus' first word out of the tomb was "Woman." He spoke it gently. Then he spoke her name, and her tears of sorrow became tears of unspeakable joy.

Good news can't be contained. The one who knows it always has to run and tell someone else. So it was with Mary Magdalene, who passed the word on. And from her testimony, the word spread around Jerusalem, across the globe, and through the ages.

The calling of Mary Magdalene is the calling of us all. Jesus still calls us by name. We, too, commune in intimacy with him when we accept the gift of abundant life and live bearing joyful testimony to the resurrection. By our testimony, we join all the followers through the centuries who can say, as Peter did, "We are witnesses to all that he did...."

—Joyce Hollyday

Second Sunday of Easter

Doubt to Faith

PSALM 150 • ACTS 5:27-32 • REVELATION 1:4-8 • JOHN 20:19-31

I LOVE THE POST-RESURRECTION STORIES: confused minds and burning hearts; Jesus walking through walls, strolling the road for a stretch, eating broiled fish, serving breakfast on the beach. It is all so human—and yet so miraculous. Dared the disciples believe?

I am most grateful for Thomas. He knew it was all too strange just to accept at face value. He needed to *touch it*—to place his fingers on the wounds and know for himself that this was indeed Jesus come back to them.

Earlier, upon hearing of the death of Lazarus—when the people were threatening to stone Jesus—it was Thomas who had boldly declared, "Let us also go, that we may die with him" (John 11:16). But of course more than one follower had found his performance falling short of his pronouncements.

Jesus honored the doubt. At the same time, he encouraged faith. He invited Thomas to see and feel the truth for himself. And he issued an invitation to all of us: "Blessed are those who have not seen and yet have come to believe."

—Joyce Hollyday

Third Sunday of Easter

Resurrection Flashes

PSALM 30 • ACTS 9:1-20 • REVELATION 5:11-14 • JOHN 21:1-19

WITH WHAT TONE OF VOICE do you imagine Peter saying, "I'm going fishing"? Why, after all that happened to them in Jerusalem, are the disciples back fishing? Why don't they recognize Jesus? This theme of non-recognition appears repeatedly (Matthew 28:17; Luke 24:13-35, 36-43; John 20:14-16). How do they know it's Jesus if they are unable to recognize him?

In Luke 5, a miraculous catch of fish rocks Peter into discipleship. In John, by contrast, it reconfirms resurrection to be, not a single eruption of eternity into time, but a series of epiphanies. These transcendental flashes in the darkness of our world do not provide a steady diet, but only an occasional fish fry by the seashore. The theophanic events of 1989-90, when every-other-day's headlines shouted the glory of God, yielded to the gloom of anarchy and economic collapse in formerly communist countries and depression at home. Those flashes will have to last us for some time, just as memory of the Exodus has fired Jewish hope these 3,000 years.

Let us remember carefully the details. Note that Peter dresses to leap in the water (?!). Count every single fish. (If you study this in a group, try acting out this story as a farce. Farce captures a quality in this story that is deliberately playful: no fish, too many fish; non-recognition, recognition; Peter swimming fully clothed; the entire fish-count, in unison; Jesus as short-order cook.)

Then sudden poignancy: Peter, do you *agapas* (the highest, self-giving love, *agape*) me? Peter: "Yes, Lord; you know that I *philo* (to have friendship, affection for) you." Jesus: "Feed my lambs." A second time Jesus asks: Do you *agapas* me? "Yes Lord; you know that I *philo* you." "Tend my sheep." A third time Jesus asks, Do you *phileis* me? Peter, grieved that this third time Jesus had adopted his word, replies, "You know everything; you know that I *philo* you." "Feed my sheep."

Why does Peter use *philo*? Why does Jesus ask three times? Compare John 18:17, 25, 27. Why is Peter grieved by Jesus' use of *philo*? Why does Jesus change to *philo*?

In this gentle scene of restitution after perfidy, we see enacted the severity and costliness of love: It breaks our heart by accepting our inability to reciprocate. Do I need to move from "liking" God to "loving"?

—Walter Wink

Fourth Sunday of Easter

I Shall Not Want

PSALM 23 • ACTS 9:36-43 • REVELATION 7:9-17 • JOHN 10:22-30

LIKE MANY OF US, I imagine, I memorized the 23rd Psalm as a child. When I was given the opportunity in Sunday school on my sixth birthday to choose a picture as a gift, I didn't hesitate. From among such familiar images as Jesus knocking on the door and welcoming children to his side, I picked Jesus holding the lost lamb.

Montessori-based religious education centers on this Jesus. Educators have discovered that a shepherd is a most comforting image for children.

But there was always one point of confusion for me as a child. In my recitations, I ran the lines of the first verse of the psalm together: "The Lord is my shepherd I shall not want." I always wondered why I shouldn't want this shepherd, especially since he was supposed to be taking such good care of me.

On the path of my faith journey since those days, I sometimes remember my early confusion and smile. Indeed, there have been days when this Jesus has been a shepherd I would rather not follow. I know his voice; but sometimes his call feels like much more than I ever bargained for.

It is impossible to follow this shepherd without walking into pain—one's own as well as that of the world. It is impossible to follow without understanding the cross and the commandment to pour ourselves out for enemy and friend.

This past week I have stood in court with battered women, prayed for a friend dying of cancer, shared bread with a community that ministers to homeless people and death row prisoners. The throng of those who suffer is immense, and likely to get worse in the days ahead.

Ours would be a lonely journey if Jesus had not walked ahead. It is a great paradox of our faith: Jesus is the shepherd—but also the Lamb that was slain. He is a guide who knows how to lead because he has been down this road before. And he still offers that intimate comfort that so touched us as children.

Revelation 7 holds forth the image of a throng gathered around the throne of this Lamb. As I read the passage, I picture faces of people I know. May we take comfort in the promise it offers for our journey:

...the one who is seated on the throne will shelter them.
They will hunger no more, and thirst no more;...
for the Lamb at the center of the throne will be their shepherd,
and he will guide them to springs of the water of life,
and God will wipe away every tear from their eyes.
　　　　　—Revelation 7:15-17

—Joyce Hollyday

Fifth Sunday of Easter
All Things New

PSALM 148 • ACTS 11:1-18 • REVELATION 21:1-6 • JOHN 13:31-35

OUR PASSAGES THIS WEEK are about new things: a new commandment, the New Jerusalem, a new heaven and earth. Old ways and old sorrows are passing away. God promises that God's saving, healing, changing work in the world is ongoing: "See, I am making all things new" (Revelation 21:5).

Perhaps most challenging for us from among this week's scriptures is the passage from John: "By this everyone will know that you are my disciples, if you have love for one another" (John 13:35). I would rest easier if the last part of the verse read "...if you live simply enough," or "...if you protest loudly enough," or "...if you help the disadvantaged enough." This commandment about loving each other is tougher.

But Jesus must have meant it. About to go to his death, he picked this as his "new commandment," among his final words to his followers. This love for each other was to be the mark of true discipleship. Jesus must have known how difficult was the task.

Those of us who are busy with trying to be the body of Christ in the world should pause over these words. How easy it is to get so consumed with the work of ushering in the kingdom that we forget to share a meal, listen to a good story, or sit on the porch with those with whom we share the work.

We can get like Peter in our fascinating Acts passage for today, so preoccupied with the details of faithfulness that we sometimes lose sight of the big picture. Peter dreams of a sheet descending, filled with beasts and birds and reptiles—all the animals good Jews are forbidden to eat. At God's command to kill and eat them, Peter stammers something along the lines of "It wouldn't be politically correct"—or perhaps religiously correct is more to the point.

But the Spirit (inklings of Pentecost) says it's time to break the rules. What matters is breaking down the barriers and distinctions between people. What matters is love.

"I give you a new commandment, that you love one another. Just as I have loved you, you also should love one another" (John 13:34). God is making all things new. Including us.

—Joyce Hollyday

Sixth Sunday of Easter
A Home for Faith

PSALM 67 • ACTS 16:9-15 • REVELATION 21:10, 22-22:5 • JOHN 14:23-29

IT IS ENCOURAGING to have the stories of two of the great women saints of the early church appear in these weeks before Pentecost. Dorcas, whose story appeared two weeks ago (Acts 9:36-43), is called "disciple"—the only occurrence in the New Testament of the feminine form of the word. She lived northwest of Jerusalem at the port of Joppa, an important center of Christianity as the faith spread across the Mediterranean. There, grieving widows looked out longingly at the sea that had claimed their sailor husbands, and the destitute scavenged on the shore for bits of rags.

Dorcas was moved to compassion by their plight. She began sewing clothes for the poor, offering all out of her generosity. She made tunics and coats, which served not only for warmth but were the mats the homeless poor slept on at night.

Dorcas' home was a center for mercy and hope. When she died, the grieving was widespread and heartfelt. The disciples sent for Peter. It was high tribute that the leader of the church came immediately.

When Dorcas came back to life, word spread quickly. The rejoicing was as ardent as the mourning had been for this beloved sister, the only person recorded to have been raised from the dead by a disciple of Jesus. So well known was her rising that many came to faith through this miracle.

Mention is made twice of "the widows" in this story. It is likely that Dorcas herself was a widow. Women took much of the lead in the early church in caring for the sick and the poor. Some opened their homes as places of prayer and the breaking of bread. Widows were both the receivers and givers of benevolence, taking care of one another and of many others beyond themselves, living joyfully in sisterhood and service, incarnating the gospel.

Some of these women had gathered by a river outside Philippi to pray when Paul came by preaching. Philippi, a city on the major overland route from Asia to the West, was an ideal location for an artisan and merchant as skilled as Lydia, who made purple dyes from a substance gathered from a mollusk. Lydia bears the unique honor of being considered Europe's first convert to Christianity.

She was clearly a woman of respect and influence. When she converted to Christianity, her entire household was baptized with her. So enflamed was Lydia with a hunger to learn the gospel, she compelled Paul and his companions to stay at her home and share their knowledge in return for her hospitality.

When Paul and Silas were released from prison in a most earth-shaking manner, they headed straight for Lydia's house (Acts 16:40). They must have known that the sisters and brothers gathered there had been in fervent prayer for their safety. Later, Paul showed his special love for those companions in Christ in his warm and heartfelt letter to the Philippians, referring to the church there as his "joy and crown" (Philippians 4:1). The seeds of that great church were found among a group of women praying on a riverbank. They first took root in Lydia, whose home became the center of the church.

These two saints, Dorcas and Lydia, gave truth to Jesus' beautiful promise: "Those who love me will keep my word, and my Father will love them, and we will come to them and make our home with them" (John 14:23). They beckon us to follow their example, offering hearts and homes for faith.

—Joyce Hollyday

Ascension Sunday

In some traditions, the Ascension Sunday texts are used in place of the Seventh Sunday of Easter.

Witnesses to Joy

PSALM 47 • ACTS 1:1-11 • EPHESIANS 1:15-23 • LUKE 24:44-53

THIS WEEK'S SCRIPTURES bring us two accounts of the ascension of Jesus. We know with what joy and hope the disciples received Jesus after his resurrection. His appearances in a house, on the shore, and on the road to Emmaus were cause for great celebration: The promises had come true.

I imagine that if I were a follower in that time, I would have wanted the celebration to last forever. Somehow, no matter what Jesus might have told me, I would have expected him to stay around for a while. Forty days would have felt entirely too short after all that had gone on.

And, like the disciples in the Acts account, I would have wanted to be assured that now all will be well. "Lord, is this the time when you will restore the kingdom to Israel?" Will the glory go on and the suffering end? Will justice finally come? Can we count on you, Jesus, to make it all right before you go?

There were no such reassurances. In fact, as we know from hindsight, the injustices continued, the persecutions escalated. To be a post-resurrection Christian meant to live in the promise while still facing the cross.

Yet, Luke tells us, the disciples—facing uncertainty without the company of Jesus—returned to Jerusalem "with great joy" after the ascension. They were "continually in the temple blessing God." They had been given the promise of a gift that would never leave them. The Holy Spirit would be with them always.

It's hard to imagine what that must have felt like to the disciples—letting go of a flesh-and-blood savior for the promise of an intangible, invisible Spirit. Yet they trusted that something remarkable was going to happen. They were going to be witnesses to marvelous signs and wonders. And they would not be alone.

Comforter, Advocate, Sustainer—the Holy Spirit would be within them and among them. They would be "clothed with power" to bear witness to all that they would see. And the overwhelming response of the followers of Jesus was not fear, or doubt, or resistance, but great joy.

Clap your hands, all you peoples;
shout to God with loud songs of joy.
For the Lord, the Most High, is awesome,
a great king over all the earth.
    —Psalm 47:1-2

—Joyce Hollyday

Seventh Sunday of Easter

In some traditions, the Ascension Sunday texts are used in place of the Seventh Sunday of Easter.

"...A Long Time Alone"

PSALM 97 • ACTS 16:16-34 • REVELATION 22:12-14, 16-17, 20-21 • JOHN 17:20-26

POET GALWAY KINNELL writes:

one knows,
after a long time of solitude, after the many steps taken away
from one's own kind, toward the kingdom of strangers,
the hard prayer inside one's own singing/is to come back, if one can, to one's own,
a world almost lost, in the exile that deepens,
when one has lived a long time alone.

—from *When One Has Lived A Long Time Alone*

WHO IS THIS "JOHN" of the mystical book of Revelation? John the Divine? John of Patmos? John the beloved disciple? John the gospel writer? John the elder? John the Baptist, high on smoked locust? All scholars agree, no one is sure. I think one thing is certain, the bulk of Revelation was written by a man called John, who had lived a long time alone.

The azure radiance of the Sea of Crete, the honey Mediterranean light that rises through the whole body until it finally reaches the eyes, the salt-encrusted air that sucks at the bones of everything living—this is the island of Patmos, off the coast of present-day Turkey, where a man called John lived a long time alone.

The book of Revelation is written in a language we no longer understand, the language of metaphor. Multivalent allegories are at work here; ancient cabal for which we don't have the key. Other scriptures are written in a language still tied (however loosely at times) to recognizable human experience. Revelation is more like speaking with whales who communicate in three-dimensional images played directly on the screen of the mind. Revelation is theater in the round.

It is filled with numerology; mythology from Zoroaster, Babylon, and Persia; ancient astrological wisdom; and Jewish mysteries. It has a backbone of four series of seven (letters, seals, trumpets, bowls) which are related to Jesus' apocalyptic discourses on the Mount of Olives (Matthew 24, Mark 13, Luke 21). The horrendous visions of destruction are bracketed with visions of God the Creator (Revelation 4 and 5) and God the Redeemer (Revelation 21). The whole book is a prophetic love letter to the persecuted Christian church.

Revelation is particularly well-chosen to close the canonical scriptures. Chapters 21 and 22 round out the work begun in Genesis with the themes of new creation, new Israel, new covenant, new temple, an eternal wedding between God and God's people. But, as there is no "last word" of revelation, so the last words of this scripture are only beginnings. "Amen! Come, Lord Jesus! The grace of the Lord Jesus be with all the saints. Amen!" This bipolar "Amen" is our Christian existence. The Risen Christ is the Alpha and the Omega. We say Amen to the future: "Come, Lord Jesus!" But we also say Amen to the present as an event of grace: "The grace of the Lord Jesus be with all the saints." Our paschal journey, which began in Lenten ashes, will rise anew in fire.

And John, who lived a long time alone, comes back to us wielding the "hard prayer" inside his own singing.

—Rose Marie Berger

The Wild Ways of the Spirit

It is the season of the Spirit. Totally dependable and utterly unpredictable, gentle and wild, challenging and comforting—this Spirit cannot be described or contained. It blows where it will, taking us along on the journey.

This is a wild Pentecost ride, to which we are all invited. Hold on to your seats—and each other. And discover that God can be found in faint whisper or fury of fire.

—Joyce Hollyday

Pentecost Sunday

Like Rushing Wings

PSALM 104:24-35 • ACTS 2:1-21 • ROMANS 8:14-17 • JOHN 14:8-17, 25-27

IT WAS BARELY DAWN, and I was still sound asleep. Then came a noise—a holy racket of sorts. Honking and calling and furious fluttering of wings. I made it to the front porch just in time to see eight huge Canada geese land in the lake on the little farm where I live. With great fanfare, they touched down and then skimmed across the water to a stop, wings still beating the air.

Red fire appeared between the trees on the eastern horizon, then slowly turned orange and finally stabbing yellow. Birds and bugs of all sorts joined in an early morning chorus of welcome to the day—humming, chirping, whistling, singing. I laughed out loud. It was the closest thing to Pentecost I'm likely to experience.

It descends on us like rushing wings, tongues of fire, a cacophony of voices. Startling. Dazzling. Unpredictable. Enough to make the neighbors think someone raided nature's wine cellar before the sun even came up.

It is good that we have this wild, unfettered, uncontrollable Spirit. We want to do good. We want to live holy and just lives. We want to get it right. But what reassurance to know that part of it is totally out of our control! The Spirit moves around, utterly oblivious to rules, more gentle and grace-filled and generous than we deserve.

We are all included in this gracious baptism, as Peter reminds us. Sons, daughters, young and old, bound and free—all are prophets, bearers of a vision as yet unseen.

O Lord, how manifold are your works!...
The earth is full of your creatures....
When you send forth your spirit, they are created;
*   and you renew the face of the ground.*
May the glory of the Lord endure forever—...
*   who looks on the earth and it trembles,*
*   who touches the mountains and they smoke.*
*   I will sing to the Lord as long as I live;*
*   I will sing praise to my God while I have being.*
                    —Psalm 104:24, 30-33

—Joyce Hollyday

Trinity Sunday

Humming With the Harmonies of God

PSALM 8 • PROVERBS 8:1-4, 22-31 • ROMANS 5:1-5 • JOHN 16:12-15

THE WISDOM OF GOD CHALLENGES the power players at the gate of the city: "O ye simple, understand wisdom; and, ye fools, be ye of an understanding heart." Sometimes those who spend a long time inside the "gated community" of power forget what it is like for those exposed outside the gate. Power players inside the gate forget where power comes from and begin to believe power is theirs alone and their right, the purpose of their lives to protect and preserve it. The Wisdom of God says, "Receive My instruction, rather than silver; and choose knowledge, rather than gold....For it is by Me that kings reign and princes decree justice."

Inside the "beltway" around Washington, D.C. (specifically in the federal ghetto around the National Mall), there is a disease of lethargy. Lethargy comes from the Greek words for "idle forgetfulness." Many of our national power wielders have abandoned the search for Wisdom—the counselor, the teacher, the mediator between earth and heaven. This Wisdom of God is the creative dynamic impulse intrinsic to all created things because She existed before all created things and brought all things into being.

The prologue of the gospel of John plays with the conceptually entwined Greek for God's logos (Word) and God's sophia (Wisdom): "In the beginning was the Word and Wisdom...." The masculine Word/logos is the history of remembrance that marked out the foundations of the earth, was preached through the prophets, was rejected by most, was accepted by a faithful remnant, and now is made flesh in Jesus Christ.

The feminine Wisdom/sophia is the internally harmonic song of God, the transcendent design of the universe that imbues all things with inherent meaning. Wisdom/sophia knows no beginning or end. Eschatologies are foreign to Her. The temporal world is not distinguished by the movement of time or history, but by how well the world reflects the pure, intrinsic, harmony of God.

In John 15, Jesus speaks to the disciples about the vine and branches, clearly connected to the logos, the history of remembrance, the foundations of the new earth. He continues in John 16, "I have much more to say to you, more than you can now bear," referring to the fragile vine which is not yet ready to bear such heavy fruit.

Jesus promises that the Spirit of Truth or Holy Spirit or Wisdom will come to them, and the vine will hum with the harmonies of God. The vine will reflect the pureness of the Spirit's song because that song is intrinsically formed in God; never, in any way, is it divided from God. Power will flow from this song, but only for those who give up everything to catch a fragment of the tune.

—Rose Marie Berger

Attending to the Feast of God

Home. It is, in its rightful incarnation, the place where you are declared safe. Home has familiar smells, familiar faces, familiar stuff, familiar food, familiar nuisances. If you have a home, more likely than not most of the time you take it for granted. If you've lost it, you mourn it like family.

The Bible is filled with wanderers in search of home. We join our journeys with theirs, not to find shortcuts, but to better understand what we seek. The Spirit leads us through wildernesses we wouldn't choose for ourselves. The promise is home.

—Julie Polter

Sunday Between May 29 and June 4

(if after Trinity Sunday)

"Yahweh is God!"

PSALM 96 • 1 KINGS 18:20-39 • GALATIANS 1:1-12 • LUKE 7:1-10

NEVER UNDERESTIMATE THE WISDOM of the people! What fun to be dropped into the middle of a Spielberg-esque scene atop Mount Carmel (1 Kings 18). Powers and principalities are waging battle through the Tishbite prophet Elijah and those bad boys of Baal. "How long," Elijah sticks it to the gathered crowd, "do you mean to hobble first on one leg and then the other? If Yahweh is God, follow him; if Baal, follow him!" Ah, but the people opened not their mouths, judiciously waiting to see which side would win before declaring an allegiance.

What follows on Mount Carmel is one of the funniest stories in the Hebrew scriptures. Single-handedly Elijah takes on all 450 of Baal's priests, challenging them at their own game. Baal has a taste for bull, so Elijah lets the Baal priest choose their best beast; they prepare it for sacrifice. Elijah shouts out, "You call on the name of your god, and I'll call on mine; the god who answers with fire is God indeed." "Agreed!" yells our pragmatic peanut gallery. The Baal boys call all day on their god, while Elijah jeers them. "Perhaps your god is on vacation, or busy. Yell louder, perhaps your god is sleeping!" All to no avail; best to let sleeping gods lie.

Elijah now gathers the people around him. He rebuilds the altar to Yahweh that has fallen into disrepair under King Ahab. He places not only the 10 stones representing the tribes of the Northern Kingdom, but two more stones for the tribes of the Southern Kingdom. The divided tribes of Jacob shall be one again and Israel shall be their name.

After all this time of drought, Elijah calls for the last of the water. Three times he has the people drench the altar. (Keep in mind that Baal is the god of rain.) Elijah then sets about winning hearts and minds: "Yahweh, let them know that you are God in Israel and that I am your servant. Answer me, so that these people will know that you are God."

Then the fire of Yahweh fell from heaven, consuming the bull, the altar, and every last drop of water in the trench. While the pyrotechnics sputter out, the people have found their voices, "Yahweh is God! Yahweh is God!" (Viewer discretion advised: The following verses contain the bloody slaughter of the prophets of Baal—all 450 of them.) Finally, Israel returns to the Lord and Elijah says, "I hear the sound of rain."

In Luke's gospel we find a Roman centurion asking Jesus to heal his dying servant. The soldier does not need to have Jesus present; he trusts Jesus' authority. "I tell you, not even in Israel have I found faith like this," Jesus tells the crowd. The servant is healed before the messengers return.

The Word of God is sent forth. It will not return empty. Blessed are those have not seen and yet believe (John 20:29)!

—Rose Marie Berger

Sunday Between June 5 and 11

(if after Trinity Sunday)

Touched by an Angel

PSALM 146 • 1 KINGS 17:8-24 • GALATIANS 1:11-24 • LUKE 7:11-17

HIDDEN IN THE ROYAL HIS-STORY of 1 Kings (16-17) is an interesting her-story: two women of Sidon (Queen Jezebel and the widow of Zarephath) and the process of conversion.

Ahab (that poor excuse for an Israelite king) had sense enough to marry the powerful Sidonian/Phoenician queen Jezebel to keep watch over his interests (1 Kings 16:31). The Phoenician monarchy is based on patron gods supporting a ruling dynasty, so Queen Jezebel is a devout follower of Astarte, goddess of sea and stars, and Baal, god of rain. (The Phoenicians' were the first to discover celestial navigation, which allowed their fearsome navy to attack enemies at night, hence their patron gods of stars and water.) Jezebel's mistake is thinking that what worked to establish a theocracy in Sidon will work in Israel. Queen Jezebel is a power wielder bent on consolidating urban kingdoms and stabilizing the status quo. Conversion to serving the Israelite God of the poor is just not in her worldview.

Out of the rural backwoods of Gilead comes this unknown prophet with the Rastafarian-sounding name—Elijah ("Jah is my God"). With little introduction (or, apparently, input from God) Elijah threatens King Ahab: "As Yahweh lives, the God of Israel whom I serve, there shall be no dew or rain these years except at my order."

The challenge works on several levels. First, Elijah sticks it to Ahab, the Israelite king, that Ahab is not serving the God of Israel. Second, Elijah chooses the threat of drought because Ahab has abandoned leadership to Jezebel, who serves the Phoenician water gods. Yahweh is stronger than these water gods. Implied in the warning is that if Ahab will convert and change his ways, the threat will be removed. Ahab has his chance, but he doesn't take it.

After Elijah's rather precocious start, God recalls Elijah for a little more training, discipling, and preparation before taking on the monarchy. In the Cherith wadi Elijah lives, fed by ravens. What did God and Elijah talk about in those desert days? Imagine having raven-angels bring you supper each night, living signs of God's constancy and care. Elijah, the Tishbite hothead, is transformed, becoming quiet and strong and holy in the desert. A conversion from zealot to man of God.

Enter now another woman of Sidon, the widow of Zarephath. She is not the great Queen Jezebel. She doesn't have time for Astartes, Baals, or Yahwehs. And she certainly doesn't have time for "men of God." She is starving to death and her son with her.

But Elijah says that Yahweh, Israel's God, has a word for her if her heart will listen. "The jar of meal shall not be spent, the jug of oil shall not be emptied," if she will make Elijah a small cake. She makes Elijah's cake and there is more to share. Elijah becomes the raven, gently feeding the widow and her son. The miracle of bread meets her immediate need; the later miracle of healing her son meets her familial and economic need; and, finally, God meets her deepest spiritual need.

She says, "Now, I know you are truly a man of God and the word of Yahweh in your mouth is truth itself." The conversion of this simple Phoenician woman is the precursor for the conversion of all of Israel.

—Rose Marie Berger

Sunday Between June 12 and 18

(if after Trinity Sunday)

In Need of Grace

PSALM 5:1-8 • 1 KINGS 21:1-21 • GALATIANS 2:15-21 • LUKE 7:36-8:3

OUR GOSPEL LESSON always raises strong feelings in me. For years I read it as a mini-contest between good and evil—the loving, needy, marginalized woman vs. the rigid, rich, judgmental Pharisee. I always followed it rather smugly to its conclusion, content in knowing that the Pharisee gets put in his place at the end. Jesus lets him know that the kingdom is for the poor and the outcast; for those who give radically of themselves; for those who know their need of God's grace.

Then one Sunday I was scheduled to preach from this passage. I was sitting on the small back porch of a Sojourners household on a Saturday afternoon, preparing my sermon. Several children walked by in the alley, and I waved hello and chatted for a while. Then my next-door neighbor pulled up in his fancy sports car, unlocked the iron gate to the fence that he had put around his property, punched some buttons on his alarm system, and walked into his house. I didn't greet him. I didn't even know his name. I only knew that he was one of the "gentrifiers"—wealthy whites who were moving into my low-income, inner-city neighborhood and displacing people who had lived there for generations.

I had trouble with my sermon after that. The message that I thought I had to preach suddenly didn't seem right anymore. As much as I might want to see myself as a Christ-like figure who would welcome the woman to the table, I couldn't get over feeling like the Pharisee.

My attitude toward the Pharisee in the story was exactly the same as the attitude the Pharisee took toward the woman: You don't belong. Perhaps the real surprise of the story for us is not that Jesus received the blessing of a "sinful" woman—but that he ate at the table of a Pharisee. He listened and taught and took the man seriously.

Many of us, it seems, find it easier to minister to people in trouble or in need than to listen to those with a different viewpoint—especially if, in our view, they are deemed among the "oppressors." Our unwillingness to engage or listen leads to just as much brokenness as theirs. Judgmentalism and self-righteousness are sin, no matter what guise they come in.

The message of Galatians is for us: We are justified by our faith in Jesus Christ, not by our works. The message of the gospel is for us as well: The kingdom is for those who know their need of God's grace.

—Joyce Hollyday

Sunday Between June 19 and 25

(if after Trinity Sunday)

The Temptations of Grief

PSALM 42 • 1 KINGS 19:1-15 • GALATIANS 3:23-29 • LUKE 8:26-39

WHEN MOM DIED SUDDENLY, in the spring before my 38th birthday, the demon of grief threatened to possess me. I knew that grief was a natural response. I was actually grateful that tears had come easily, from the very first news she'd gone into a coma, at the decision to take her off the respirator, through the hour or so afterward in which we prayed and read scripture and sent her to heaven, and nearly daily in the weeks that followed.

I didn't mind the tears, but I felt uncomfortably close to the cliff edge. I imagined disappearing from my present life, choosing to live anonymously someplace where I could be alone with my grief. I turned to William Stringfellow's *A Simplicity of Faith: My Experience in Mourning* for understanding and guidance, and his wisdom has shaped my experience since.

First, I was encouraged to know that there could be a positive aspect to my urge to "disappear." In reflecting on the loss of his closest companion, Anthony Towne, Stringfellow wrote, "...in the midst of both grief and mourning I yearned, more than anything else, to be alone, to return to myself, so to speak, to conserve myself for awhile, to be freed of entanglements."

But the destructive temptations of grief I'd experienced were confirmed as well in Stringfellow's reflections. "Deep calls to deep," the psalmist writes. In Stringfellow's words:

There was more implicated here than a matter of the temptation of a bereaved person to live in the past, and more than the vanity of indulgence in self-pity. There was, as well, the issue of allowing grief, the atmosphere and activities of grieving, and the effort of grief, to define my living. If I allowed this, the power of death would not only have claimed Anthony in the grave but would also seize me—prematurely, or without sufficient pretext.

The 1 Kings reading for today, well-known passages about Elijah's meeting with God at Horeb, speaks to these themes. God gives us the sustenance we need for life's journeys—even in the wilderness—and when we are faithful, God comes in the "gentle whisper" or the "sound of sheer silence."

—Karen Lattea

Invitations to Faith and Freedom

In the hot, "lazy" days of July and August— maybe just when we're ready for that vacation— God lets us know that there is no "down time" where faith is concerned. Our summer lectionary is a short course in the prophets: Elijah and Elisha, Amos and Hosea, Isaiah and Jeremiah all appear, speaking with clarity and force about the demands of faithfulness. Above all, they sound a clarion call for justice.

Our gospel lessons are drawn from Luke, who had his own preoccupation with the sufferings of the poor. His summons to compassion and simplicity is complemented with the beautiful images of restoration and joy found in the Psalms. The texts are rounded out with the cosmic, poetic invitations to faith and freedom that dance through the Epistles.

Summer is a bold season. Though we may long mostly to retreat to the shade with a tall glass of lemonade and a good book, it's a time to plunge into deep waters and attack life with gusto. But if you must lose yourself in a book, try the Bible. These texts are as likely to refresh as to challenge.

—Joyce Hollyday

Sunday Between June 26 and July 2

Life on the Fringe

PSALM 77:1-2, 11-20 • 2 KINGS 2:1-2, 6-14 • GALATIANS 5:1, 13-25 • LUKE 9:51-62

LUKE PORTRAYS JESUS now beginning his journey to Jerusalem, via Samaria. Samaritans, according to Josephus, not infrequently refused to quarter Jews on pilgrimage from Galilee to the Jewish high festivals. The disciples, whose lack of faith is already legendary in the gospels, are suddenly quite sure of their power to call down fire from heaven like Elijah did (2 Kings 1:9-12). Jesus rejects their violence-driven response. Yet he is determined to stay with Samaritans. He just goes on to the next village, where ostensibly they find shelter. He rejects the insider/outsider, Jew/Samaritan, clean/unclean divide. A verse not found in the better manuscripts at Luke 9:56 perfectly captures his intent: "You do not know what manner of spirit you are of; for the Son of Man came not to destroy lives but to save them."

Jesus was, according to Luke's tradition, born in a borrowed manger and buried in a borrowed tomb; his last meal was in a borrowed house in Jerusalem, which he had entered on a borrowed ass. Even foxes and birds do better! Nor does he make it easy on those who wish to follow him. One says, "I will follow you wherever you go," and Jesus says, Hey, wait a minute, take this a little more seriously. Then, when he calls two others, they say, Hey, wait a minute, this is pretty serious, give us some time to settle our affairs and then we'll catch up—and Jesus says, No, you have to drop everything and follow now.

One prospective disciple's father is on the verge of death (had he already died, the son would scarcely have been with Jesus); Jesus will not give him time to see him dead and grieved for. By then Jesus would himself be dead. Discipleship may even mean violating the fifth commandment ("honor your father and mother").

Who or what is this "human being" ("son of man" is a Hebrew idiom simply meaning a person) who exists on the fringe of society, not belonging, rejected, censured, finally executed, yet most certainly "taken up" (Luke 9:51)? Why is Jesus demanding of those who follow him that they too take up this wanderer's existence? If the "human being" that was incarnate in Jesus were to be awakened in us, what excuses would we give? What would it mean for you to leave behind every normal or collective security for God's domination-free order?

—Walter Wink

Sunday Between July 3 and 9

Reaping the Harvest

PSALM 30 • 2 KINGS 5:1-14 • GALATIANS 6:1-16 • LUKE 10:1-11, 16-20

I RECALL ONE SUMMER—my first in the country after 15 years of inner-city living—which was the season of the priceless tomato. Despite a serious lack of experience, I decided to plant a garden. I read up on gardening, talked with veteran gardeners, and plunged in. I got seeds and seedlings, tools and tomato cages, truckloads of manure and topsoil and lime. But I planted late, in a spot that wasn't sunny enough, and quickly lost interest in weeding. And then the goat got loose.

I managed to salvage one scrawny tomato plant from the goat attack. I moved it to a pot on my very sunny porch, watered it regularly, and kept a close watch. A few weeks later I had one marvelous, plump, juicy, red tomato. I calculated that that tomato cost me $42.87.

Our scriptures today are about sowing and reaping. In the agricultural society of biblical times, these images were particularly rich with meaning. You cannot harvest what you have not planted. You receive only from that which you have carefully watched and tended. You reap only what you sow.

Those who sow violence, reap violence. Those who scatter peace will find peace springing up all over. Those who water the earth with tears of compassion will be embraced by a harvest of healing and love.

"So let us not grow weary in doing what is right, for we will reap at harvest-time, if we do not give up" (Galatians 6:9).

—Joyce Hollyday

Sunday Between July 10 and 16

"To Suffer With"

PSALM 82 • AMOS 7:7-17 • COLOSSIANS 1:1-14 • LUKE 10:25-37

THIS TIRED PARABLE is the wet noodle with which Christians flagellate themselves into acts of mercy. We thus become as deeply mired in works-righteousness as the lawyer who put the question. As if there were anything one could do to inherit eternal life!

Two fiendish Princeton sociologists exposed the whole game. They put a group of seminary students in a room, read them this parable, then asked them to go at varying intervals, one at a time, to a building next door, where half would give extemporaneous sermonettes on the parable and the other half would talk about ministry as a vocation. An actor was planted beside the sidewalk who feigned distress. The real test was to see how many of these Christians, their heads full of this parable of compassion, would actually stop. Only 40 percent did.

Ingenious. This study proves that people are not compassionate because ordered to be so by religious law. They are, on the contrary, compassionate most often when they see themselves as the victim beside the road. Com-passion—"to suffer with." The Samaritan was not a better person than the priest or levite or lawyer. We call him "good" though we know nothing about his life. He may have been a shyster. He simply knew what it was like to be unable to get decent accommodations as a hated half-breed. He knew that, if he had been mugged, no one would stop. He identified with the victim.

Jesus invites the lawyer to do the same—to see himself in the ditch, to watch his own religious leaders pass him by, to see a Samaritan approach, to undergo the choice. Do I let this accursed person render me unclean, or do I let him save my life? Then Jesus makes the Samaritan his role model: Go and do likewise. Not to inherit eternal life. But because he sees himself in the sufferer.

It is as we identify and find healing for our own wounds that we are able to become wounded healers for others. As we openly share our woundedness, others are enabled to bring their wounds into the open for healing. Do a picture of your wounds—the ways you have "fallen among robbers." If you are in a group, share your picture.

—Walter Wink

Sunday Between July 17 and 23

A Vision for Our Time

PSALM 52 • AMOS 8:1-12 • COLOSSIANS 1:15-28 • LUKE 10:38-42

WOMEN IN JESUS' DAY were not full members of the covenant. They were saved through their men (father, husband) and through bearing male heirs. They were taught only the negative commandments of the Law; the positive ones were reserved for men. The Mishnah states, "If any man gives his daughter a knowledge of the Law it is as though he taught her lechery." The logic is impeccable. To teach her lechery is to cause her alone to sin; to teach her Torah is to break down the division between male superiority and female inferiority, and to threaten male dominance.

Rabbinical texts reveal that some women persisted, nevertheless, in trying to learn the Law. One such in the gospels is Mary, whose sister Martha complains to Jesus that Mary refuses to help serve the dinner, but is instead seated at Jesus' feet—the prerogative of a male disciple of a teacher. However much we might wish that Jesus had gotten up and helped to serve the meal and to clean up afterwards—a role to which he seems not to have been averse (Luke 12:37; in John 21:9-14 the risen Jesus confirms his identity by cooking breakfast for the disciples, a task normally reserved for women and servants)—the fact remains that Jesus and Mary were transgressing on a deep-seated prohibition from which Martha could not free herself.

Martha projects her own authority on Jesus: You tell Mary. Her anxiety and agitation reveal her as caught in a gender role from which Mary has extricated herself. As the failed struggle for the Equal Rights Amendment showed, it is often women who most profoundly oppose liberation from male supremacy. This issue very much survives today, in both Christianity and Judaism, in the question of the ordination of women.

But we must not split Mary and Martha into good and bad, but look for both within ourselves. What is the one thing needful for me? What is the source of my anxiety? How do I perpetuate collective definitions of myself as woman, as man? Redo this story in a role-play that carries the story forward to address our more recent concerns for full equality between women and men.

—Walter Wink

Sunday Between July 24 and 30

On Prayer

PSALM 85 • HOSEA 1:2-10 • COLOSSIANS 2:6-19 • LUKE 11:1-13

WATCH THE IMPERATIVES! Jesus' teaching on prayer is impertinent, rude, a theological embarrassment. He understands nothing of Christian etiquette. Prayer as he describes it is effrontery. He commands us to command God. We are to hammer on the door until God, out of pure irritation, answers our need. Like the widow haranguing the judge, we are to persist in prayer like a dog worrying a bone (Luke 18:1-8). The squeaky wheel gets the grease.

All this seems a bit beneath our sophistication about prayer. After all, God is God. Who are we to order God around like a lackey? We should rather surrender ourselves to the inscrutable will of God and be willing to receive whatever God sends. God is immutable, and cannot be changed by our incessant implorings.

Oh yeah? That's Stoicism, pure and simple. Jesus, and the entire Bible with him, teach prayer as jawboning. Abraham haggles with God like a merchant in a bazaar (Genesis 18). Moses makes God repent (Exodus 32). God, it appears, wants relationship, not unapproachable authority and power. God, it seems, is creating history with us, alongside us, and wants, needs, cannot do without, our input. The limp passivity of what so often passes as Christian prayer is anathema to the Bible. When we pray, we are to be totally energized beings staking everything on God's future for the world.

Hence the imperatives. "Hallowed be"—imperative. It is not something we do, but that God does through us (compare Ezekiel 36:22-23). We are commanded to command God to hallow God's name: Come on, God, be God! "Your kingdom come"—imperative. We are ordered to order God to bring on God's domination-free order. Are you ready to receive it? We are permitted, as children of the Abba, to demand (imperative) our daily bread, and to insist (imperative) that we be forgiven and shielded from temptation.

What would we have to give up to pray this way? What would it require of us? How would it alter our picture of God? Do we care enough to pray thus? Role-play the parable in Luke 11:5-8. Alone or in a group, shout the Lord's Prayer at the top of your lungs in order to grasp its imperative force.

—Walter Wink

Sunday Between July 31 and August 6

The Lie of Violence

PSALM 107:1-9, 43 • HOSEA 11:1-11 • COLOSSIANS 3:1-11 • LUKE 12:13-21

VIOLENCE IS EASILY the most often mentioned activity and central theme of the Hebrew Bible. This violence is in part the residue of false ideas about God carried over from the general human past. It is also, however, the beginning of a process of raising the problem of violence to consciousness, so that these projections on God can be withdrawn. For in scripture, for the first time in all of human history, God begins to be seen as identified with the victims of violence. But these occasional critiques of domination in the Hebrew Bible continue to alternate with texts that call on Israel to exterminate its enemies now or in the last days.

The problem of violence could not have been discovered in a nonviolent society. It had to be gestated at the very heart of violence, in the most war-ravaged corridor on the globe, by a repeatedly subjugated people unable to seize and wield power for any length of time. The violence of scripture, so embarrassing to us today, became the means by which sacred violence was revealed for what it is: A lie perpetrated against victims in the name of a God who, through violence, was actually working to expose violence for what it is and to reveal the divine nature as nonviolent.

How do we continue to perpetuate that lie today?

—Walter Wink

Sunday Between August 7 and 13

Keeping the Faith

PSALM 50:1-8, 22-23 • ISAIAH 1:1, 10-20 • HEBREWS 11:1-3, 8-16 • LUKE 12:32-40

THE LAST THREE SUNDAYS in August bring us the marvelous passages on faith from the Letter to the Hebrews. The best definition of faith I've ever heard begins the 11th chapter: "Now faith is the assurance of things hoped for, the conviction of things not seen."

Today's passage goes on to recount the faithfulness of Abraham and Sarah, Isaac and Jacob. It includes these disturbing—and comforting—words: "These all died in faith, not having received what was promised" (11:13). Disturbing, because these ancestors in the faith never reached the promise but only "greeted it from afar." Comforting, because we know we have company in our efforts, which, like theirs, aren't always "successful" by the world's terms.

Penny Lernoux was a journalist who was converted by the deep faith of the suffering people she met in Central America. These are the closing words of her last book, *People of God:*

> *The People of God will continue their march....And the Third World will continue to beckon to the First, reminding it of the Galilean vision of Christian solidarity. As a young Guatemalan said a few months before she was killed by the military, "What good is life unless you give it away?"—unless you can give it for a better world, even if you never see that world but have only carried your grain of sand to the building site. Then you're fulfilled as a person.*

We're building a new city—one where justice and peace replace hatred and violence. I may only add the 57th brick in the third row of the left wall of the garage for the second house from the corner. It may seem like little. But if we all work together—and keep the faith—a world more grand than our greatest imaginings will one day appear.

—Joyce Hollyday

Sunday Between August 14 and 20

Cloud of Witnesses

PSALM 80:1-2, 8-19 • ISAIAH 5:1-7 • HEBREWS 11:29-12:2 • LUKE 12:49-56

TODAY'S PASSAGE FROM HEBREWS lists more of the history of the people of faith: the Red Sea crossing; the tumbling walls of Jericho; the valor of warriors up against enemies and lions; suffering of the faithful by torture, jail, and death. These also did not receive what was promised. This passage adds an interesting twist. It tells us why: "Since God had provided something better so that they would not, apart from us, be made perfect" (11:40).

Cleo Fields of Louisiana, who at 25 was the youngest state senator in the country, said during the 1988 presidential campaign: "Booker T. Washington started to teach so Rosa Parks could take her seat. Rosa Parks took her seat so Fannie Lou Hamer could take her stand. Fannie Lou Hamer took her stand so Martin Luther King Jr. could march. Martin Luther King marched so Jesse Jackson could run."

Each step forward in the civil rights struggle depended on the faithful step of someone else. The same could be said of every movement for freedom and justice everywhere. Those who take the initial and middle steps may not see the promise, but they have moved the world that much closer to it.

And their perfection depends on us. The vision only keeps moving forward as long as we pick up the ball and run. The efforts of all those who went before us end in failure if we don't do our part. "Therefore, since we are surrounded by so great a cloud of witnesses, let us also lay aside every weight and sin that clings so closely, and let us run with perseverance the race that is set before us" (12:1).

Historian Vincent Harding describes these witnesses as "a great cheering squad for us. In the midst of everything that seems so difficult, that seems so powerful, that seems so overwhelming, they are saying to us: 'We are with you,' and 'There is a way through....Don't give up!'

"No excuse for drooping—at least not for long. No excuse for not running—or at least walking strong....'Cause we are surrounded, folks. So, let's...get down with some real long-distance walking and running—and maybe even some flying like eagles, in due time. That's our tradition. That's our destiny. That's our hope. So go right on, brothers and sisters....There is a city to build."

—Joyce Hollyday

Sunday Between August 21 and 27

Vessels of God's Love

PSALM 71:1-6 • JEREMIAH 1:4-10 • HEBREWS 12:18-29 • LUKE 13:10-17

JEREMIAH'S CALL MAY be unsettling if we have the notion that the life of faith is a smooth sail. The Lord called Jeremiah to "pluck up and to pull down, to destroy and to overthrow, to build and to plant." And in Hebrews, the God who called Jeremiah is described as a "consuming fire"! It's important to learn, or to be reminded, that not only do we Christians encounter storms, sometimes we'll be the ones to cause them.

The gospel reading carries similar powerful images, even for our modern times. We can easily picture this crippled woman—"She was bent over and could not straighten up at all" (Luke 13:11)—because many suffer from back, hip, or knee ailments. Stairs, subcompact cars, and cheaters in the handicapped parking all become major obstacles.

What's hard to imagine is how she endured this condition for 18 years. Empathy with her suffering might be enough to cause us to "break the rules" as Jesus did.

Psalm 71 describes the foundation in God—our "rock of refuge," our "strong fortress"—from which we find the strength to take such action. It is from just this source that Jeremiah learned to speak. The Lord said, "You must go to everyone I send you to and say whatever I command you. Do not be afraid of them for I am with you and will rescue you."

Not everyone will listen, and not everyone will agree. And sometimes we'll be wrong in our pronouncements, having let our own agenda get in the way of truly being a vessel of God's love. But I wonder if that's all part of God's plan. We must learn how to get along, especially in the body of Christ, even when we disagree. And most important, we must learn to rely on God, and God only.

Jesus explained to the leader of the synagogue why he had healed the crippled woman on the Sabbath. He and his opponents weren't convinced. Christians of every perspective, even honestly seeking the way of Jesus, won't be easily convinced of others' interpretations of doctrine, history, and scripture. But whatever common ground we can find might start the world "rejoicing at all the wonderful things Jesus was doing" (Luke 13:17).

—Karen Lattea

The Extraordinary Within the Ordinary

*W*e are settling deep into the long stretch that the church calls "ordinary time." Our readings span the "Twenty-second Sunday in Ordinary Time" to the "Thirtieth Sunday in Ordinary Time." That feels like enough to get a yawn out of anybody. No startling birth, no earth-shaking resurrection, no wild Pentecost wind to stir us up these days.

But the pocket of earth in which most of us reading this live is about to enter its most beautiful season, by my estimation. Leaves are turning, birds are moving, an expectant chill is setting in. Our task this season is to see the truly extraordinary within the ordinary; to know that behind the splashes of color and crispness of days is the invisible hand of a God who lovingly keeps it all in motion—and who calls us always to faithfulness.

—Joyce Hollyday

Sunday Between August 28 and September 3

A New Kind of Banquet

PSALM 81:1, 10-16 • JEREMIAH 2:4-13 • HEBREWS 13:1-8, 15-16 • LUKE 14:1, 7-14

IS THIS TONGUE IN CHEEK? Go to a banquet and take the lowest place. I've tried it, and they left me there. He must be talking to people with more standing. Is this just a way to get yourself exalted? Hardly. The Symposiarch, or president of the banquet, was assigned the task of figuring out the pecking order of the guests. One's honor and prestige rode on where one was seated. To deliberately flout the pecking order is to negate it altogether.

Jesus also counsels not inviting friends, brothers, relatives, or rich neighbors, but rather a very different quartet made up of the poor, crippled, lame, and blind. Is he just being perverse? Hardly. If he is seriously intent on overthrowing the domination system, then such hierarchies must go. They shame the less prosperous and desirable, and exclude altogether whole classes of people.

Worship leader Marilyn McDonald had a 13-person group do this exercise: "You have been invited by a host who really cares for you. Eyes shut, you stand at the door to the banquet. You know that there are seats of honor at the right, seats of less honor to the left. The host is occupied elsewhere. Find the chair that seems to suit you."

All four men went to the right, seven women went to the left, one woman to the middle, only one to the right. And these were professionally trained women! The power of patriarchy is incredible. Studies show that 80 percent of conversational interruptions are men interrupting women. Our hierarchies are still intact, and deeply internalized. How do you catch yourself still demanding status? In what situations do you find yourself pulling rank? Needing to be noticed? Who are the poor, maimed, lame, and blind whom you excluded from notice, inclusion, and concern?

—Walter Wink

Sunday Between September 4 and 10

The Cost of Discipleship

PSALM 139:1-6, 13-18 • JEREMIAH 18:1-11 • PHILEMON 1:1-21 • LUKE 14:25-33

IF CATASTROPHE FACES a people, a nation, a species, and the sentinels fail to warn those under their care, the blood of the people will be required at the hand of the sentinel. Perhaps the people will not listen; then their blood will be upon their own heads.

We live in such a time. Global warming, ozone depletion, overpopulation, massive starvation, air and water pollution, topsoil erosion, the death of the coral reefs and oceans, extermination of species, the continued threat of nuclear radiation from leaks, dumping, and accidents: Catastrophes threaten us on every hand. Our politicians are all but worthless; our president lacks conviction, vision, or concern. At a time when every human resource should be trained on surmounting these crises, torpor reigns.

And for good reason. Americans have a lot to lose from a more just and sustainable order. We are now slowly waking from a sleep of several thousand years to the realization that Jesus' most stringent commands are not calls to a superhuman piety, but the foundation of human survival. We are told to count the cost of discipleship before we make the plunge, because what God now requires of us is not halfway measures and limp compromise, but responses equal to the urgency of our gathering catastrophes.

To take up our own crosses means breaking free of the socialization that keeps us complicit with a profligate and ecologically unsustainable system. Consumerism, possessions, hoarding, the fascination of ever-new technologies—all these seduce us from living simply so that others may simply live. "None of you can become my disciple if you do not give up all your possessions" (Luke 14:33). Does Jesus really mean this? Is it even possible?

This is more than we can hear. Yet it is gospel: good news. It offers hope of survival. The cost is painful. But we will pay it voluntarily, now, or involuntarily, later. We still, barely, have a choice.

—Walter Wink

Sunday Between September 11 and 17

Ready to Forgive

PSALM 14 • JEREMIAH 4:11-12, 22-28 • 1 TIMOTHY 1:12-17 • LUKE 15:1-10

THESE READINGS FOCUS ON EXTREMES—in the midst of great adversity, God can do even greater good. Paul describes himself as the foremost sinner, who therefore received the utmost patience from Jesus. The psalmist says, "You evildoers frustrate the plans of the poor, but the Lord is their refuge." The Jeremiah reading ends with, "For thus says the Lord: The whole land shall be a desolation; yet I will not make a full end."

In the gospel reading, Jesus has created the greatest comparison—between himself and "tax collectors and 'sinners'"—leading the Pharisees to grumble, "This man welcomes sinners and eats with them." Sinners. All of them. For any reason. Jesus is completely undiscriminating.

In the parables of the lost sheep and coin, it seems like the way to please God is to be a wild sinner and then repent, rather than to live a life of faithful seeking with no big mistakes. But the message here is much different.

Jesus is teaching about God's forgiveness. It is remarkably wide and deep, this forgiveness, when a person truly repents. As Luke 15:10 says, "There is rejoicing in the presence of the angels of God over one sinner who repents." Since we should be able to identify both with the sinner who seeks forgiveness and the one who has been sinned against, the deeper message here is about our ability to forgive others as God forgives us.

Do we ostracize sinners—those with membership in certain groups with which we disagree, in certain occupations with which we're uncomfortable, with lifestyles we can't abide? The point here isn't that we should have loose values and morals, it's that we must be ready, in a heartbeat, to forgive when a person repents or seeks the space to explore another way.

Think about your own experiences of repentance. They don't always occur overnight. Sometimes what's required is a process of repentance. And when you first showed a willingness to look at a difficult area of your life, were there Christians around who were patient enough to walk with you through the process?

Many outside of the church see us Christians as too quick to judge, acting like we have all the answers or that the answers are simple, and never struggling with difficult choices. In an effort to be a witness to the world, to stand for righteousness, Christians can end up with an unforgiving spirit, sitting in judgment over right and wrong.

Jesus' message stands in contrast: He welcomed everyone into relationship, and trusted the love of God to bring out the best in them. Can we say the same about the modern church's ability to build bridges—among ourselves and with those who don't yet know the love of God?

—Karen Lattea

Sunday Between September 18 and 24
Apostasy From the Gospel

PSALM 79:1-9 • JEREMIAH 8:18-9:1 • 1 TIMOTHY 2:1-7 • LUKE 16:1-13

IN HOSEA, GOD LAMENTS Israel's proclivity to sacrifice to the Baals and offer incense to idols. "My people are bent on turning away from me." Yet God cannot turn away from them. God's love trumps God's anger; mercy overwhelms wrath. But only after the consequences of apostasy have played themselves out.

We can watch apostasy being played out in the first epistle to Timothy. This is a text many avoid. First there is the supine acquiescence to the political order. Not that it is wrong to pray for those in high positions. We should be praying far more aggressively and persistently than we have been. But the reason Timothy gives for doing so is suspect: "that we might lead a quiet and peaceable life in all godliness and dignity." Our prayers are no longer mighty intercessions that aim to transform the powers that be, but meek petitions for safety and even prayers of thanksgiving for the benevolence of kings and magistrates.

As if that were not enough, we also avoid this text because of its attitude toward women. Gone here is the radicalism of Jesus, who in every encounter with a woman in all four gospels violated the mores of his time regarding women. Now all the talk is of reinserting them back into patriarchy. How do you feel about this text?

We cannot duck the issue. Here scripture violates itself. As in the case of slavery, scripture is not always faithful to the gospel. When it is not, the gospel can still be heard and proclaimed—by pointing out the truth. Those who were repatriarchalizing and domesticating the gospel have left their fingerprints all over the text. The gospel of Jesus exposes them as the apostates that they were. We do not do honor to Jesus by defending texts of terror as inspired, even though they dehumanize women and bring the church into docility before earthly authorities. God speaks through such texts nevertheless—to denounce them as apostate. Even then, these texts can bear witness to the Word of God, who is not a book, but a Being.

—Walter Wink

Sunday Between September 25 and October 1

Love of Money

PSALM 91:1-6, 14-16 • JEREMIAH 32:1-3, 6-15 • 1 TIMOTHY 6:6-19 • LUKE 16:19-31

NO MISSING THE POINT this week. We encounter that unsettling and uncomfortable story about the rich man and poor Lazarus. The rich man arrayed himself in purple, the color of royalty, and feasted sumptuously every day. I picture him as a rotund man, draped in a bright robe with big cuffs, smacking his lips as he polishes off another turkey drumstick. Poor Lazarus lies outside his gate, hungry, covered with sores that the stray dogs lick.

Both men die—Lazarus likely of starvation, the rich man of a heart attack or stroke or other fat-and-cholesterol-induced condition (read "microcosm of today's world"). Lazarus goes to heaven; and the rich man, well, he goes to that place of torment and fire.

"Send Lazarus," he cries out, "to dip the tip of his finger in water and cool my tongue; for I am in agony" (Luke 16:24). No go. Lazarus has found rest and isn't going to be anybody's lackey. And there is this insurmountable problem of a chasm between the two men that cannot be crossed.

In an apparently uncharacteristic burst of altruism, the rich man worries about his five brothers back on earth and asks that Lazarus be allowed to go and warn them about what has happened to him. No to that, too. If they aren't willing to listen to the prophets' calls for justice, scaring the hell out of them (or into them, as the case may be) won't do any good. It's a little jab at the "fire and brimstone" preaching that seems to be so in vogue where I live these days, in the South's Bible belt. Invitations to mercy and justice always speak louder than shouts designed to frighten.

As Lazarus was stuck with his lot in life, so the rich man is stuck with his lot in death. His sin? He refused to cross the chasm between him and Lazarus in their first life. His inability to walk outside his gate, to share his abundance, doomed him forever. He kept himself apart, and such is his sentence for eternity. He became what he loved.

Paul addresses the same issue directly: "We brought nothing into the world, so that we can take nothing out of it; but if we have food and clothing, we will be content with these. But those who want to be rich fall into temptation and are trapped by many senseless and harmful desires that plunge people into ruin and destruction. For the love of money is a root of all kinds of evil, and in their eagerness to be rich some have wandered away from the faith and pierced themselves with many pains....They are to do good, to be rich in good works, generous, and ready to share, thus storing up for themselves the treasure of a good foundation for the future, so that they may take hold of the life that really is life" (1 Timothy 6:7-10, 18).

—Joyce Hollyday

Sunday Between October 2 and 8

We Have Enough Faith

PSALM 137 • LAMENTATIONS 1:1-6 • 2 TIMOTHY 1:1-14 • LUKE 17:5-10

THE APOSTLES SAY, "Increase our faith." Examine their presuppositions. They feel they don't have enough yet. That whatever the crisis, it will require more. That Jesus had more. That he could give them more. That faith is quantitative.

But how much would be enough? That whole way of looking at it puts the accent on our doubts. Would 51 percent faith be enough? 65 percent? 90 percent? Will we ever have enough? Will we ever be good enough?

Jesus' response demolishes their presuppositions. If you have any faith at all, you can do stupendous miracles. (Note the present tense; he is not slamming them for having no faith. After all, they had gone out healing and exorcising on several missions.) Move trees into oceans, or mountains into oblivion. All it takes is a minuscule amount, no more than that symbolized by a tiny mustard seed.

For faith is not quantitative, but qualitative. It is not a matter of how much you have, but of having any at all. Even the slightest amount can be overwhelmingly effective, because it is not faith in our own faith, but simply faith in God, faith that God is God, that God is able to act in the world. If we believe in God even just a little bit, it is enough.

Truth is, we always have faith. The problem is that we have faith in the wrong things. We believe in money, or power, or seduction. We trust that things will turn out bad. And our faith becomes, to a degree unknown to us, self-fulfilling. What are your negative beliefs?

If, in all that welter of negative faiths, we have even an inkling of trust in God and the brazenness to exercise it, that, says Jesus, will be enough to change the very face of reality. Do you have evidence in your own life that this is true?

—Walter Wink

Sunday Between October 9 and 15

Divine Source, Human Means

PSALM 66:1-12 • JEREMIAH 29:1, 4-7 • 2 TIMOTHY 2:8-15 • LUKE 17:11-19

THE HEALING OF THE LEPER is packed with insights about healing. First, Jesus is not afraid of contamination. He does not regard holiness as separation, as did the Pharisees and Essenes. He understands it rather as the mighty power of God to heal. He rejects the notion that external things defile or pollute a person's essential being (Mark 7:15; Matthew 15:11).

In contrast to the traditional view, Jesus regards holiness/wholeness—not uncleanness—as contagious. Thus Jesus touches the leper, the unclean, women, the sick, without fear of contamination. Holiness is not something to be protected; rather, it is God's numinous transforming power.

Second, Jesus does not use healing to bring others under the spell of his own charisma. He merely sends these lepers on their way to the priest. Their going, their trust, their acting on his command activates their healing. He is not content merely to heal, but to restore their own sense of power: "Your faith has made you well."

Third, there is healing, and then there is wholeness. Only one leper, recognizing his healing, returns to give thanks and praise. There is an aching sadness in Jesus' question, "But the other nine, where are they?" He had empowered them, and they think they healed themselves. So quickly they forget! They are still spiritual lepers. Why was it the lone Samaritan among them that returned? What is the difference between being cleansed (v. 14) and being made whole/well/saved (v. 19)?

Who are the people in your life who have been agents of healing for you? Have you glorified God for your healing? Have you thanked the people? Would a letter be appropriate?

—Walter Wink

Sunday Between October 16 and 22

Persistent Widows

PSALM 119:97-104 • JEREMIAH 31:27-34 • 2 TIMOTHY 3:14-4:5 • LUKE 18:1-8

IN 1976, A MILITARY JUNTA took over rule of Argentina. Soon men in unmarked cars began arriving in the night at homes, restaurants, and workplaces to take away people involved in the struggle for peace in that nation. Before long there were thousands of people among the ranks of the "disappeared."

Lines began to form in front of government offices. Mothers of the missing came day after day, begging for information about their sons and daughters. When they were turned away, they got together and drew up a petition, listing the names of their disappeared children and demanding that they be returned. When the government refused their petition, they began a silent, illegal protest.

Every Thursday they marched in a circle in front of the government offices that ring Buenos Aires' Plaza de Mayo. Each mother wore a white handkerchief embroidered with the names of her missing children. Many carried pictures. As the number of disappearances grew, so did the group of silent, walking women. Despite beatings and arrests, the mothers persisted. Their vigil went on for years.

In 1952 in South Africa, 20,000 women converged on the prime minister's office in Pretoria, demanding justice. In the decades since, mothers have marched, compiled affadivts of torture and murder, and helped children into safe exile—all under the rallying cry, "You have struck the women, you have struck the rock."

In El Salvador, mothers and widows fasted at the tomb of the late archbishop Oscar Romero and occupied the cathedral in San Salvador, demanding an end to repression. In Detroit, mothers whose children were gunned down in the streets have banded together to demand gun control and an end to drug violence.

All these mothers display the persistence of the widow in today's gospel parable. They confront the "unjust judges" of today—whether they come in the guise of prime ministers or police, mayors or military officers. These women demand to be heard. And they invite us to join them in taking a stand for justice.

"And will not God grant justice to his chosen ones who cry to him day and night?" (Luke 18:7).

—Joyce Hollyday

Sunday Between October 23 and 29

The Bounty of God

PSALM 65 • JOEL 2:23-32 • 2 TIMOTHY 4:6-8, 16-18 • LUKE 18:9-14

THE PARABLE OF THE PHARISEE and the tax collector brings to mind a conversation I had with Blake Byler-Ortman at the Jubilee Partners community in Comer, Georgia. Blake and his wife, Sue, had spent several years in El Salvador working with refugees before moving to Georgia. They often participated in base-community style worship in which everyone was invited to offer their reflections on scripture.

In that context, Blake had an eye-opening encounter with Matthew 25, the passage that recounts the nations being separated into sheep and goats, based on their treatment of the "least of these." Those who fed, clothed, and visited the hungry, naked, and imprisoned are ushered into eternal life with the sheep; those who neglected Jesus by neglecting these works of mercy go with the goats to eternal punishment.

Blake was near Santa Cruz Berlin, a town where a month earlier a group of refugees had fled from an army scorched-earth operation, carried out with the help of U.S. military aid. The refugees had constructed shelters with leaves for roofing and had almost nothing else. Soon another group of refugees arrived, fleeing heavy bombing in a nearby area. Though the first group had only two weeks' worth of food left and no assurance that they could get more, they began sharing their tortillas with the new arrivals.

Blake and others were there investigating the bombings, and the refugees also shared their food with them. "They were ashamed," Blake says, "because all they had was tortillas for us. Their response afterward was, 'I'm sorry we have nothing to give you.'" Within a week, about $10,000 worth of food, used clothing, and tin roofing arrived from U.S. churches.

Reflecting on it later, Blake said, "I can see the refugees before Jesus getting in the wrong line—the goat line—because they didn't have anything to give away. They gave away all they had, but they'll feel bad. The scary half is that I can see myself and those churches saying, 'Look, we sent a lot of help down there'—and we'd get in the wrong line, too. And Jesus would ask us, 'Who paid for the bombs that fell on their houses?'"

The parable of the Pharisee and the tax collector is about recognizing and confessing sin. It's about avoiding self-righteousness and not taking pride in such gestures as turning over a tenth of one's income to God's service. It's about the reality that "all who exalt themselves will be humbled, and all who humble themselves will be exalted" (Luke 18:14).

—Joyce Hollyday

Reformation Day

In some traditions, Reformation Day is celebrated the last Sunday in October.
See Appendix 1, "Reformation and All Saints' Days."

All Saints' Sunday

All Saints' Day (November 1) may be celebrated the first Sunday in November.

The Christ Over All Powers

PSALM 149 • DANIEL 7:1-3, 15-18 • EPHESIANS 1:11-23 • LUKE 6:20-31

SOUTHERN WRITER REYNOLDS PRICE once said, "It is the height of arrogance for us to think that we can understand the world as the characters in the Hebrew and Christian scriptures did, that we can compare our experiences to theirs. Do we see demons, spirits, and angels, crowding us in every room? Are we yanked and pulled by the whims of capricious gods?"

Who of us would dare slip into the virtual reality of the book of Daniel? Every way we turn horned beasts are ripped apart; iron-teethed demons are gnashing their way toward us. They feed on violence, getting stronger and more powerful. Brother Daniel wakes with (literally) one hell of a headache and goes in search of someone who can tell him the meaning of his dreams. The news is not good.

The book of Daniel is the last expression of Messianic prophecy in Hebrew scriptures. Written 167-164 B.C., during Antiochus Epiphanes' bloody attempts to Hellenize the Jews, Daniel sets the stage for the Maccabean revolt, under the command of Judas Maccabeus—the Lion of Judah. It is a classic piece of resistance literature, depicting a monstrous oppressor, the sacrifice that will be required from those in bondage to break free, and, ultimately, the handing over of the "kingdom" to the "saints of the Most High."

Two hundred and thirty years later our brother Paul is, once again, in chains for the Lord. Life in Roman jail for a turncoat Jew had its own nightmarish qualities. Yet Paul takes the time to continue writing, reflecting, praying, evangelizing, and guiding the fragile faithful. He turns his thoughts toward Ephesus, addressing the problem of those following the Jesus Way who are putting celestial and cosmic powers (understood as part of Jewish mythology) higher than Jesus Christ. He does not say that these powers do not exist, only that they should be seen as preparatory to the coming of the Anointed One in Jesus who establishes a new order in which the Christ is over all powers—celestial, cosmic, angelic, and earthly.

—Rose Marie Berger

Sunday Between October 30 and November 5

Passing Through

PSALM 119:137-144 • HABAKKUK 1:1-4, 2:1-4 • 2 THESSALONIANS 1:1-4, 11-12 • LUKE 19:1-10

WHO IS ZACCHAEUS? The more we think about Luke's little man up a tree who runs ahead to welcome Jesus to his home, the less we might want to have to do with him.

As a chief tax collector in Palestine, Zacchaeus was an extortionist for an occupying power. The fact that Zacchaeus is rich tells us he extracted taxes ruthlessly from other Jews. The pun on his name—Zakkai means "the righteous"—is bitingly ironic.

Zacchaeus is the kind of enemy of the people whom the prophet Habakkuk is crying out against: "O Lord, how long shall I cry for help, and you will not listen? Or cry to you 'violence!' and you will not save?" (Habakkuk 1:2).

But has Luke set us up in today's gospel before we even get to Zacchaeus? What about the unobtrusive introduction, "He entered Jericho and was passing through it"? Who is this passing through Jericho?

It is a man whose namesake is Joshua. (Yeshua is a late form of the Hebrew Yehoshua.) Joshua also once passed through Jericho—in his case "massacring them all, men and women, young and old, even the oxen and sheep and donkeys" (Joshua 6:21). Is Luke recalling Joshua and Jericho, the prototypes of holy genocide?

A charismatic leader on his way to Jerusalem, whose name identifies him with the charismatic leader whose forces exterminated one enemy people after another, doesn't just "pass through Jericho" without raising expectations. It is not surprising that the crowd grumbled at Jesus suddenly being welcomed into the sumptuous home of a chief tax collector for Rome. These people knew how little tolerance the original Joshua would have had for such a collaborator.

So how are we "passing through Jericho"? Are we conscious of the continuing preparations for nuclear genocide and the ongoing genocide of the two-thirds world, much of it done in God's name?

As we deepen in our understanding of such radical evil, are we then duplicating it by our murderous disdain for the Zacchaeus ("the righteous") whom we see doing evil?

Or are we willing to run ahead and welcome, as Zacchaeus himself did, the all-inclusive "Human Being" who has come "to seek out and to save the lost"?

—Jim Douglass

Sunday Between November 6 and 12

Totally Transformed

PSALM 145:1-5, 17-21 • HAGGAI 1:15-2:9 • 2 THESSALONIANS 2:1-5, 13-17
• LUKE 20:27-38

CERTAIN HISTORICAL EVENTS carry such consequences that humanity is never the same afterward. The discovery and development of nuclear energy with its awful capacity for destruction was such an event; the Resurrection is another. Jesus highlights the totally transformative nature of resurrected human life in Luke's gospel today.

A group of religious leaders who deny resurrection ask him a wildly speculative question. Jesus replies by opening to them the vision of a transcendent human condition that could not have been imagined before. "Those who are deemed worthy to attain to the coming age and to the resurrection of the dead neither marry nor are given in marriage. They can no longer die for they are like angels; and they are the children of God because they are the ones who will rise" (Luke 20:35-36). Some have taken Jesus' words as a repudiation of marriage. Far from that, they point to the coming of God's kingdom, that final state where God is all in all.

On a much more worldly, though no less religious plane, a prophet in Israel, this time Zechariah, once again holds kingdom values high above those of ritual. Confused returnees from the cataclysmic experience of Israel's exile from the land and the Temple ask if they must continue their 70-year practice of periodic fasting in reparation for the destruction of that sacred place of worship. In answer the prophet speaks for God: "Render true judgment, and show kindness and compassion toward each other. Do not oppress the widow or the orphan, the alien or the poor; do not plot evil against one another" (Zechariah 7:9-10). Tragically, the people refused to listen.

Finally, Paul links the vision of resurrected life and the need to remain faithful as he admonishes his community at Thessalonica: "God has called you through our gospel to possess the glory of our Lord Jesus Christ. Therefore, brothers and sisters, stand firm and hold fast to the traditions that you were taught..." (2 Thessalonians 2:14-15).

—Joe Nangle, O.F.M.

Sunday Between November 13 and 19

Jerusalem, Jerusalem

PSALM 118 • ISAIAH 65:17-25 • 2 THESSALONIANS 3:6-13 • LUKE 21:5-19

PAUL IS OFTEN CRITICIZED for placing himself in front of his writings, offering himself as the model, an example for others to follow. In virtually every line of his letters, the apostle writes in the first person, a style that jars us. In today's passage, however, this technique strikes the reader as acceptable, even necessary. The apostle reminds the community that he did not burden them financially while he was with them, choosing rather to earn his own livelihood "in toil and drudgery, night and day."

Paul goes on to use that example as a lesson to those in the community who would sit around idly waiting for the Second Coming: "If anyone is unwilling to work, neither should that one eat." He pushes the lesson still further, advising the community to refrain from associating with those who refuse to work.

The lesson has serious implications for Christian communities today. There come times when a member is deemed incorrigible, out of the pale, incapable—at least for the moment—of reform, be the problem laziness, or any attitude which violates the common good. The community has the right, indeed the duty, to separate that member from its number, hard as that may be and un-Christian as it may appear. The Shakers have a precise word for this kind of ultimate warning. They call it "shunning."

In the gospel today, Luke continues the theme of the promise of God's reign, citing the many evils that will surely befall those who guide their lives by that covenant. No matter the severity of the test or the harshness of the persecution; no matter who is doing the wrong to us, including "parents, brothers, relatives, friends"; even should death itself ensue, Jesus assures us "by your perseverance you will secure your lives" (Luke 21:16,19).

So many followers of Jesus are living in belief of the promise today, in places such as South Africa, Peru, Haiti, and America's inner cities.

—Joe Nangle, O.F.M.

Sunday Between November 20 and 26

The King on the Cross

LUKE 1:68-79 • JEREMIAH 23:1-6 • COLOSSIANS 1:11-20 • LUKE 23:33-43

IN LUKE'S GOSPEL on this final Sunday of the church year, the Feast of Christ the King, three different antagonists challenge a dying Jesus with the same question. First the leaders, then the soldiers, and finally one of the criminals all taunt him, "Are you not the Messiah of God, King of the Jews? If so, save yourself and us" (Luke 23:39).

An executed messiah. A powerless king. What kind of king winds up on a cross at the place called The Skull?

Whether it is the first or the 20th century, redemptive violence is the ruling myth.

The messiah or superhero in this myth saves himself and us from death at the hands of evil enemies. The means of redemption from evil is killing, massively if necessary.

How does a king with no army who dies on a cross fit into our myth?

He doesn't.

The king on the cross, the gospel tells us, is the only one who can save us from the myth of redemptive violence. Jesus saves us from the willful illusion that we will be freed from evil by killing our enemies. He leads us into the opposite end of killing: suffering and dying, which are the body of nonviolence; love and forgiveness of enemies, which are its soul. The messiah can't kill evil. But by dying to evil he can transform it through love.

As Paul sums up that transformation in his letter to the Colossians, "through him God was pleased to reconcile to himself all things, whether on earth or in heaven, by making peace through the blood of his cross" (Colossians 1:20).

—Jim Douglass

APPENDICES

APPENDIX 1
Holy Days and Seasons

While the reflections in the body of Living the Word *address specific readings, the short seasonal and holy day articles included in this appendix offer a theological, liturgical, or historical look at the various seasons and the ordering of the lectionary readings.*

The church year is divided into three cycles—Christmas (inclusive of Advent, Christmas, and Epiphany), Easter (inclusive of Lent and Easter), and Pentecost (primarily Ordinary Time). Space does not allow a comprehensive examination of each of these seasons, but short perspectives are presented here.

Significant holy days in the church year, which usually do not fall on Sunday, are also included. Because most communions have worship services on Ash Wednesday, Maundy Thursday, Good Friday, and Thanksgiving Day, the significance of these days are considered. Some congregations also have special services for Pentecost, New Year's Day, and Reformation Day, so those three days are also examined.

These articles are meant to illumine further the reflections offered in the main body. We encourage their use and hope they are helpful in deepening the worship experiences of all who use this resource.

—The Editors

Advent Season

Make Room!

WHEN I WAS GROWING UP, the time of preparation for Christmas was ceremonially launched with the reverencing of Thanksgiving Day football games on television. The next day was the solemn ritual of spreading Christmas lights through the house, testing every bulb to find out which one was making a string blink frenetically like a neon sign outside a strip joint. Sniping, yelling, complaining, and threats of strangulation marked the day. And so began the season that would culminate with the celebration of God's ultimate gift of love and grace.

As is often the case with the seasons of the church, Advent moves at a rhythm different than our frenzied culture. Advent is a season of expectation and preparation. But unlike the jangly, insistent good cheer, high stress (and big profits) bandwagon that may be going down the cultural Main Street, the liturgical Advent is marked with pause and quiet, and an acknowledgment that uncertainty and hope, fear and longing, abide together.

Advent is observed from the eve of the fourth Sunday before Christmas until Christmas eve. We seek light—but, in the Northern Hemisphere at least, the darkness and cold are growing, the days are shortening. We feel in our hearts and bodies the tension between hope and doubt.

Likewise, during Advent the scriptures anticipate both joy and judgment. John the Baptist rants and Mary sings, and the prophets proclaim the wonders and justice, consolations and terrors that come with God's chosen one.

THE WORD "advent" comes from the Latin *adventus*, "an arrival," but also incorporates a sense of approach as well as the reaching of the destination, the now and not yet of God-with-us. We catch a glimpse of the power and glory of God; we wait for it to be revealed in fullness. We dream of how the injustices of the world could be overturned; we await a new order. We know we are in exile from our own hearts, people, and God; we await judgement and reconciliation.

Advent is a season of humility and penitence, for to be healed we must acknowledge our wounds; to experience the full joy of Christmas, we must acknowledge our sin and need for God. Purple, a color also liturgically associated with the other penitential season, Lent, is used for church sanctuaries and vestments during Advent.

There are many ways to "make room" for the coming Messiah. Churches might clear a space in the sanctuary at the beginning of Advent for a nativity scene and leave it empty until Christmas. (The same might be done at home with the area that will hold a creche or Christmas tree.) A series of simple Advent vespers services or prayer gatherings can encourage a faith community to pause and reflect in the midst of a perhaps inescapably busy season.

Many traditions incorporated fasting into Advent, but it is also truly appropriate to share simple meals with friends or new acquaintances during this time. This way we remember that we are not waiting alone, but as members of the far-flung and close-at-hand people of God. Seasonal preparations such as making Christmas cards or ornaments, baking, or even house cleaning can also become opportunities for helping one another and making the season both more holy and communal.

The Advent wreath is probably the most familiar symbol of this season. The evergreens represent the life that is found in Christ. Four candles are set in the wreath, with one more candle lit for every week of Advent, symbolic of the nearing of Jesus, the living light of the world.

A less well-known Advent tradition is a Jesse Tree. Read together scripture stories of Jesus' ancestors (see Matthew 1:1-17, which traces Jesus' lineage back to David, son of Jesse, and augment this list with women who are not listed there, such as Sarah, Rebecca, and Rachel). Then make symbols by which to remember the person in the story, and hang them from a small tree branch stood upright in a coffee can or other container.

There is not a single "correct" way to observe Advent. What is most important is an openness to the tension and longing expressed in the scripture readings during these weeks, and being unafraid to step a bit out of the social swirl. If we follow that lead, we will find ourselves expecting the unexpected. We will name the dark and yet pray confidently for the light.

—Julie Polter

The Season of Christmas
The Nativities of Our World

CHRISTMAS SEASON IS the 12-day period between Advent Season and Epiphany Season. The Christmas cycle encompasses Advent, Christmas, and Epiphany, with the birth of Jesus as the defining event. Most denominations play out this drama over three, or sometimes four, worship services.

Christmas Eve is the breakthrough point from our Advent-watch into labor pains. We are invited into the stable as strangers to witness a painful, bloody, and yet magnificent birth. Finally the promise of Advent is to be fulfilled.

On Christmas Day, we join the heavenly host in singing praise for God's gift—God-become-human. Although singing Christmas carols—a practice originated by St. Francis of Assisi—is now normal during Advent (shopping malls play the tunes interminably, hoping to encourage the "Christmas" spirit in consumers), some congregations now are trying to save the familiar songs until the Christmas Season.

Whatever joys or pains we bring to this celebration, our cultural symbols are inevitably incorporated. For example, Northern Europeans, having made pine wreaths and trees almost synonymous with the Christmas celebration, decorate them with bulbs, lights, and candles—signs of the synchronicity with the solstice celebrations and their emphasis on light.

Mid-December's Saint Lucia Day celebrates light in countries where darkness reigns supreme for most of the winter months. (Lucia was, according to tradition, an Italian princess who chose chastity and faithfulness to God over her own eyesight. This victory of light over darkness captivated early Swedish Christians.)

Other festivals of light are also celebrated during the Advent and Christmas seasons. Kwanzaa, an African-American celebration tied to the reverse-season harvest of the Southern Hemisphere, emphasizes cultural values such as family, community, and sharing. (In Swahili, kwanzaa means "first fruits.") For seven days a candle representing a different principle is lit in a kihara, or candelabrum.

Chanukah is the Jewish celebration of the defeat of the Greeks by Judas Maccabaeus. The traditional menorah is replaced by a candleholder with eight or nine branches, commemorating the ever-burning candle that saved the Jewish rebels.

The God whose first act as creator was to make light has sent that creation a Light in this Christmas season. The light of Christ warms our hearts in this surprising birth narrative.

FROM YEAR TO YEAR, the Christmas Season has either one or two Sundays. Because of this irregularity, the lectionary readings vary for each communion.

The common lectionary readings, in addition to those already presented in the Christmas readings for Cycles A, B, and C (see appropriate pages in this resource) are as follows:

- Christmas Eve: Psalm 96, Isaiah 9:2-7, Titus 2:11-14, Luke 2:1-10.
- Second Sunday After Christmas: Psalm 147:12-20, Jeremiah 31:7-14, Ephesians 1:3-14, John 1:1-18.

In the Nativity readings, the author known to scholars as First Isaiah identifies hope in the being of the God of Israel, even in the midst of the despair of Assyrian exile. That hope for Christians is given flesh and blood as the transcendent and the imminent become one: In Jesus the cosmic and the particular are united, giving creation reason to hope.

News Year's Day texts (see page 130) occasionally are used for the Second Sunday of Christmas, but there are specifically assigned texts. In these we are reminded of the continued activity of God in creation: Jeremiah says God will redeem the remnant from captivity; John reminds us that the Word which existed at the time of creation has walked with us, offering the world another redemption. (When the John reading has been used for a service prior to the Second Sunday of Christmas and when the New Year's Day texts are not used, Matthew 2:1-12 may be substituted.)

But in their infinite wisdom, the constructors of the church calendar don't allow us to become too carried away with the excitement of Jesus' birth. The feast days after Christmas include remembrances of St. Stephen the Martyr (December 26) and the Holy Innocents (December 28). Thus we are immediately reminded of the inevitable outcome of this radical birth; we are on the road to crucifixion. And as the Christmas Cycle ends, we begin the cycle—Easter—that leads to great suffering. The joy of birth is tempered by the sting of death. Thus is the way of the one true God.

—Bob Hulteen

New Year's Day

In God All Things Are New

NEW YEAR'S DAY is an interesting celebration for Christians. Its theme of new beginnings makes it almost a secular Easter. Its proximity to the celebration of Christmas encourages birthing imagery also of a secular nature. (Grandfather Time gives way to the innocent Baby New Year.) And yet, since Christian folk already have liturgical opportunities to talk about "newness," New Year's Day is something different.

The transition from New Year's Eve to New Year's Day is a reflective time, an opportunity to contemplate the direction and passage of our life. Whereas Easter is about the radical change of death to life, and the paradigm of sin and redemption, New Year's is a time of transition that causes people to reflect on the disappointments and hopes of their lives. Both of these patterns help to fulfill the yearnings of the human heart.

The scriptures for New Year's Day, the same for Cycles A, B, and C, all point to the stages of life. As our society continues to discuss the care of children and elderly parents, as adults increasingly look at job changes, as the migration away from place of origin continues; the opportunity to reflect on where we are, where we are headed, and whether our direction truly fits our calling is of ever more value. As we reflect, it is good to remember that our God has walked with us, is walking with us, and will, in fact, continue to walk with us.

—Bob Hulteen

A New Earth

PSALM 8 • ECCLESIASTES 3:1-13 • REVELATION 21:1-6 • MATTHEW 25:31-46

I WAS ONCE PART of a writing group that met every month. Most of us were writers of prose and gave easy affirmation or advice about one another's essays and short stories. But there was one among us who was a poet. And whenever she read her contributions, we were speechless. "Nice imagery" was about all we could muster to say, after some awkward silence. And pretty soon it became a bit of a joke, this repetition of the compliment "Nice imagery." It was the response of people inspired and in awe of the beauty of poetic creation.

"Nice imagery" fits our passages this week. What a way to start the year! We begin with the poetic affirmation that there is a time for all things—a time for planting and harvesting, weeping and laughing, speaking and keeping quiet; a time for birthing and dying. Life goes on, seasons change, God is lovingly in charge. Time to rest, renew, and rejoice.

Psalm 8 puts us in our place—crowned with glory and honor, not God but made in God's image. Trusted with care of the earth and all that lives on it. Sheep and oxen, sparrows and trout, daisies and oak trees—all living under sun and moon and stars, according to God's plan. Good work, God. Nice imagery. How majestic is your name! Thank you.

God is the beginning and the end, the Alpha and the Omega, creator of a new heaven and a new earth. And in this new world there will be no more death. God will reach down and, with a mother's care, wipe away every tear.

But we are not there yet. There are still many of us who are hungry and thirsty, naked and cold, alone and afraid, sick and dying. The old earth still groans and makes its claim: feed, clothe, visit, heal. There is much to be done.

And Jesus, the Word Made Flesh, reminds us that we will find him there, among the lonely and suffering ones. More than just a metaphor or creative poetic image. He is there. And—make no mistake about it—our salvation is at stake in how we treat him and his sisters and brothers.

—Joyce Hollyday

Epiphany Season

The Appearances of Jesus

O N THE 12TH DAY of Christmas...is Epiphany. The basics are familiar to us: The coming of the Magi, taking down the tree, putting away the decorations.

But there's more to the story than "We Three Kings." In the early church, the celebrations of what we now call Christmas and Epiphany were wrapped up into one celebration—some authorities hold that they weren't separated until as late as 813 A.D. (although most place it in the fourth century). In the Eastern church, Christ's birth was remembered on January 6, the date of an Egyptian solstice festival, and the focus was as much on Jesus' baptism in the Jordan as on the visit of the Magi.

Other traditions, and readings for the season, feature three of Jesus' "epiphanies"—the word means appearance or manifestation—including (along with the Magi's visit and the baptism of Jesus) the wedding feast at Cana, where Jesus first manifested his power and began his public life.

Epiphany has been a traditional opportunity for focus on evangelism and missions; the visit of the Magi—the first non-Jews to pay homage to Jesus—symbolizes the universal extension of the reign of Christ. While Judaism is the religion of a people (i.e. the people of God), Christ's following—like the Magi—is made up of all those who seek after him.

Who were these Magi? While folklore, paintings, and Christmas carols refer to them as kings, the gospel doesn't. Scripture calls them "wise men" or "astrologers," those who study the stars for portents of earthly destiny. The notion that they were kings may derive from Psalm 72, another traditional Epiphany reading: "...the kings of the Arabians and of Saba shall bring gifts; all kings of the earth shall adore him; all nations shall serve him." But Epiphany is really not so much the feast of kings as it is the feast of the kingship of Christ.

THE THREE WISE MEN are popularly depicted as one European, one African, and one Asian. Their search for Jesus and homage to him are thereby a sign and symbol that Christ's salvation knows no boundaries; the Epiphany story provides an occasion for sermons on reconciliation across racial, ethnic, national, and other boundaries.

The Christian-Jewish link is prominent. Augustine wrote that Christmas and Epiphany are like two sides of an arch, representing "our Jewish and Gentile inheritance"—Jewish shepherds visited him at birth, and Gentile Magi came soon thereafter.

The story of the Magi's visit has other, more-disquieting implications, mostly ignored in contemporary churches—perhaps because the deadly undercurrents are out of sync with the jingle-bells and ho-ho-hos of modern American Christmastide celebrations. Herod's duplicity and cruelty is observed at another time, the feast of the Holy Innocents, but it belongs in the context of the Magi's story.

The elements are familiar. Soon after the visitors arrive in Jerusalem, they're summoned to Herod's court. Herod, of course, claims that he, too, wants to pay homage to the newborn child, and asks them to report back to him. Fortunately, the wise men practice direct civil disobedience to Herod's order, and they and the holy family escape Herod's wrath; not so the children of Bethlehem. The lessons are stark and clear: While kings may come to bow down to Jesus, some come to kill. And who knows: If the wise men were indeed kings, would their response to Jesus have been similar to Herod's if the Christchild had been born in their back yards? Power being universally reluctant to yield its monopoly, wariness of secular authority seems the proper stance.

But this season is not Herod's; it rightly belongs to the one who incarnates the living God. It is a time of triumph and hope—a hope made tangible and abiding because God loved us enough to send his only son. In that epiphany, all things are made new.

—Jim Rice

Ash Wednesday
Redemption in the Ashes

EVEN BEFORE the time of Jesus, people anointed themselves with ashes as a sign of repentance or mourning. In the wearing of ashes, the outside of the body reflects the inside; ashes on the forehead are a sign of sadness or sin in the heart. Early Christians continued the practice of wearing ashes, and in Rome they designated a day 40 days before the beginning of Easter as a time for penitents to wear ashes (one step in their re-admittance to the community of believers). This practice gradually evolved into Ash Wednesday, the first day of Lent, on which some Christians put ashes on their foreheads as penance or a reminder of their own mortality.

While ashes are a valuable sign for the day, it is possible to commemorate the day without using them. Putting on ashes is one of the few Christian rituals that is not a re-enactment of an event in Jesus' life. Communion, foot washing, baptism, fasting, and feasting are all activities we have record of Jesus doing, but not anointing with ashes. (We do, however, have stories of Jesus fasting and mourning, as well as numerous Old Testament stories of anointing with ashes.) The important ingredients in an Ash Wednesday service are not the ashes themselves, but confessions of sin and the call to repentance.

When the Old Testament prophets put ashes on their forehead, they usually did so not for their own personal sins, but for the sins of Israel. Over the centuries, the focus of Ash Wednesday has become personal sin, rather than institutional sin. It is valuable to use Ash Wednesday to remember the sins of our community, nation, and world, in addition to our own sins. In recent decades, some Christians have used Ash Wednesday as a day of protest, calling on various structures to repent.

FOR CHURCHES THAT use ashes in a traditional Ash Wednesday service, small bits of ash are smeared on each participant's forehead in the shape of a cross, so that the ashes are simultaneously a sign of sin and Jesus' atonement for our sins. In the Roman Catholic and some liturgical Protestant traditions, the ashes are given with the words, "Remember that you are dust, and to dust you shall return." Other traditions use different phrases, such as "Turn from your sins and return to the gospel."

Any simple message about human sin or mortality is appropriate, as long as the same phrase is used for every single person in the congregation. When we reflect on our sinful or fallen nature, it is an enormous comfort to remember that all of the people around us are in the same situation.

Traditionally, in the Roman Catholic church, Ash Wednesday ashes are made by burning palm leaves that were blessed and distributed on Palm Sunday the year before. This connects the ashes with Jesus' triumphal entry into Jerusalem. Like the practice of putting the ashes on in the form of a cross, burning palm leaves reminds us of God's power to redeem us.

For churches that do not have leftover palm leaves available, however, there are many liturgical options. It is very powerful to ask members of the congregation to write on slips of paper sins or bad habits they would like to be free of, then to collect and burn these papers as part of the Ash Wednesday service. The fire is a reminder of God's ability to destroy sin, and the ashes are another reminder of God's glory.

—Jan Degges

Lenten Season

Fasting and Repentance

EASTER IS A SPRINGTIME holiday. Altars covered with new flowers remind us that God's power is present in the renewing of creation, just as that power was evident in Jesus' resurrection from the dead and the Holy Spirit's renewal of our hearts.

The journey toward Easter begins in the winter, however, with the cold and sometimes painful season of Lent. This time of self-reflection and self-denial gives us an opportunity to give up an idolatrous habit, take on a new discipline of faith, or spend time with our community in a new way.

The Lenten season—the six-and-a-half weeks between Ash Wednesday and Easter—grew out of two pre-Easter traditions in the early church. The first tradition included a time of fasting and repentance, particularly for people who had committed sins that separated them from the kinship of other Christians. These "notorious sinners" spent a period of weeks or months doing penance before being re-admitted to worship with other believers at Easter.

The second tradition involved the preparation for converts, who were baptized the night before Easter. Gradually the preparations for re-admittance of sinners and the admittance of converts grew into a time of fasting, prayer, and study observed by all Christians.

Lent is usually described as lasting 40 days, a number that reminds us of Jesus' 40 days of fasting and temptation and the Hebrews' 40 years of wandering in the desert before arriving in the Promised Land. The 40-day count does not include Sundays in Lent, however, in part because every Sunday has been seen as a "little Easter," and therefore a time to rejoice, not fast.

In the Western church, modern observance of Lent is concentrated in the Catholic and more liturgical Protestant (principally Lutheran and Episcopal) denominations. Communions that observe Lent usually omit the word "alleluia" from all services, and use purple altar cloths and hangings.

In medieval Roman Catholic Europe, meat and some comforts were entirely forbidden throughout Lent. After the Second Vatican Council, strict fasting requirements for Lent were considerably relaxed. The Orthodox churches still encourage a strict regimen of fasting. Fasting by entire faith communities can bind Christians closer together.

ASIDE FROM LITURGICAL observances, Lent can mean many things to individuals and communities. Many people remind themselves of the season's original fasting by restricting a food, activity, or habit. "Giving something up" for Lent can help us experience Christ's 40 days of temptation, and can also loosen the grip that "thing" may have on us. We are reminded of God's "intrusion" in our lives.

Lent can also be a time to take on an observance, such as dedicating oneself to reading the Bible daily, doing community service, or simply slowing down to experience more of God's world. Six weeks seems like a manageable length of time, and many people feel more comfortable committing to a Lenten activity than to something longer term.

Because of this, Lent is an ideal time to organize a short Bible or book study. Christians interested in issues of social justice and reform have also used Lent as a time of increased action and prayer.

A Lenten change of lifestyle bears fruit even after the season is over. Having given something up, we may decide that we don't need that thing in our lives, or we may return to it with a different perspective. New knowledge of God gleaned from increased prayer and study stays with us and may inspire us to continue with that discipline. Friendships formed in a Lenten action group may continue to nourish our lives. Ideally, after walking more closely with Jesus through Lent, we can rise with him on Easter and continue our journey together.

—Jan Degges

Maundy Thursday
At the Table With Jesus

MAUNDY THURSDAY—the commemoration of Jesus' last night with his disciples before the crucifixion—is at once one of the most joyful and most sober days in the liturgical year. On this night Jesus gave his followers the sacrament of Communion, reminded them to love each other, and illustrated this love by washing their feet. Yet on this night his followers' love failed him, as they could not stay awake to keep vigil with him, and he was betrayed by Judas and denied by Peter.

This evening ended with Jesus' greatest act of love: his submission to the arrest he knew would lead to humiliation, torture, and death. The crucifixion is an occasion of painful sorrow and grateful joy.

Traditions associated with Maundy Thursday reflect the day's dual nature. Maundy Thursday is named after Jesus' words spoken at the Last Supper: "I give you a new commandment, that you love one another." (The word "maundy" comes from the Latin *mandatum*, meaning "commandment.") Services usually focus on Jesus' actions at the Last Supper; some traditions also commemorate his time in the garden and his arrest.

Since Maundy Thursday was Jesus' initiation of Communion, a eucharistic meal is normally at the center of the worship service. (Some Roman Catholic parishes schedule children's First Communion for Maundy Thursday.) The Communion celebration can be preceded by a common meal, like the one the disciples shared with Jesus. Since Jesus' last meal was a Passover seder, the Jewish sacred meal which commemorates deliverance from Egypt, some congregations replicate this. A Maundy Thursday meal can just as easily be a simple dinner or a potluck, however. Sometimes church leaders serve such a meal to the congregation, emulating Jesus' role as a servant.

Foot washing—another of Jesus' activities at the Last Supper demonstrating his servanthood—can also be a part of a Maundy Thursday service, reflecting Jesus' commandment that we love one another. While some denominations regularly practice foot washing, others do so only on Maundy Thursday. Again, it is appropriate for ministers and lay leaders to wash the feet of members of the congregation.

(In the past few decades, some parishes have substituted hand washing for foot washing. Hand washing may not feel as servile, but its symbolism may be more accessible to modern Westerners.)

MANY TRADITIONS END Maundy Thursday services with Communion, focusing on the joyous side of the holiday. Other churches continue reading the gospel lesson through to Jesus' prayers in the Garden of Gethsemane and his arrest. After the full account has been read, the liturgists dim the lights in the church, stripping the altar and sanctuary. Linens, candles, books, and hangings are removed. The church is left as bare as possible, evoking the theft of Jesus' garments. In traditions that keep consecrated bread and wine stored in the sanctuary, the elements are entirely consumed during the Communion service, leaving the church without Jesus' presence. After this stripping, the congregation leaves in silence.

I have attended churches that hold an all-night vigil in the sanctuary after the conclusion of Maundy Thursday services. Members of the congregation sign up to pray in the church for blocks of time throughout the night. Staying up to pray—even for one hour—reminds us of Jesus' request to the disciples to pray with him in Gethsemane, as well as the fact that he was denied sleep the night before the crucifixion.

This prayer vigil is especially meaningful (and effective!) if each participant agrees to focus on one particular topic. A congregation can organize an all-night prayer vigil for the health of the parish or the community in which it is located, or for an issue of national or international concern. A prayer vigil of this type can be an excellent way to prepare individuals and communities for Good Friday.

—Jan Degges

Good Friday
The Paradox of Life Through Death

WHAT'S SO GOOD about Good Friday? That's often the first question asked by people unfamiliar with this holy day. It may seem like an easy question to those well-versed in the Christian tradition; but the more deeply one thinks about it, the more difficult it becomes to offer a simple explanation. The paradox of Good Friday lies at the very heart of our faith: Our life comes through Christ's death.

Good Friday is the commemoration of our Lord Jesus being beaten and mocked; of him being forced to drag the instrument of his own execution through the streets and out of Jerusalem; of Jesus being stripped of his garment—his only worldly possession—and seeing Roman soldiers gamble for it. Good Friday is the day Christians remember the bloody nailing of their Savior to the cross, his crucifixion between two thieves, his last words and expressions of abandonment, and finally his death and burial in a donated tomb. Surely these things, if taken at face value, can hardly be considered "good" by those who love and follow Jesus.

Yet, this Friday before Easter also marks the day the veil that separated the people from the most intimate place of God was symbolically rent in the temple, "and the graves were opened and many bodies of the saints which slept arose" (Matthew 27:51-52). As foretold in Isaiah 53, on this day Christ took on our griefs and sorrows, offering us healing through his own wounds. On this day Christ died for our sins, making sin dead to us—a reality that becomes complete with the triumph of Easter Sunday resurrection.

This combination of the pathos of death and the profound joy of liberation saturates the world of many Christians on Good Friday. For many it is the most serious and solemn day of the liturgical year, a day of reflection about the tremendous price that was paid for our salvation and the commitment to which this sacrifice calls us. Many believers observe traditions of fasting, abstinence, and prayer on Good Friday.

FOR ROMAN CATHOLICS, Good Friday is one of two days (along with Holy Saturday) in the year when no Mass is held. Instead, many congregations, both Catholic and Protestant, hold silent vigils or other extra-liturgical services on that day. One of the most popular devotional practices on Good Friday is the "Way of the Cross" (*Via Cruces*), which is a public procession of believers with the cross. It is based on Jesus' journey from Pilate's house, where he was condemned, to Calvary, where he was crucified. Early Christian pilgrims to Jerusalem first observed the Way of the Cross ceremony, which over the years has spread around the world.

From the Capital Mall in Washington, D.C., to the mountain paths of the Peruvian Andes, Christians gather on Good Friday to follow the cross and recreate Christ's final journey in ways that reflect their own context and experience. In a Mexican indigenous village, I've seen the crowd beat a member of their community who had the honor of representing Jesus on Good Friday. Bloodying his nose, kicking him to the ground, and drawing blood with their whips before tying him to a cross, and leaving him there until an ambulance arrived to take him away. The blood, sweat, and tears shed by the "Jesus" in this "dramatization" was for them a communal prayer of penitence which lifted the sins of the whole village up to God.

In Washington, D.C., members and friends of Sojourners gather with others doing ministry in our neighborhoods and follow the cross in silent procession to each of our worksites. Together we reflect on the scriptures and pray, stopping at a neighborhood center that provides children with safe space after school, at a church that offers language classes for refugees, at a sanctuary that opens its space to local community groups struggling to make a difference without sufficient resources, and at a school of discipleship that trains servant leaders. We end at Malcolm X Park, which overlooks Washington and is across the street from Sojourners' office. In this way, we offer witness to both the pain and the hope of Christ that is found among the rich and poor, gay and straight, African-American, Latino, Asian, and European-American women and men of our community.

In whatever way you observe Good Friday, dig deep and open your heart and soul to our God and Savior on this day, remembering both the pain of Jesus' death on the cross and the eternal salvation of the Creator that flows through it. Pray, together with other believers, "Into your hand I commit my spirit; you have redeemed me, oh Lord, faithful God" (Psalm 31:5). Truly, this is a good Friday.

—Aaron Gallegos

Easter Season

Freed to Follow

JESUS' RESURRECTION is a reality that puts forward a choice—and guarantees the freedom to make it. Confronting the risen Lord may prompt nearly as many fears as it calms. The community of disciples is shaken to its roots as much by Easter as by Good Friday; the Living God asks them to begin again.

Any number of the resurrection experiences, beginning with Mary and the other women, then variously the other disciples, have the effect of re-stating the call to discipleship: "Behold, he is going before you"; "Go, therefore, and make disciples of all nations." None, however, is more explicit than the passage from John's epilogue (21:14-19) where the risen Christ says straight out to Peter, "Follow me."

There is a stark simplicity in this original call of disciples. They drop everthing and go. There is no record that they had previously heard him preach, mulled over the message, and then, ripe for an invitation, finally met him by the sea.

Jesus does not lay out the details of what they might expect: "You'll join a vagabond community and live by begging. Eventually we'll go up to Jerusalem to confront the authorities. You will betray me and deny me and scatter. I'll be arrested, tried, and executed. Come, follow me." No such thing is said.

It's simpler, if no less surprising, in that first go around. He offers neither program nor predictions, but himself.

After Easter, however, there is a little more water under the bridge. When Peter is called to follow in the resurrection, he knows a good deal more about what that means, where it leads, and even who he is himself: To meet Jesus, crucified and risen, is at least to face your own death.

IN THE EARLY WEEKS of the Eastertide lectionary, a series of texts from the first three chapters of Acts appears, addressing the costs of discipleship. It is a shame to read these piecemeal, for the chain of events deserves to be read as a single story.

EASTER is the highest and most holy day of the Christian year. Beyond the miracles of Jesus' birth, baptism, and ministry; beyond his parables, transfiguration, and Passion; the resurrection of Jesus Christ is the defining moment in Christian history.

Easter's promise of new life is celebrated in many ways around the world, from brilliantly colored eggs to liturgical direct action. In the Northern Hemisphere, creation itself reflects the power of the resurrection with spring's renewal of light and warmth out of winter's darkness and cold.

Yet the season's real celebration takes place within, in the heart of each believer, when we realize anew the eternal life that Christ has wrought for us. In the midst of all our struggles of faith and doubt, Easter is a season of celebration. Because Christ is risen, we have the victory. This truly is a season to rejoice and be glad. Indeed!

—Aaron Gallegos

Peter and John, on their way to temple prayers, heal a man begging at the Beautiful Gate, leading to a sermon from Peter on resurrection. Here, two healings have come together. The healing of the beggar was in fact his call to discipleship in the resurrection. He is already faithful to that.

Peter's call to discipleship in the resurrection was also his own deep healing. Following his arrest for healing the abovementioned man, Peter makes it his business to tell the intellectual, ecclesial, and economic leadership exactly who the disciples are in relationship to Christ. He pulls no punches and the man born lame stands beside him. Peter—and the other disciples—certainly recalls his own denial in this affirmation.

The disciples have met that healing freedom personally face to face, in their hearts and in their bones. Now they are exercising that freedom publicly, which is to say, "politically." They laugh out loud with God. The "public works," or liturgy, of Easter is to celebrate all such things.

Eastertide marks the renewal of discipleship. We are healed in it. Unflinching honesty about our weakness and frailty gives way to our rehabilitation in the call. We follow and follow again.

To keep the season is to embrace and proclaim the sovereign freedom of God in history. In spite of—and against the overwhelming claims of—power, disciples announce and enact the freedom. There is no shortage of opportunity on that score.

To keep Easter is to rejoice—all the way to jail and, for the time being, home again. Our celebration is neither flip, for we know the cost and the long haul, nor morose, because we're in on the joke. We rejoice, even in suffering, in our own healing, in our freedom, and for the presence of God in Christ.

The powers have had their day.

—Bill Wylie-Kellermann

This meditation is adapted from Seasons of Faith and Conscience: Kairos, Confession, Liturgy, *by Bill Wylie-Kellermann (Orbis Books, 1991).*

Festival of Pentecost
Storming Heaven

LOOKING FROM MY back stoop across the tops of row houses, I watch lightning do its flashdance over the northern cityscape. A storm has been building all day, each layer of the storm cell doing its part. The thunderheads are too far away for sound yet, but the wind is beginning to rock the trees, and the hair on my arms stands up with static. Is this what Pentecost was like?

Bible scholar Ched Myers gives another view of that first descending of the Holy Spirit. In a new reading of Genesis' Tower of Babel story and Acts' Pentecost, Myers explores the theme of language in the "divine project" of God.

From heterogeneous Eden to the Fall, from Cain and Abel and the flood to Noah and the covenant, humanity has been through a cycle of participating in God's project and revolting against it. Genesis 10 gives the "begats," telling us that diverse populations and nations are returning post-flood. "These are the clans of Noah's sons [and, presumably, their wives], according to their lines of descent....From these, the nations spread out over the earth after the flood" (Genesis 10:32). The model from the Noah story is diversity. The earth is filled with a great variety of people, creatures, languages, arts, sciences, and social contracts.

In Genesis 11:1, the revolution against God begins again: "Now the whole world had one language and a common speech." This is a drastic jump into centralization! What do we know about "one language"? In our own world, languages are dying almost as quickly as the rain forest because of the imperial projects of the rich and powerful. Five hundred years ago in North America there were thousands of languages in a diversified, decentralized culture. Now there is one dominant language as a result of the U.S. colonial project. Monolingualism is one of the tools of imperialism. The more coherent the society is, the easier it is to control.

The building of the Tower in Genesis 11 is a Babylonian imperial project bent on consolidating power in an urban center, specifically through the use of Hebrew slaves. God's "divine counterstrategy" is to reconstruct diversity through the "confusion of languages" and the scattering of colonizers to all the ends of the earth.

JUMP NOW SOME 2,500 years to the occupied urban center of Jerusalem. Acts 2:1—"When the day of Pentecost came, the disciples were all together in one place"—echoes Genesis 11. The disciples were from a variety of lands, but in Jerusalem they spoke only the lingua franca of the empire, Greek.

With the onrush of a mighty wind, "tongues" were distributed among this remnant of the Jesus sect, and each disciple spoke in "other" languages as enabled by the Holy Spirit. The Holy Spirit then sets afire each one to revert to speaking in her/his native language or tongue! Acts 2:9 is the redistribution of cultural power through language ("Parthians, Medes, Elamites..."), harkening back to Genesis 10 and the table of nations.

Israel has become an imperial nation (see 1 Samuel 8:5). But when God's divine counterstrategy arrives through the Holy Spirit, the church born is not an imperial project, but an arrangement based in rich cultural diversity bringing people together around the works of God!

The storm now hits my house full force, rain driving in through open summer windows. The Salvadoran kids from the apartment building dance in the street with a soaked cat. Myung and Yoon Her lay down flattened boxes at the entrance of their corner store to keep the mud from being tracked too far inside. Next door Reggie listens to the baseball game in his car. Is this what Pentecost was like?

—Rose Marie Berger

Ordinary Time
Of Sabbath and Summer

IN FLANNERY O'CONNOR'S classic story *The Violent Bear It Away*, a character says, "Love cuts us like a cold wind, and the will of God is plain as the winter. Where is the summer will of God? Where are the green seasons of God's will? Where is the spring and summer of God's will?"

From Advent to Pentecost, we turn through the complete cycle of our faith, churning up the whole soil of our soul—except the last piece, the seventh day, the rest. In the liturgical year, this "spring and summer of God's will" is called "Ordinary Time." Maybe we can call it "fallow time" or "Sabbath time," when God invites in us a fallow heart.

Actually, God extends such an invitation to us every evening and morning—to rest and rejoice in God. The old children's prayer reminds us, "Now I lay me down to sleep. I pray the Lord my soul to keep"; and with the dawn, "Now I wake and see the light. Thy love was with me through the night." One friend enjoys falling asleep and waking by remembering special places where she felt God very near: the peacefulness of a West Virginia cabin, quiet nights on the back porch.

Sabbath time also comes each week with Saturday evening endings and Sunday morning beginnings. When Jesus healed on the Sabbath and "broke" Sabbath laws, he wasn't rejecting the Sabbath, only the idolatry that placed rules over genuine needs of people.

IN CATHOLIC TRADITION, Sundays and holy days are for "abstaining from any servile work." The implication, of course, is that most people have to do "servile work" during the week. The word "servile" comes from the Latin for slave, or to be "humbly submissive before a master." For immigrant Catholics who helped build this country, "servile work" was what was available. Now we call it working in the "service sector"—fast food, day labor construction, door-to-door sales—and it is still the work of immigrants, slave descendants, and poor whites.

When we explore ordinary time from this perspective, we come up against the politics of rest. For the "service sector" work force to set aside Sundays or seasons for rest and renewal in God goes directly against the ever-increasing demands of our market economy. When the prophet in Ecclesiastes says, "There is nothing new under the sun," he's not succumbing to fatalism but shouting out a word of resistance against propaganda that uses slave labor and the working poor to build the next great "new" project, an economy that treats people like cogs in a machine.

When I was growing up, my family escaped the valley heat each August to the mouth of the Klamath River on the Northern California coast. (Both my parents were teachers in the public school system.) We parked the trailer on the end of a sand spit. The Pacific crashed behind us and seals and steelhead swam in the river out front. We picked wild blackberries and Mom made cobbler, smoked fresh perch, maybe a salmon, and cob corn over an open-pit fire. I roamed the beach for hours knee deep in tide pools, testing the springiness of moss in fern forests, watching otters play in the surf.

Where do you rest in the "green seasons of God's will"?

—**Rose Marie Berger**

Reformation and All Saints' Days
Celebrating Wheat and Chaff

God of unity, we pray for your church. Fill it with all truth and peace. Where it is corrupt, purify it; where it is in error, direct it; where in anything it is amiss, reform it; where it is right, strengthen it; where it is in need, provide for it; where it is divided, reunite it.

THIS ECUMENICAL PRAYER, adapted from the World Council of Churches' *In Spirit and In Truth: Prayers to the Holy Spirit* (1991), hits the nail on the head; and that nail might even be from the same batch as the one Martin Luther used in 1517 to hang his 95 Theses on the Wittenberg door. Luther saw a church lost, and he offered theological direction. Though the immediate result was fissure, a slow and arduous process began of reformation of the very institution that was Jesus' body.

Many events today reinforce the awareness that the church is as susceptible to corruption and exploitation as any other human institution. The church is comprised of people who are sinners, as well as saints, and so can be polluted. The principalities and powers Jesus warns of are present in all human institutions and social structures; the church is no exception. But on Reformation Day we are called to renewal of our church and our world.

The pericope (texts) assigned for Reformation Day is the same for Cycles A, B, and C: Psalm 46, Jeremiah 31:31-34, Romans 3:19-28, and John 8:31-36. In these scriptures, we are reminded of the limitations of structures and the unlimited resourcefulness of God. Although we cannot be justified by works, God's grace is large enough to be offered to us freely. We simply need to recognize that it is not our acts, deeds, or feats that so impress God that we become justified; it is the gospel's transformative power that still renews the church. Surely, the truth sets us free.

EVEN AS THE CHURCH is in need of constant renewal, so it is still the home of people who attempt to live their lives with integrity, and to point to God's New Creation in the way they live. All Saints' is a feast day to remind us that we all carry that saintly spark: True, we may be sinners who can corrupt the church, but we are also moral beings who can bring light into the darkness of the world and seasoning to that which is tasteless.

The origin of All Saints' is not firmly established, though it originally was a day of recognition of the martyrs of the faith. Over the years, minor saints—those without their own feast day—were honored in total on this day. And eventually many church people began to see that all who share the faith are in fact saints.

All Saints' became a liturgical opportunity to remember those of the faithful who have recently departed this life, as well as those who have modeled the faith for us. It allows us to place ourselves in the great stream of believers by recognizing those who have gone before, as well as the value of our witness for those who follow.

Reformation Day and All Saints' Day are recognized primarily in the more liturgical traditions. In those communions that commemorate Reformation Day, its readings are substituted on the last Sunday of October. All Saints' Day readings are used on the first Sunday of November, in place of the regular readings in traditions where All Saints' is celebrated.

Although the customs around All Saints' and Reformation Days vary according to tradition, the theological gem can be gleaned by all. In grace, God has made us all the children of God. We are one family. And though corruption and fissure are both very real, God constantly calls the body to unity and the people of God to truth.

—Bob Hulteen

Thanksgiving

How Big is Our Table?

Thanksgiving is a holiday in decline in the United States. Though its origins are part of American mythology, similar celebrations predate the meal shared by the Puritans and the Massasoits. In England, and in most areas of the world, a harvest festival is celebrated as the gardens and fields are put to rest for the winter season.

For Christians inclined toward biblical concerns for justice, Thanksgiving is the locus of many interwoven themes. Perhaps best known, albeit irregularly acknowledged, is the theme of racial harmony. Although stories vary, the Puritans, hoping to make peace with the American Indians surrounding them (likely for ambiguous reasons), hosted a feast which included the tribe. And the table was full.

Much like the feeding of the 5,000, tradition maintains that there was abundance out of scarcity. The celebration of a completed growing cycle was upset by the growing guest list. Where did the extra food come from? Did the Massasoit bring deer and maize? Stories vary, but it is clear that the road to "enough" was through "each other." (Still, we must remember that though peace reigned for a while, a war resulting in the near-genocide of the original residents of this country was waged for several hundred years, making repentance an important subtext of this holiday.)

The choice of hospitality over hostility is a model for our time. Neither Puritan nor Indian responded to the common meal by asking what the need of the other was; neither seemed especially concerned with charity, if legends be true. But both responded hospitably and gratefully out of what had been given. Perhaps this vision can infect current debates over such issues as welfare in this country.

THE ASSIGNED TEXTS for Thanksgiving are as follows:

- Cycle A: Psalm 65; Deuteronomy 8:7-18; 2 Corinthians 9:6-15; Luke 17:11-19.

- Cycle B: Psalm 126; Joel 2:21-27; 1 Timothy 2:1-7; Matthew 6:25-33.

- Cycle C: Psalm 100; Deuteronomy 26:1-11; Philippians 4:4-9; John 6:25-35.

Consistent themes herein are God's faithfulness and the wholeness that comes to us in our gracious response to God's initiation. Paul says, "God lavishes gifts on the needy....You will always be rich enough to be generous" (2 Corinthians 9:10-11). In our abundance (even if it appears to be scarcity), in our hospitality, we can imitate God. Paradoxically, we gain our health in this free response. "Those who sow in tears will reap with songs of joy," the psalmist posits.

Thanksgiving is a lost opportunity for many of us. Can we interweave the themes of abundance, hospitality, and racial justice into our liturgical calendar? In so doing, are we open to the fact that our lives will be changed?

A Thankgiving litany of All Nations Church in Minneapolis can be a litany for our lives:

ONE: Great Spirit, for the bitterness and sweetness that come to us as we live in the human family;

MANY: We acknowledge the joy and pain that connections have brought us.

WOMEN AND GIRLS: Empowering Justice, for all the ways, big and small, that people have stood side by side as allies with those facing different oppressors;

MANY: We acknowledge that strength that solidarity has brought us.

MEN AND BOYS: God of Hope, for the millions who have maintained some dignity for themselves and their neighbors in the face of crushing circumstance;

MANY: We acknowledge the courage that integrity has brought us.

ONE: Creator of Life, for the trees planted, the species sheltered, the cans recycled, and the spiders carried outside instead of squashed;

MANY: We acknowledge the restoring planet that conservation efforts have brought us.

WOMEN AND GIRLS: Source of Compassion, for the many who have reached out to us in our pain, even amidst their own burdens;

MANY: We acknowledge the grace that caring has brought us.

MEN AND BOYS: Gentle Tenderness, for all that is tender, for all that is full and rich and varied, for all that is a witness to your love incarnate in the world;

ALL: We gather in gladness and give you thanks.

And so it should be. Thank you, O God of wonder, warmth, and willful hearts. Amen.

—Bob Hulteen

APPENDIX 2: Index of Lectionary Readings

*T*his appendix provides assistance in locating scriptural passages as they appear in the lectionary cycles. Since the weekly reflection may not give specific attention to every passage in the week's readings, this appendix may also be used to coordinate a given passage with related scripture while not necessarily giving explicit comment on each reading.

APPENDIX 3: Contributors

We are grateful to the following people for their work on this resource.

ROSE MARIE BERGER grew up in the Central Valley of California, located in the flood plains of the Sacramento and American Rivers. Raised in radical Catholic communities heavily influenced by Franciscans and the Catholic Worker movement, she currently serves as pastor of Sojourners Community Church in Washington, D.C., is director of Sojourners Internship Program, and has been a member of Sojourners Community since 1987. She is a poet, works on a landscaping crew, and keeps house with a Flat-coat Retriever named Milagro.

JAN DEGGES was raised Episcopalian and has worshiped regularly with Quaker and United Methodist congregations. She studied religion at Oberlin College and spent a year as an intern with Sojourners.

YVONNE V. DELK is a *Sojourners* contributing editor and the chair of the Sojourners Board of Directors. She is executive director of the Community Renewal Society in Chicago, as well as a United Church of Christ pastor, a member of The Churches' Anti-Violence Network, and a member of the Programme to Combat Racism, World Council of Churches.

JIM DOUGLASS is a Gandhian Catholic who lives and writes in Birmingham, Alabama. He is the author, most recently, of *The Nonviolent Coming of God* (Orbis Books).

SHELLEY DOUGLASS, a *Sojourners* contributing editor, was raised an eclectic Protestant and now claims the Catholic faith. She lives and works at Mary's House, a Catholic Worker residence in Birmingham, Alabama.

VERNA J. DOZIER, a native of Washington, D.C., is an educator, lay theologian, and member of the Episcopal church. She is the author of *The Dream of God: A Call to Return* (Cowley Publications) and *The Authority of the Laity* (The Alban Institute).

AARON GALLEGOS is an assistant editor of *Sojourners* and a member of Sojourners Community in Washington, D.C. "Place" has been influential in his theological perspective. He spent his childhood in the Latino barrio of East Los Angeles, where his family has a long history, then in the Mojave Desert as a teen, and was an active member of a Pentecostal church in Santa Cruz, California. Most recently, he has been involved in founding the Washington, D.C. chapter of Barrios Unidos, a gang-alternative group working with Latino youth.

JOYCE HOLLYDAY's spiritual formation began in the First United Methodist Church on Chocolate Avenue in Hershey, Pennsylvania, and she was an associate editor of *Sojourners* for 15 years and a contributing editor since 1994. Her most recent book is *Clothed With the Sun: Biblical Women, Social Justice, and Us* (Westminster/John Knox Press). She is currently in the Master of Divinity Program at Candler School of Theology, Emory University, in Atlanta, and at work on *Then Shall Your Light Rise*, a book exploring social witness as a spiritual discipline.

BOB HULTEEN is an associate editor of *Sojourners*, a board member of Longfellow United for Youth and Families, and a member of the National Steering Committee of the Lutheran Volunteer Corps. A member of Holy Trinity Lutheran Church and the Community of St. Martin's, he lives in Minneapolis, Minnesota.

KAREN LATTEA has been managing editor of *Sojourners* since 1983 and a member of Sojourners Community Church in Washington, D.C., since 1986. Raised United Methodist in the D.C. suburbs and then trained in inner-city community organizing at college, she works to build bridges among people, communities, and ideologies through the practice of a biblical, grassroots theology.

Continued on next page...

JOE NANGLE, O.F.M., worked as outreach director at Sojourners in 1990-94. Previously he had spent 15 years in Latin America, where he participated in the early development of liberation theology. On returning to the United States, Joe worked at the U.S. Catholic Conference in the office for international justice and peace, and for the Conference of Major Superiors of Men in a similar capacity. Currently, he is executive director of his Franciscan order's overseas lay missionary program and a member of Assisi Community, made up of lay and religious men and women, in the inner city of Washington, D.C.

JULIE POLTER lives in Washington, D.C., where she is an assistant editor of *Sojourners* and a frequent preacher in Sojourners Community Church. She attended (and was baptized in) a Free Methodist church in West Unity, Ohio, as a teen-ager and joined the United Methodist Church in college. She has a master's of theological studies from Boston University School of Theology and is convinced that theology without paradox is usually wrong, or at least boring.

JIM RICE is an associate editor of *Sojourners*. He was raised Catholic in Richland, Washington, the bedroom community of the Hanford Nuclear Reservation, where he played sports for the Richland Bombers. After stints with an Assembly of God congregation, the Jesuit Volunteer Corps, and Pax Christi's Washington, D.C. chapter, he came to Sojourners in 1982 as a peace organizer. He is a member of Circle Community Church in Mt. Rainier, Maryland.

NANCY HASTINGS SEHESTED is a little-b baptist from the South. After 14 years of pastoring Baptist churches, she is now a retreat leader, itinerant preacher, and writer in Lake Junaluska, North Carolina. She is married with two daughters and attends an ecumenical house church.

KARI JO VERHULST grew up in Canada, where her father served as a pastor with the Christian Reformed Church Home Missions. After studying at Calvin College in Grand Rapids, Michigan, she moved to Washington, D.C. She works at Sojourners and worships at Washington Community Fellowship, where she serves as a worship planner and leader. Madeleine L'Engle, Annie Dillard, Anne Sexton, Frederick Buechner, and Garrison Keillor have shaped her theology, and she thinks John Calvin was on to something with his ideas about the depravity of humanity and the sovereignty of God.

DAVID A. WADE is director of marketing at Sojourners and pastor of The House of the Lord faith community in Maryland. Having spent many years in a charismatic, conservative evangelical environment, he now works to preserve the best of those traditions while seeking alternatives to their excesses and shadows.

WALTER WINK is professor of biblical interpretation at Auburn Theological Seminary in New York City. With his wife, June Keener Wink, he conducts workshops aimed at a transformative encounter with the biblical text. She leads the group in body movement, meditation, and art, and he facilitates Socratic dialogue about the texts. They live in the Berkshire mountains of Western Massachusetts, where they attempt to live the complicated and time-consuming "simple" life. He is the author of many books, including *Engaging the Powers* (Fortress Press).

BILL WYLIE-KELLERMANN is a United Methodist pastor who has served inner-city parishes in Detroit and is currently appointed to teach at Whitaker School of Theology, an Episcopal diocesan school. A native Detroiter and a graduate of Union Theological Seminary in New York, Bill is a *Sojourners* contributing editor and book review editor for *The Witness*. His books include *Seasons of Faith and Conscience: Kairos, Confession, Liturgy* (Orbis) and *A Keeper of the Word: Selected Writings of William Stringfellow* (Eerdmans). He is currently working on a book about the principalities, *Powers That Be*.